Crenshaw, James L.

BS
1455   Old Testament
.C67   wisdom

Old Testament Wisdom

OLD TESTAMENT WISDOM

an introduction

JAMES L. CRENSHAW

John Knox Press
ATLANTA

Library of Congress Cataloging in Publication Data

Crenshaw, James L
   Old Testament wisdom.

   Bibliography: p.
   Includes index.
   1. Wisdom literature—Criticism, interpretation, etc. I. Title.
BS1455.C67   223'.06   80-82183
ISBN 0-8042-0143-9
ISBN 0-8042-0142-0 (pbk.)

© copyright John Knox Press 1981
10 9 8 7 6 5 4 3 2 1
Printed in the United States of America
John Knox Press
Atlanta, Georgia 30365

To Jerry and Hazel
and those dearest to them (Allan, Regina, Scott)
and the new generation

Preface

This book took shape in the classroom at Vanderbilt Divinity School, where for over ten years I have joined my students in trying to understand Old Testament wisdom. That common task was made more difficult by the lack of an adequate introductory textbook. With the publication of this present volume, I hope that need will finally be met. I have written this book as preparation for a more ambitious project, a study of the art of persuasion in Israelite wisdom, which I hope to complete in the near future.

Two grants, from The Association of Theological Schools in the United States and Canada and from the Graduate Research Council of Vanderbilt University, made possible a year's sabbatical study at Oxford University during 1978–79. I am deeply grateful for that opportunity to complete the writing of this book in such pleasant surroundings.

Several individuals have assisted me in the final stages of this work. Special thanks go to my colleagues, Walter Harrelson and Douglas Knight, and to the following students who have kindly read the manuscript and made helpful suggestions: Victoria Lynn Garvey, Andrea C. Barach, Thomas H. Lanham, and Laura Kelly York. I wish also to express appreciation to my wife and to Aline Patte, both of whom greatly assisted me with typing the manuscript.

This volume is dedicated to my brother and his wife, together with their larger family. My hope is that each of them will enjoy the search for wisdom as much as I have.

Contents

Introduction:
On Defining Wisdom

Students of Israelite wisdom have at their disposal a number of significant studies dealing with particular aspects of the phenomenon, but no really satisfactory introduction exists at this time. Among older studies, three deserve mention here. Orvid S. Rankin, *Israel's Wisdom Literature*,[1] focuses attention upon the problem of reward and retribution and discusses the growth of belief in life after death and the presence of God in personified wisdom. Harry Ranston, *The Old Testament Wisdom Books and Their Teaching*,[2] views the biblical texts against the background of Hellenistic thought. J. Coert Rylaarsdam, *Revelation in Jewish Wisdom Literature*,[3] pursues the theme of divine grace as it gradually evolves among the sages who lost confidence in their own resources.

Gerhard von Rad, *Wisdom in Israel*,[4] concentrates upon the liberation of knowledge and the resulting problems, particularly the dynamics associated with faith in God and attack upon the deity's justice. Walter A. Brueggemann, *In Man We Trust*,[5] highlights the neglected side of biblical wisdom, specifically a strong faith in the power and goodness of human beings. R. B. Y. Scott, *The Way of Wisdom in the Old Testament*,[6] places Israelite wisdom within its larger cultural setting and attempts to isolate sapiential, that is, wisdom themes within the entire Hebrew canon, while offering a sustained analysis of wisdom in revolt. Roger N. Whybray, *The Intellectual Tradition in the Old Testament*,[7] examines the vexing problem whether a special class in Israel who were known as the wise actually existed, and in so doing gives comprehensive studies of putative sapiential vocabulary. The prolegomenon to my anthology, *Studies in Ancient Israelite Wisdom*,[8] deals with three major issues which have plagued research: affinities between wisdom and other types of literature, the literary forms used by Israel's sages, and the intrinsic structure of wisdom thinking, particularly with regard to creation theology.

Not all attempts to clarify biblical wisdom have addressed the scholarly community. Several valuable treatments of Israelite sapiential literature have presented the findings of research in language that ordinary laity could easily understand. Roland E. Murphy, *Introduction to the Wisdom Literature of the Old Testament*,[9] introduces readers to Egyptian and Mesopotamian texts which resemble biblical wisdom, and discusses the essential characteristics of Israel's wisdom. John Paterson, *The Wisdom of Israel*,[10] and James Wood, *Wisdom Literature*,[11] emphasize the religious dimensions of the individual books which derive from Israel's sages.

Those who develop an interest in wisdom literature, whether students or laity in general, will find several competent translations of Egyptian and Mesopotamian texts. James B. Pritchard, ed., *Ancient Near Eastern Texts Relating to the Old Testament*,[12] contains numerous examples of the several literary forms employed by ancient sages. In addition, W. G. Lambert, *Babylonian Wisdom Literature*,[13] and William K. Simpson, ed., *The Literature of Ancient Egypt*,[14] provide expert translations and explanatory notes to this informative literature. The pioneer study in this area, Adolf Erman's *The Ancient Egyptians*[15] still has much of value if one makes allowances for the somewhat archaic language which nevertheless often captures the spirit of the ancient text.

The wish to illuminate Israelite wisdom by means of a careful examination of Egyptian and Mesopotamian literature seems proper, but one could even make a case for spreading the net wider still.[16] The urge to secure human existence through the use of reason is universal. As we shall see, that striving to discover what is good for women and men expressed itself in many ways: the study of the observable universe; the analysis of animal and human behavior; the posing of ultimate questions about life's meaning, especially in the face of undeserved suffering; the composition of succinct proverbs and extended treatises; and the teasing of the imagination through enigmas.

Some cultures, like the Chinese,[17] excelled at this type of thinking, while most peoples have left a rich legacy of proverbs and riddles. For example, in Africa proverbs were so highly regarded that they even functioned in judicial proceedings.[18] A few African proverbs suffice to demonstrate the pervasiveness of sapiential thinking.

1. The earth is a beehive; we all enter by the same door but live in different cells.
2. Where there is more than enough, more than enough is wasted.
3. The journey of folly has to be traveled a second time.
4. Today's satiety is tomorrow's hunger.
5. Sticks in a bundle are unbreakable.[19]

The boundary between Bantu riddles and proverbs is often difficult to perceive.

6. Big-nose has not blown his nose; big-feet has not softened the road.
7. Though you sweep the hut in a sand flat, the sand will not disappear.
8. A little bird does not fly into the arrow.
9. A highway does not have grass on it; a highway does not grow mushrooms.[20]

Occasionally, riddles were used as a form of greeting, and the answer was given upon departing.

These particular examples of proverbs and riddle-like sayings derive from close observation of human beings within their immediate context. The first recognizes the essential oneness of all persons, but acknowledges varying lifestyles. The sixth example warns against assuming that a notorious individual is responsible for every crime, and the ninth observes that sexual profligacy militates against having a family. Numbers two through four, together with seven, resemble biblical proverbs which rest upon long experience. The similarity to Israelite wisdom is especially striking in numbers five and eight. The fifth recalls the saying in Ecclesiastes that a threefold cord is not easily broken (4:12), and the eighth uses imagery which Ben Sira, the author of Ecclesiasticus, selected to depict indiscriminate sexual activity, although in his case the blame is placed upon the woman who readily opens her quiver to receive any arrow.

It should be obvious that human survival depends upon an ability to study the complexity of human relationships and to cope with reality as it presents itself in the ordinary circumstances of daily existence. Generation after generation acquired fundamental insights into the difficult problem of male-female relationships, and these discoveries were etched into the collective memory through careful formulation of unforgettable sayings. Similarly, young people learned their parents' legacy concerning correct speech, proper table manners, control of one's temper, diligence, and the many things that enhance life.

To be sure, not every mystery in life has lent itself to convincing solutions. The suffering of innocent individuals has posed a vexing problem from time immemorial, for it has defied every effort at rational explanation. We shall see how this difficult problem evokes one of the masterpieces of the religious spirit, the book of Job. Indeed, the tension between divine freedom and human claims to justice pervades much more than that book, so that this single issue looms large in any significant analysis of biblical wisdom.

Although it may seem that the meaning of Israelite wisdom is beyond dispute, that is not the case. The highly informative passage and the most problematic in the wisdom literary corpus is chapter 31: Job's defense of his ethical conduct is a moral code which soars to lofty heights not even surpassed in the Sermon on the Mount.[21] This is a good text to use in an effort to define wisdom.

SAPIENTIAL ETHICS

Having given up hope of attaining a hearing from his inept comforters, the suffering Job took his case to a higher court. In form the remarkable declaration of innocence approximates an Egyptian execration oath in which wronged individuals pronounced a curse upon themselves if they had done anything amiss. Accordingly, they enumerated every conceivable offense and swore innocence with regard to it, on penalty of dire consequences. The comprehensive, ideal character of Job's declaration detracts little, if at all, from its actual representative capacity—nothing appears in this enumeration of misbehavior that did not apply to every Israelite or Edomite.

Job's list of offenses covers external deed and inner disposition, abuse of humans and affront to deity, active misdeeds and passive acquiescence in wrongdoing. Outright adultery and its secret counterpart, seething lust, stand alongside one another as equally heinous conduct in Job's eyes. Without a moment's hesitation, he drew back the curtains to his heart and revealed uprightness with respect to avarice and deceit, as well as singleness of devotion before God. Devoid of deception, greed, and idolatry, Job refused to hoard his possessions for selfish ends, but distributed his goods to needy persons. He championed his servant's cause; clothed, fed, and sheltered widows, orphans, and the poor; provided hospitality to strangers traveling the dusty roads. Naturally, such a person acted out of his own understanding of justice rather than fear of the crowd, and possessed sufficient power to correct injustice. Even the land had no complaint against Job, who understood the necessity of allowing soil to replenish its nutrients. What is more, Job had never rejoiced over his enemy's misfortune.

The crucial question is not whether Job pulled the wool over the eyes of his companions, or even if he managed to trick God into thinking his servant was so pure that he had windows in his heart. Of course we all know that nobody can be completely without fault. What really matters is that the poet describes his or her understanding of the *ṣaddiq* (righteous or upright person). This is what it means to be good, the poet writes, and proceeds to enumerate vices in such a manner as to indicate what he or she regards as virtue. The result constitutes a code of ethics.

But is the code Israelite and is it sapiential? Nothing in the catalog of vices falls into the category of distinctive wisdom behavior, and every item could appear in a non-Israelite declaration of innocence. Thus there is a fundamental problem at the outset: how can one determine what is distinctive of Israel's sages in the area of ethics, particularly when the wise share the general world view that pervades the entire Hebrew scriptures as well as Egyptian and Mesopotamian literature?

Our difficulties do not stop with shared viewpoints within the separate portions of the Hebrew Bible. What if the book of Job does not belong to wisdom literature? After all, chapter 31 has the form of Egyptian ritual texts. As a matter of fact, a case can be made against Job as a wisdom writing.[22] None can deny strong affinity between Job and complaints within the book of Psalms and related laments in Mesopotamian texts. The book can certainly be viewed as an example of an answered lament, a model for the appropriate manner of responding to suffering.[23] It also has the form of disputation, specifically, a mythological prologue, a debate, and a divine resolution. In addition, the book freely incorporates material from prophetic literature, especially Isaiah 40—55, and traditions concerning the divine self-manifestation.[24] The ending to the poetic dialogue, specifically God's approach to humans, belongs to prophetic and narrative texts but is ill at home within wisdom contexts.

At the same time, the book bears a striking resemblance to discussion literature in Mesopotamian wisdom, which in itself differs greatly from Israelite sapiential texts. This thematic continuity with wisdom concerns elsewhere, despite formal departure from the customary, poses an urgent question: are form and content inseparable, or can one divorce the two? For the present, we shall assume the two are separate. Job 31 represents wisdom ethics, but not exclusively so. The latter qualification means that Amos or Hosea could subscribe to Job's standard of conduct without reservation. So could the Egyptian sage Amenemopet and his Mesopotamian counterpart.

To understand how it is possible to include Job 31 within sapiential ethics, we need to define biblical wisdom. While there are various attempts to catch wisdom's essence—wisdom is "the ability to cope," "the art of steering"; it is "practical knowledge of the laws of life and of the world, based on experience"; wisdom constitutes "parents' legacy to their children"; it is "the quest for self-understanding and for mastery of the world"—no single definition suffices because of the variety of phenomena that employ the

Hebrew word *ḥokmah* and similar ideas in the ancient Near East.[25] Still, a beginning step toward an adequate definition can be taken.

The first point concerns a scholarly convention. Wisdom signifies a literary corpus. In the Bible the following works are almost universally acknowledged to belong within a collection of Wisdom texts: Proverbs, Ecclesiastes, Job (with reservations), Sirach, and Wisdom of Solomon. However much these literary productions differ from one another, they retain a mysterious ingredient that links them together in a special way. This bond is so powerful that it prompts interpreters to use these works as a norm by which to connect certain psalms with the sages, despite the present context within which the "wisdom psalms" occur.

The same point applies beyond Israel's borders. Certain Egyptian texts identify themselves as "Instructions," that is, advice to prospective administrative officials from wise counselors.[26] Some texts stand apart from other literature by their subject matter, whether skeptical questioning of life's value or rhapsodic proclamations to live it up *(carpe diem)*. Similarly, in Mesopotamia both subject matter and identifying vocabulary set off a significant body of literature that deserves the name "wisdom," even if certain features of that literary corpus differ sharply from Israelite and Egyptian wisdom. These are omen texts, which endeavor to regulate life so as to avoid activity which falls under ill omens and to encourage business when favorable signs are visible, and the magical foundation upon which Mesopotamian wisdom stood.[27]

The second observation about defining Israelite wisdom is that ancient Near Eastern parallels furnish an important clue that assists one in determining precisely what constitutes wisdom. Like all clues, this one must be interpreted, lest it thrust one along winding paths that lead astray. Distinctions within cultures must be honored if one wishes to profit from comparative analysis. For example, not a single example of omen wisdom has survived in Israel,[28] and the putative nature wisdom in Job and Sirach scarcely resembles its Mesopotamian prototype.[29] Still, something unites these widely divergent texts.

The third point: wisdom is a particular attitude toward reality, a world view. That stance survives through time and reaches from one end of the Fertile Crescent to the other. It persists in Israel from clan existence, through court circles, and into scribal settings. The prevalent attitude toward reality survived the collapse of the First Kingdom in Egypt (about 2200 B.C.E.) and the disappearance of Sumerians beyond the Euphrates (around 1750 B.C.E.). That way of looking at things begins with humans as the fundamental point of orientation. It asks what is good for men and women.[30] And it believes that all essential answers can be learned in experience, pregnant with signs about reality itself. That world view assumes a universe in the deepest and richest sense of the word. The one God embedded truth within all of reality. The human responsibility is to search for that insight and thus to learn to live in harmony with the cosmos. In a sense the sage knows the right time for a specific word or deed. It follows that optimism lies at the center of wisdom. This confidence in the world and human potential gives rise to profound skepticism, of course, but such a heart-rending cry bears eloquent testimony to a grand vision of what ought to be, a vision that persists even though despair has overwhelmed the sage.[31]

A fourth observation surfaces from such discussion of attitudes characterizing ancient sages: wisdom expresses itself with remarkable thematic coherence. Wise men and women address common problems, whether the dangers of adultery, the perils of the tongue, the hazards of strong drink, the enigma of undeserved suffering, the inequities of life, or the finality of death.[32] In addition, these sages clothe their intuitions, confirmed by experience, in recognizable dress (proverb, sentence, debate, instruction). As time passes, the style of the sages changes noticeably. Early brief maxims and sayings give way to instructions which in turn are eclipsed by dialogue. The perspective of teachers also varies from the parental admonition to the courtier's political counsel and ultimately to religious dogmatism. Here, too, the supreme honor is bestowed upon wisdom: she gradually assumes separate existence. Dame Wisdom moves freely within two societies; she is truly a citizen of two worlds, the heavenly and the earthly.[33] A caution is in order at this point: many of the above-mentioned themes appear also in patently non-sapiential contexts. The circle is complete; once again the student of wisdom stands before the problem of form and content.

The conclusion reached from this multifaceted approach to defining wisdom is that formally, wisdom consists of proverbial sentence or instruction, debate, intellectual reflection; thematically, wisdom comprises self-evident intuitions about mastering life for human betterment, gropings after life's secrets with regard to innocent suffering, grappling with finitude, and quest for truth concealed in the created order and manifested in Dame Wisdom. When a marriage between form and content exists, there is wisdom literature. Lacking such oneness, a given text participates in biblical wisdom to a greater or lesser extent.

The situation is no less complex when reflecting upon the underlying premise of ancient wisdom. The fundamental assumption, taken for granted in every representative of biblical wisdom, consisted of a conviction that being wise meant a search for and maintenance of order.[34] Propriety, then, is an essential ingredient in wisdom—the right time and place for each deed or word. It follows that the good act constitutes the appropriate one for a given situation. In truth, "for everything there is a time." The universe itself depended upon appropriate human conduct. A word untimely spoken or an act out of sequence threatened the harmony of nature, thus strengthening the forces of chaos that hovered over all creation.

It naturally follows that human actions had cosmic implications. This fact alone gave utmost seriousness to the search for insight, together with the dissemination of that valuable lore from generation to generation. At some moment in remote antiquity God had created the universe orderly, bestowing upon that creation the necessary clues to assure its continued existence. From then on the Creator left human survival to its own devices. Those who used their intelligence to learn the universe's secrets and to live in accord with those secrets fared well; those who refused to do so suffered grievous consequences. In such a world, grace played no role;[35] indeed, to ask for special consideration approached blasphemy, since individuals had the necessary equipment to assure their well being.

Such an understanding of reality produced strong pragmatism. Life in harmony with the principles of the universe eventuated in the good things of society: health, wealth, fame, honor, longevity, progeny. Hedonism in its classical sense received divine sanction. Those who acted in such a way as to secure for themselves the above good things were pleasing God at the same time, for they demonstrated their approval of the creative act. Consequently, asking the important question, "What can I do to achieve happiness?" transcended self-centeredness. In fact, such egocentricity constituted genuine spiritual devotion.

In a society where pragmatism enjoyed religious undergirding, one could expect considerable emphasis upon moderation. The sages did not want anyone to rock the boat. Accordingly, they encouraged any means that would mollify anger, and they refused to become involved in efforts at social reform. Powerless themselves, the sages quickly learned their place in the social world, and recognized the usefulness of bribes, obsequiousness, and general "yesmanship."[36]

Restraint prevailed in other matters as well and assisted greatly toward character formation. The wise saw the dangers of excessive drink and gluttony, just as they realized how readily too much talk could destroy individuals. Good things carried to excess became evil in their consequences. That included piety, which like all virtues carried, imbedded within, a seed of self-importance that could burst forth destructively in due time. As Job knew from personal experience, and Qoheleth surmised, extreme piety came to no good end. It is difficult to tell whether Israel's sages thought punishment for exceptional virtue or vice came from God or humans; perhaps both sources of evil were envisioned.[37]

In some circles of the wise, the fear of Yahweh functioned as the compass point from which they took moral readings. Originally this idea meant "religion," but in time it assumed a technical, restricted sense. Fear of the Lord thus stood at the beginning of all knowledge, and perhaps served as the crowning achievement in wisdom as well. In time torah, that is, revelatory knowledge, became a legitimate subject for study, inasmuch as this sacred deposit contained all truth vouchsafed to Israel.

So long as wisdom represented human achievement, the authority granted counsel and sapiential reflection lacked divine

backing.[38] This does not imply that the sages' observations had no
authority, for they carried the weight of parental standing and
compelled assent through logical cogency. When patriarchs spoke,
children listened. Similarly, when teachers summoned students to
attention, the youngsters obeyed or suffered harsh treatment. To be
sure, proverbs by their very nature compel assent; they ring true,
and one wonders why it took so long to discover such transparent
truth.

That is why the wise refused to reinforce their teachings by
appealing to the doctrine of creation. They could easily have said,
"Do this because God created you and certain actions naturally
follow." Instead, they appealed to a sense of self-interest and relied
upon a capacity to reason things out. To assist others in recognizing
the truth of sapiential discourse, the wise developed a rich
repertoire of rhetoric. Whether admonition or warning, dialogue or
sentence, narrative or poetry, the stylistic device adopted by sages
enhanced the teaching and heightened its authority.[39]

Let me illustrate this point with reference to Proverbs 6:20-35.
This textual unit focuses upon the threat posed by loose women, a
favorite topic of Israelite sages whose blood ran hot like that of most
cultures. Here we have a discourse in which a teacher appeals to
parental authority and invokes *torah* as well. Still, when he wants to
make his point decisively this sage quotes a proverb; that is, he relies
upon consensus, appealing to what all know to be true. His
argument runs as follows. Do not cavort with an adulteress, for
unlike a common whore, she pursues a costly goal: life itself. Can a
man carry live coals in his vest pocket without burning his clothes?
Can one walk barefoot upon hot coals and not burn his feet?[40] The
obvious, though unspoken, answer is "no." Then neither can one
commit adultery without suffering the consequences of such folly.
Again the sage pushes the argument home: do we not despise a thief
who steals even if starving? how much more the hungry lecher will
be stripped of all he has. With remarkable adroitness, the sage plays
on the obscene meanings of fire, food, thief, go in, touch. In
addition, he returns to the beginning by a clever pun on the
similarity between the Hebrew words for woman and fire; otherwise
the redundant reference to a man's commiting adultery *with a*

woman violates Hebrew syntax as grievously as an adulterer violates a marriage.

From Proverbs 9:13-18 it appears that Dame Folly had learned something from the sages' method of argument. In any event, she deigns to press her case with a vacillating individual by quoting a proverb: "Stolen water is sweet, and bread eaten in secret is pleasant." If the sage has given an accurate portrayal of this wanton, we can conclude that she chose to rely upon commonly accepted knowledge. In truth, stolen water and bread signify sexual congress—as any fool knew. The simpleton also knew that forbidden fruit tasted better, at least in fantasy. In this particular unit, the sage has chosen to challenge the insight preserved in proverbial form. This time he appeals to personal authority achieved by means of fuller knowledge.

This appeal within an appeal demonstrates the sages' willingness to defy tradition when the evidence warrants such action. If true wisdom consists of the appropriate deed for the moment, then different situations called for varied responses. In this sense, biblical wisdom is immensely historical despite its complete disregard, until Ben Sira, for special moments in the history of Israel.

Anyone who is only remotely familiar with the content of the biblical book of Proverbs may wonder why I have ignored what occupies the center of the stage there—lengthy discussions of family relations, sexual ethics, political ethics, and general social relations. Without a doubt, the sages have bequeathed to us a comprehensive code of conduct, which they never tired of promoting by every available means.

The family was the most important institution in ancient Israel. Here values were acquired, and character was lovingly shaped. Respect for parents, obedience of their every command, and caring for them in old age functioned as cement to hold a complex society together. Discipline freely rendered signified the importance of learning and learner alike; a father disciplines those he loves. In such a closed social structure, brothers played a significant role. Any act that threatened fraternal peace was anathema. At the same time, the sages knew that friends could be closer than brothers. This perception prompted them to view every true friend as a potential brother or sister in difficult times. The chief threat to the family was sexual; the adulterer was loathsome because of the complete disregard for familial solidarity.

The wise never tired of discussing the dangers of sexual license. The foreign woman, who seems to combine features of ancient fertility religion and common adulterers, posed a health risk for young men, who seemed especially vulnerable to her blandishments. As an antidote to this sickness, the sages suggested reflection upon the teachings; when all else failed, they resorted to poignant portrayal of the awful fate that befell victims who placed themselves in the hands of foreign women. Since the sages concentrated upon sexual deviancy, we must glean from that discussion what was taken for granted. Marriage was the norm, departure from which is never mentioned except for eunuchs.[41] The latter were the subject of genuine sympathy in Sirach, where they are described as embracing lovely women and groaning, and where they are promised special favor in God's sight to compensate for their grievous loss. Naturally, the goal of marriage was procreation.

A definite bias against women permeates biblical wisdom. Women are responsible for perverting a good creation, and they "drink from any available fountain or open their quiver for every arrow," to paraphrase Sirach. At the same time, women are a gift of God and deserve praise from husbands and children, particularly because good wives enhance the reputation of a man in the community.[42]

The latter point calls attention to the larger society within which life unfolds. The sages enjoined social responsibility for justice and encouraged truthful testimony. They conceded that bribes work effectively, and warned against heroic stands in the presence of powerful rulers. Life at court placed great demands upon young men, who had to learn proper table manners, discreet silence, and the art of eloquent reply. In general, the sages taught charity when one had sufficient means, but warned against involvement that might place one in financial jeopardy. They seem not to have objected to monarchy, although the wise knew that kings were subject to baser human emotions, leading to devastating fury.

A union of religion and ethics characterized ancient wisdom. The dichotomy between secular and sacred did not exist in the biblical world. Every act bore religious consequences and arose from a religious understanding of reality. Life with people was at the same time existence in God's presence. Whatever enriched one context enhanced the other; ethical behavior thus assumed ultimate significance.

The brief account of sapiential ethics concerning the family, sexual relations, politics, and so forth, came last in this introductory analysis because nothing in it is exclusively wisdom. Although preserved within wisdom literature, such views were shared by all Israel. Prophets, priests, and lay persons alike endorsed these teachings. So did biblical sages. Once again, a solid wall presents itself: the points of continuity between sages and the rest of society. Thus, the reason for beginning with observations about Job 31, a text that introduces the fundamental problem with which one struggles throughout any attempt to understand sapiential ethics.

What, then, characterizes wisdom's ethic as opposed to shared understandings? Belief in order, though pervasive and highly significant to sages, cannot qualify as distinctively sapiential. What does is a conviction that men and women possess the means of securing their well being—that they do not need and cannot expect divine assistance. From this humanistic stance they achieved an amazing breakthrough: the recognition that virtue is its own reward. Disinterested righteousness emerged as a reality in biblical wisdom. If in truth this perception does capture the distinctive feature of wisdom, that understanding exploded all bounds, for it surfaces in rare texts outside the wisdom corpus.[43] Conversely, the gracious wooing of subjects by the Creator intruded upon wisdom's self-sufficiency, until at last a wedding of Yahwism and wisdom took place. On the other hand, complete skepticism seems also to have characterized biblical wisdom. In this case, no comfort from beyond intrudes; instead, warm arms suffice until death silences one and all.

It follows that wisdom is the reasoned search for specific ways to assure well-being and the implementation of those discoveries in daily existence. Wisdom addresses natural, human, and theological dimensions of reality, and constitutes an attitude toward life, a living tradition, and a literary corpus. Perhaps in the long run one can say about wisdom what a noted critic remarked with regard to a proverb, specifically that it possesses a certain indescribable quality.[44] This book is an attempt to clarify that "certain indescribable quality."

THE PLAN OF THE BOOK

Chapter one will examine the world of wisdom, its language and literary forms. Did Israel's sages see themselves as a distinct group, and if so, what specific features characterized their self-understanding? Naturally, this investigation will concentrate on the wise as an elite class, and it will ask whether this group influenced others within Israelite society.

The second chapter will focus upon the sapiential traditions, hoping to discover central emphases which survived the several stages through which biblical wisdom passed. Since Solomon occupies center stage in this lore, we shall study his supposed role in composing and preserving canonical proverbs. In addition, we hope to demonstrate the way in which important themes arose and assumed increasing significance, especially the notion of personified wisdom.

Chapters three through seven will provide an analysis of the literary corpus: Proverbs, Job, Ecclesiastes, Sirach (Ecclesiasticus), Wisdom of Solomon, and Wisdom Psalms. Each of these discussions will treat the central themes of the book, characterize the chief literary features within each one, and attempt to place the book within the larger context of ancient wisdom.

The eighth chapter will isolate certain abiding contributions of biblical wisdom, specifically the insistence upon a fundamental realism which tests all convictions by experience itself, and the radical skepticism that kept the sages honest and enabled them to cope with every eventuality.

The final chapter will place Israelite wisdom within the ancient Near Eastern setting. This discussion will examine sapiential texts from ancient Egypt and Mesopotamia. Its location at the end of the book suggests that such material functions best in Old Testament scholarship when it *helps to clarify biblical wisdom,* rather than serving as the *norm* by which all else is judged.

CHAPTER 1

The World of Wisdom

One can scarcely imagine a time when the adjective "wise" (*ḥakam*)[1] did not function in ancient Israel. The same is true of the several related terms for sagacity, understanding, prudence, and insight. By their actions certain people demonstrated wisdom, cleverness, skill, while others just as surely exemplified folly. To designate these individuals wise and foolish was not to identify them as members of a distinct class of professional sages or simpletons.

As one might expect, the word "wise" and similar adjectives occur when signifying general ability or special skill at some craft. Those who possessed natural talent and who acquired expertise in weaving, shipbuilding, mourning, metal work, and the like are designated "wise." Such persons possessed wisdom to accomplish a particular task. Similarly, animals are called "wise" because of their instinct for survival which leads them into profitable courses of action. Such uses of *ḥakam* and its derivatives have nothing whatsoever to do with a professional class of "the wise."

In some cases *ḥakam* seems to occur in contexts which imply a more narrowly defined clientele, as if to designate the special domain of a distinct group of people in Israel. According to Jeremiah 18:18, "the law shall not perish from the priest, nor counsel from the wise, nor the word from the prophet." Many critics have seen in this statement an allusion to three classes of leaders in ancient Israel: priests, prophets, and sages.[2] The essential function of each professional group is thus captured in a single word. Priests promulgate instruction (*torah*), prophets proclaim the divine word (*dabar*), and sages give counsel (*ᶜesah*).

A PROFESSIONAL CLASS

The existence of a professional class of sages in Israel has been postulated for various reasons: analogy with Egypt and Mesopotamia, the presence of a literary corpus which reflects sapiential concerns, attacks upon the wise within prophetic texts, and general probability, that is, the likelihood that a royal court would need the particular talents which sages possessed. Although such arguments are hardly decisive, they lend considerable weight to the hypothesis that a special class of sages did exist in Israel.

To be sure, a professional class of courtiers arose quite early in ancient Egypt and Mesopotamia. In Egypt these sages instructed the children of pharaohs and other potential bureaucrats. Their insights concerning proper speech, correct etiquette, and interpersonal relationships proved indispensable to aspiring rulers. Consequently, a system of private education developed, and instructors soon composed texts which survived for centuries in a tradition-oriented culture. Similarly, temple schools became the instrument by which Sumerian and Babylonian scribes acquired special skills which enabled them to assist the government in its various projects, and to provide numerous services for wealthy private citizens.[3]

Such dependence upon sages to carry out the ordinary requisites connected with business transactions was due in large measure to the complex systems of writing in these two countries. Ancient Hebrew presented fewer obstacles to any reasonably intelligent person. For this reason, the argument from analogy lacks real cogency, especially when one takes into consideration the relative simplicity of the Israelite court. Fundamental differences loom large—for example, the significant function of Babylonian sages, interpreting omens, is wholly missing from the Hebrew Bible.

The existence of a body of literature which reflects specific interests at variance with Yahwistic texts in general seems to argue strongly for a professional class of sages in Israel. Within Proverbs, Job, and Ecclesiastes one looks in vain for the dominant themes of Yahwistic thought: the exodus from Egypt, election of Israel, the Davidic covenant, the Mosaic legislation, the patriarchal narratives, the divine control of history and movement toward a glorious moment when right will triumph. Instead, the reader encounters in these three books *a different thought world,* one that stands apart so impressively that scholars have described that literary corpus as an alien body within the Bible.[4]

What is more, that literary corpus has achieved a high degree of artistic merit. Both the quality of the reflection and the beauty of expression testify to studied composition and arrangement. Now such accomplishment demands a unified world view and ample leisure to master sapiential traditions. For this reason alone, several interpreters insist that a professional class of "the wise" must surely have existed in Israel.[5]

This hypothesis that the quality of wisdom literature requires a distinct class may receive some support from the fact that certain prophets direct harsh criticism at "wise" persons who refuse to acknowledge God's control over political events.[6] On the other hand, nothing within these texts *requires* the assumption that the references have a special class of sages in mind. It may be that such passages inveigh against folly which masquerades as wisdom, and thus have nothing to do with a professional group of "the wise."

Still, the several arguments seem to justify the conclusion that a group of professional sages existed in ancient Israel. That verdict does not rest upon the identification of counselors within the Davidic court. Even if Ahithophel and Hushai functioned solely as political advisors, which is probable, the subsequent appearance of "the men of Hezekiah" suggests that a distinctive class of sages existed in the eighth century. At least one function of these men must certainly have been the collecting of proverbs which expressed their own understanding of reality. One noteworthy feature of these proverbs concerns their general applicability: the narrow concerns of the royal court have given way to more universal interests.

CONSCIOUSNESS OF DISTINCTIVENESS

Within the literary corpus preserved by the sages one discovers a strong conviction that "the wise" constitute a distinct group. The starting place in addressing this problem must surely be the comparison between the wise and persons engaged in other pursuits (Sirach 38:24—39:11). With painstaking care, the poet describes the manner in which farmers, craftsmen, smiths, and potters carry on their work. Farmers concentrate singlemindedly on the care of oxen, the means of achieving straight furrows, and the best way to get maximum effort from animals. Similarly, craftsmen and designers labor until late at night, endeavoring to discover the right engraving and to obtain an exact copy of a desired image. So, too, smiths work long hours under intolerable conditions, hoping to achieve the correct pattern once the clamor of hammering is silenced and the intense heat has died away. Likewise, potters crouch over their wheels and race against time to achieve the required quota, and then tarry to clean up the furnace.

This important text does not demean such workers. On the contrary, it admires them for their expertise and praises them as the mortar that holds civilization together. Nevertheless, these persons do not occupy positions of honor, even if by work and prayer they maintain the fabric of the city. Others sit in judgment within the governing assembly, and discuss the complexities of legal proceedings or daily experience as reflected in maxims.

In contrast to these specialists in farming, craft, metals, and pottery, a scholar studies sacred literature, here described as law, wisdom, and prophets. This person "preserves the sayings of famous men and penetrates the intricacies of parables." He also "investigates the hidden meaning of proverbs and knows his way among riddles" (39:3). As a result, he will advise rulers, and frequent travel to faraway places becomes one of many rewards bestowed upon him. Such persons will not keep secret what they have learned, but will transmit it to succeeding generations, both orally and in writing. Ultimately, these individuals will live in the memory of others, who recognize that they were a rare treasure —one in a thousand, to use a phrase preferred by sages.

According to this passage, the crucial difference between sages and persons in other occupations is leisure. Only those who have ample free time can afford to concentrate upon intellectual pursuits. Taking this observation as their clue, several interpreters have suggested that Israel's sages belonged to the upper social class.[7] As wealthy owners of estates they possessed sufficient capital to enable them to cultivate the mind. If this observation is correct, wisdom remains an elite phenomenon. The wise do not possess political power, hence their perceptions about justice cannot be implemented in the face of violence, nor do they claim membership in the oppressed class. When concern for justice surfaces in their teachings, it either registers a protest to God or merely observes the harsh facts of life. The slightest hint of prophetic outcry is wholly lacking in proverbs and maxims.

At the very least, Israel's sages see themselves as a distinct group standing over against fools. This consciousness of radical differences between wise persons and foolish ones has its corollary in the claim that the former are good, the latter, wicked. According to the wise, all people belong to one group or the other, for there is no middle ground. Although this sharp division into two distinct camps may have grown out of antithetical parallelism, the preferred stylistic device characteristic of older proverbial collections, it persists relentlessly in sapiential thought. In fact, at least one modern scholar has viewed this feature of Israelite wisdom as distinctive within ancient Near Eastern texts which are related to the canonical wisdom literature in form and content.[8] It should be noted, however, that the contrast between the silent one and the passionate one in Egypt functions in a comparable manner to the Israelite contrast between wise and fool, good and evil.

THE SAGES' GOAL

Another means of discovering the self-consciousness of Israel's sages is to analyze their stated goal in compiling a body of literature. Precisely what did they hope to achieve by coining proverbs and formulating observations about reality in all its mystery? A host of texts comment upon the aim which motivated the wise.

The canonical book of Proverbs has been given a carefully worded introduction which functions to set the several collections into a common framework. This valuable section (Proverbs 1:2-7) uses many different words to characterize those who master the Solomonic proverbs: wisdom, instruction, understanding, intelligence, righteousness, justice, equity, discretion, knowledge, prudence, learning, and skill. This heaping together of numerous ideas without further elucidation has been appropriately called stereometry. Those who truly listen detect multiple voices competing for attention, each of which rewards close hearing. Every pregnant concept triggers multiple images within the students' imagination, which perceptive individuals grasp to their utter delight.

This passage mentions four kinds of sapiential teaching that students must understand: proverbs, parables, sayings, and riddles. The first of these, the proverb (*mašal*) refers to a basic similitude or likeness,[9] wherein a given phenomenon is set alongside another as illuminating it in some significant fashion. Perhaps, too, the original sense of the word shines through, signifying that proverbs are powerful expressions of truth. The second word, parable (*m^elişah*), seems to point in the direction of sayings which carry a sting hidden within their clever formulation, and may by extension refer to admonitions and warnings. The expression "wise sayings" seems to function as a sort of general category, and consequently serves to identify certain collections within the present book of Proverbs. The final word, riddles (*ḥidoth*), designates enigmatic sayings and perhaps even extensive reflections on the meaning of life and its inequities.[10]

Two further features of this programmatic introduction deserve comment. The first concerns an implied distinction between wisdom and learning, intelligence and skill. It follows that learning is an art, and that one can become expert in the craft, so to speak. The other point I wish to make is that hearing plays an important role in sapiential education, so much so in fact that "the hearing heart" becomes synonymous with sage in ancient Egypt. In Israel, the appeal to a proper hearing or attention occurs with great frequency.

In still another passage within canonical Proverbs a father reflects upon the continuity of the wisdom tradition and his role in that important enterprise (Proverbs 4:1-5). Wisdom almost constitutes a legacy transmitted from parents to children. Appealing to his son for a hearing, the father recalls his own instruction at the feet of his dad, and repeats the earlier promise of long life and warning against deafness. One could almost say nostalgia surfaces, and direct quotation functions to demonstrate the value placed upon paternal teaching.

> He taught me, and said to me,
> "Let your heart hold fast my words;
>   keep my commandments, and live;
>   do not forget, and do not turn away from the words of my
>   mouth."
>
> (4:4-5)

The glance backward employs a formula of self-abnegation ("I, too, have been a father's son"). This particular device recurs in King Solomon's pious self-revelations within Wisdom of Solomon, but he extends the formula in the direction of marital imagery, claiming that God endowed him with a pure soul and boasting that he had consequently wooed Dame Wisdom for his bride.[11]

The reference to a mother within the text under consideration suggests that the words "father" and "sons" function in their natural sense here, although an Egyptian text does exist in which a school boy is said to have been the recipient of tender maternal care.[12] That is, school contexts do not necessarily rule out mention of a mother. While scholars generally assume that "father" and "son" come to mean "teacher" and "student" in canonical Proverbs, nothing prevents a normal understanding of these terms. Even the admonition to acquire wisdom at great cost (Proverbs 4:7) does not invariably point to tuition, and thus to a school setting.[13] It could just as easily suggest the rigors facing anyone who wishes to become wise.

The book of Ecclesiastes closes with some brief observations about the intention lying behind the teacher's work (12:9-12). In this instance, the comments derive from someone other than the author of the sayings attributed to Qoheleth. The description of the Speaker's activity attempts to make his conclusions somewhat more palatable to the larger community.[14] Qoheleth taught what he knew to be true, this epilogue observes, and devoted considerable energy to packaging his teaching. Here we note the desire to present truth in pleasing form; perhaps the mere hint of aesthetic interest on the part of Israel's sages justifies the expenditure of effort to recover the fruits of such endeavor. In any event, the art of persuasion in Israelite wisdom will be dealt with in another volume.[15] In the opinion of the person commenting on Qoheleth's work, the sayings retain their sting even when clothed attractively. In fact, he seems uncertain whether to praise the sayings of one Shepherd, or to warn against further efforts at writing or at grasping the complexities of what stands written. Still, the accuracy and sufficiency of Qoheleth's sayings are attested, inasmuch as they direct those assembled before him.

With regard to conscious articulation of pedagogic goals, Sirach makes up for what is lacking in Job. The translator's preface compiled by Sirach's grandson who rendered the work from Hebrew into Greek so as to make its teachings available to Jews in Alexandria, acknowledges that students of the Bible owe a debt to the outside world. Interestingly, this explanation for Sirach's intellectual effort breathes the same spirit as the book itself, where wisdom categories mingle with legal ones. While the themes accord with concerns of earlier sages (discipline and wisdom), the means of achieving proficiency is said to be adherence to the law, thus signaling a new note in sapiential texts.

The sufficiency of divine commandments prompted Sirach to warn against idle speculation about subjects which God had chosen to keep secret (3:17-24). Here one comes upon an astonishing attitude toward intellectual pursuits: do not try to discover the meaning of things that are too difficult for you, for what God withholds is of no concern.

Do not meddle in what is beyond your tasks,
> for matters too great for human understanding have been shown
> you.
For their hasty judgment has led many astray,
> and wrong opinion has caused their thoughts to slip.

(Sirach 3:23-24)

Apparently, danger from apocalyptic movements and Greek philosophical speculations caused Sirach at this point to lose all contact with a legitimate stream within ancient wisdom, the probing of riddles and all kinds of enigmas. Elsewhere he opposes the practice of predicting the future by means of dreams, but the effectiveness of his observations suffers through a qualifying concession that dreams sent by God do possess great significance. Omen wisdom, which had thrived in ancient Mesopotamia, now threatens to invade biblical wisdom in disguise. Sirach's warning against this threat, like so many other teachings, never really achieves consistency. In 14:20, for example, he declares the one who ponders wisdom's secrets to be happy indeed.

In another setting Sirach reflects upon the long line of tradition by which fathers pass their teachings along to their children (8:8-9). In this instance he focuses upon the high office of counselors to princes, which befalls those who master the art of appropriate reply. Learned maxims should be studied diligently, inasmuch as they embody truths which past generations have tested and found reliable before transmitting them to succeeding ones. Elsewhere he concedes the fact that much effort has gone into the formulating of proverbs (13:26), a point forcefully put forth in the epilogue to Ecclesiastes.

Sirach's contrast between scholars and persons in other occupations, which we discussed earlier, concludes with a glowing description of the advantages enjoyed by sages (39:1-11). Students of the entire Hebrew canon, here presented in the unusual sequence "Law, Wisdom, and Prophets," with wisdom occupying the second rather than third position, Israel's sages preserve the sayings of famous men and penetrate the intricacies of parables; "they investigate the hidden meaning of proverbs and know their way among riddles" (39:2-3, altered). The terminological affinities between this text and the prologue in Proverbs indicate a desire to demonstrate continuity with past scholarship. With justifiable pride, Sirach writes that God willing, the devout sage will be inspired to pour out his own wise sayings, something which Sirach takes pains to demonstrate by his own life and teachings. More than once he confesses that his own wise sayings threaten to overflow their banks like a raging flood. Having finished his inspired utterance, he proceeds to identify himself and to urge attention to his book just as one would study the other sacred texts (50:27-29). Only here do we encounter an expression comparable to our pride of authorship. All previous wisdom books in Israel remain anonymous to this day, with the exception of two foreign treatises which have been attributed to Agur (Proverbs 30:1-4) and Lemuel's mother (Proverbs 31:1-9). For the rest, it sufficed to call them "Solomonic" or to ignore the issue of authorship altogether.

The concluding thanksgiving prayer in Sirach (51:1-12) trails off into a long self-congratulatory account in which he connects piety and wisdom in such a way as to present himself as a worthy teacher. Naturally, Sirach invites prospective students to dwell in his house of learning so that their thirst would be slaked without going on a long journey to acquire wisdom, perhaps to Alexandria. This is the first reference to an actual school in Israelite literature; whether this institution had newly arisen in Sirach's time remains a disputed point. The possible objection to the high cost of tuition and lodging may have prompted the reminder that gold will come in return for silver expended. The religious dimension echoes throughout this highly mundane appeal for means of livelihood. Demonstrating his familiarity with Scripture, Sirach alludes to Deutero-Isaiah's great invitation to "buy without money" and to quench their thirst (Isaiah 55:1-2).

LITERARY FORMS

If we are correct in assuming that the wise constituted a distinct class within Israel, we may make another assumption: that these sages used a characteristic mode of discourse. It follows that the literary forms within Job, Proverbs, Ecclesiastes, Sirach, and Wisdom of Solomon comprise a special world of communication which can only be understood in terms of its own categories. What were the peculiar wisdom forms? We shall examine eight literary categories: proverb, riddle, allegory, hymn, dialogue, autobiographical narrative, noun lists, and didactic narrative (poetry and prose).[16]

The simple saying registers a conclusion which has arisen through observation of nature, animal behavior, or human conduct. Its form is succinct, epigrammatic, and metaphorical. Such *proverbs* need not include a pedagogic intent, since the desire to teach others seems to have arisen at a secondary stage in the process of proverb composition. Once the impulse to teach became dominant, syntax was altered so as to include motivation clauses, warnings, and the like. In the process, a distinct type of proverb emerged: instruction. Both sentence and instruction aimed at brevity and placed a premium on their capacity to be remembered. Imagery which made a lasting impression ranked high in the eyes of those who composed proverbs; naturally, similes possessed a remarkable power to linger in the memories of those who valued instruction. Who could easily forget the comparison of sluggards upon their bed with a door upon its hinges, or the likening of a beautiful woman lacking discretion to a pig with a gold ring in its snout?

Although no pure *riddle* has survived within the wisdom corpus, there can be little doubt that ancient sages coined enigmas. We have seen that Ben Sira thought the solving of riddles belonged to the essential tasks of the wise. The ingredients of a riddle are (1) cipher language that (2) simultaneously informs and conceals. It follows that riddles function both as clue and snare. Within wisdom literature certain vestiges of cipher language have survived, particularly in allegorical contexts.

Two *allegorical* texts stand out as worthy links with riddles; these are the poignant description of old age in Ecclesiastes 12:1-8 and the exquisite advice about marital fidelity in Proverbs 5:15-23, where a wife is likened to a cistern from which one drinks life-giving water. In both instances ciphers function on two levels at the same time, so that one must distinguish between general and special language. Cistern, for example, has two distinct meanings, and only those who possessed special knowledge grasped the cipher's full sense.

Although the sages did not invent the category of *hymn*, they fashioned their own particular kind of song about Dame Wisdom or about the inaccessability of wisdom. The latter exalts humans in remarkable fashion, since they explore the inner recesses of the earth while searching for rare metals, but at the same time the hymn recognizes human limits. Thus it concludes by praising God who alone has access to wisdom. The hymns concerning God's self-revelation through personified wisdom resemble those hymnic texts throughout the Hebrew Bible which rejoice in God's goodness and power. In the case of wisdom hymns, emphasis falls upon the role of wisdom in creation and in making known God's will to humans. Similarly, prayers take on special features when sages utter them, particularly in those cases where the acquisition of wisdom is under discussion.

Perhaps the supreme achievement of sapiential rhetoric was the *disputation,* or *dialogue.* Its peculiar characteristics, in distinction from prophetic disputes, include a mythological introduction and conclusion, the dialogue proper, and a divine resolution. Of course, the book of Job has all three of these formal features, which also characterize comparable discussions of the problem of undeserved suffering in ancient Babylonia. One text, *I Will Praise the Lord of Wisdom,* lacks a dialogue between friends, but this feature occurs in *The Babylonian Theodicy.* A variant of the disputation, imagined speech, occurs frequently in Israelite wisdom literature. Once again, prophetic texts have similar passages, although the content differs notably from the sapiential texts.

The sages developed a special type of *autobiographical narrative* which allowed them to communicate a lesson from personal experience. Wisdom's firm roots in experience provide the occasion for profiting from what one sees, even if that object lesson is played out in someone else's life. The sages pass by and observe significant features of the environment and portentous behavior on the part of human beings; later these teachers put that knowledge to effective use.

The literary category known as *noun lists* has not survived as such in the Old Testament, but certain numerical proverbs indicate that the type of thinking which produced exhaustive lists of flora, fauna, and the like has given rise to a secondary stage in which this information has been put to work in the service of instruction concerning morals. To be sure, some critics think the divine speeches within the book of Job contain echoes of ancient noun lists, and the same goes for the description of the different types of work in Sirach.[17] Evidence for viewing these texts as a late form of noun lists is scant, even if they represent the same kind of encyclopedic thinking that produced comprehensive lists of various phenomena.

Another important literary form which the sages adapted to their own purposes is the *didactic narrative*. An exquisite example of the story-sermon exists in Proverbs 7:6-23, where a seductress leads an unfortunate young man to his ruin. The author of such texts uses every available means to heighten the impact of the story. Naturally, appeal to personal experience and superior knowledge occurs with regularity. Didactic poetry aims at the same kind of edification, although it often shows signs of real personal struggle, especially where divine justice is concerned.

This brief discussion of sapiential literary forms has indicated the difficulty of isolating specific categories which were the peculiar domain of sages. The difficulty is exacerbated when one tries to identify exclusive sapiential vocabulary. Since Israel's sages did not dwell in isolation, and consequently spoke the language of everyday usage, such attempts at discovering the special terminology of the wise inevitably abort. For this reason, we shall not try to identify sapiential vocabulary. In truth, all such investigations stumble over their own circular reasoning,[18] for the favorite expressions in wisdom literature also functioned in a non-technical manner throughout Israelite society. This observation applies, above all, to such words as wise, intelligent, understanding, knowledge, and the like.

WISDOM INFLUENCE

The attempt to recognize wisdom influence in canonical texts other than Proverbs, Job, and Ecclesiastes encounters the same problems. Since that pursuit of a larger sapiential corpus has made far-reaching claims in recent literature, we shall describe that endeavor, without trying to be exhaustive.

Within certain liturgical passages in Isaiah (9:6; 11:2, 9), but also in non-liturgical texts (28:23-29; 31:2) emphasis falls upon wisdom and understanding, so much so that some interpreters have thought that Isaiah was originally a member of the sages,[19] but submitted to a prophetic summons and turned his back upon old friends. Not all critics who recognize wisdom influence upon Isaiah assume that he once was a professional sage; instead they claim that the prophet has made free use of sapiential vocabulary, especially with regard to agricultural data and the torah.[20]

Similar conclusions have been reached concerning Amos, whose home town is said to have been a center of wisdom.[21] Various types of argument have been mustered to place Amos squarely within clan wisdom: linguistic phenomena, such as the peculiar kind of numerical sayings; theological emphases, for example, the universalistic message which submits all peoples to God's judgment; special vocabulary, like Sheol, "right," and so forth; unusual rhetorical devices, for instance the "woe" sayings. This sort of reasoning has also led to the claim that Micah should be understood against the background of clan wisdom.[22] Similarly, Jonah is thought by some to have been written under wisdom influence, since its message endorses universalism and the entire book wrestles with the problem of divine justice. Moreover, the literary form which the book takes, that of a *mašal,* is at home among sages.[23]

Within historical literature, the succession narrative (2 Samuel 9—20; 1 Kings 1—2) has been attributed to a wisdom writer who sought to illustrate the teachings of various proverbs by telling a story in which eternal truths find embodiment.[24] The same goes for the Yahwistic narrative, which at least one author thinks constitutes a conflation of wisdom and history.[25] Such an astonishing conclusion derives much of its inspiration from the claim that the Joseph narrative was composed by a sage in the royal court who sought to provide a model for professional courtiers.[26] The association of court tales and wisdom has also led to the observation that Esther was written by a sage who wished to demonstrate the rewards which accrue to those who combine wisdom and integrity.[27]

Even the primeval history (Genesis 1—11) has been broken up to make way for wisdom influence in specific units, especially the story of the fall, which alludes to a tree of knowledge and refers to the knowledge of good and evil.[28] One interpreter has gone so far as to see the entire primeval history as a product of the sages.[29]

Beyond these larger units, wisdom influence has been found in numerous verses and individual chapters. For example, the majestic description of God's attributes in Exodus 34:6-7, which is alluded to in Jonah, is thought to derive from a sage.[30] This trend has caught on so widely that the entire Hebrew canon is in danger of being swallowed. For example, the book of Deuteronomy, which reeks with covenantal language and election categories, has been attributed to sapiential authorship,[31] and the claim has arisen that wisdom gave birth to apocalyptic.[32] Clearly, such widening of the net threatens to distort the meaning of wisdom beyond repair. In every instance these claims rest upon circular reasoning. Therefore, this discussion will restrict itself to those literary works which are widely acknowledged to comprise the legacy of the sages.[33] That legacy constitutes a tradition that Israel's sages endeavored to conserve and to transmit from generation to generation.

CHAPTER 2

The
Sapiential Tradition

The thesis that Israel's sages comprised a distinct professional class gains further support from a consciousness that the wise were transmitting a valuable tradition. Job's friend, Eliphaz, interjects the following remark:

"I will show you, hear me;
    and what I have seen I will declare
(what wise men have told,
    and their fathers have not hidden . . .)."

(Job 15:17-18)

This sense of urgency which prompted a desire to pass along vital lore underlies the father's plea for a hearing which occurs frequently in Proverbs. Even a sage like the author of Ecclesiastes, who stands in open opposition to "school" tradition,[1] finds it impossible to *ignore* that sapiential tradition. The central figure in that tradition was King Solomon. In what follows, we shall examine the traditions about Solomon as Israel's greatest sage. Clarification of this significant elevation of a royal figure should enable us to grasp the manner in which other sapiential traditions emerged.

SOLOMON AS SAGE PAR EXCELLENCE

Tantalizingly enigmatic language characterizes the story describing the unnamed Queen of Sheba's visit to Jerusalem for the purpose of testing Solomon's wisdom *bᵉḥidot* (by means of riddles, 1 Kings 10:1-13). Certain phrases tease the imagination in extraordinary fashion. Drawn by the legendary language of hyperbole, the references to gold, precious stones, spices, and the allusion to "the half has not been told," Jewish weavers of fantasy readily seized upon these provocative expressions and turned Solomon into a king on the make.[2] The summary statement, "And King Solomon gave to the Queen of Sheba all that she desired," explodes with eroticism when set alongside the comment that "There was no more strength in her" and "there was nothing hidden from the King." Later fantasy substituted a son for the Queen's squandered energy, and identified him with Israel's notorious enemy, Nebuchadnezzar.

The Queen's loyal subjects engaged in flight of fantasy too, hoping to capitalize on the result of honor's compromise. In their lore Solomon had his way with the Queen through subterfuge, and the son born to their brief union brought divine favor and presence with him to Ethiopia. Two different traditions tell of the deceitful way Solomon gained access to the Queen. In both she agreed to share Solomon's bedroom if he would not force her, but promised that if she ate anything during the night he could cohabit with her. Each story describes Solomon's treachery. In one, he served an exceedingly salty meal, making her thirsty for some water conveniently placed by her bed. In the other, he suspended some honey from the ceiling, and its fragrance eventually enticed her to reach out for it. The young son born from Solomon's act of lust and deceit later visited his father; after a short stay at the court of Jerusalem, he returned to Ethiopia accompanied by a retinue of Hebrew sages who were so impressed by Solomon's son that they followed him to Ethiopia and took along the sacred ark.

Arabic and Christian legend embellished the story even more, now at the expense of Sheba's Queen. In these stories she appears as a demon, and Solomon used his wits to discover her true nature. In some versions he applied a special depilatory and removed ugly hairs from her feet; in others the ass-footed demon refused to cross a bridge because she knew that its wood would eventually form the cross upon which Jesus was to be slain. In medieval legend riddles were supplied for the story, and the scene depicting the

Queen's visit adorns tapestries and tavern walls throughout
Europe. Even the oldest collection of Germanic riddles, the
Strassburg Book of Riddles,[3] contains a woodcutting that depicts
Solomon and the Queen of Sheba. The latter presents him with two
bouquets of flowers, one real and one artificial, asking him to
identify each. Hovering over the genuine flowers is a bee, a
messenger of truth to Solomon.

An impregnable mountain called Fantasy stands between
biblical interpreters and the historical Solomon.[4] In all his glory
King Solomon compares unfavorably with lilies of the field, but
none born of woman can compel him to stand aside when awards for
fame are passed out. If Solomon were to accompany Inanna into the
underworld, perhaps we could finally observe the real Solomon,
stripped of all trappings of wealth.[5] Sheol, unfortunately, is not
peopled with creatures whose function is the removal of pieces of
apparel. The task, it follows, is to scale the mountain of tradition.

Disregarding the aforementioned Jewish, Ethiopic, Christian,
and Arabic legends, we come to yet earlier speculation about
Solomon's wisdom, a theme running through the apocryphal
Wisdom of Solomon. The association of his name with a text written
in Greek is a derivative tradition. The legend, by this time full
blown, prompts talk about a marriage between Solomon and
Wisdom, now understood as divine hypostasis, the earthly
expression of God's intelligence. "I loved her and sought her from
my youth, and I desired to take her for my bride, and I became
enamored of her beauty" (Wisdom 8:2). Here and throughout this
section is a midrash upon a legend in 1 Kings 3:3-14, God's
unlimited offer to Solomon and the young king's request for
wisdom. Another book, Eccelesiastes, halfheartedly attempts the
literary fiction of Solomonic authorship, although the name is never
given. Instead, the author adopts the title Qoheleth, perhaps with
reference to Solomon as a gatherer of women, and speaks of himself
as "the son of David, king in Jerusalem" (Ecclesiastes 1:1). In this
same vein, Solomon's name is associated with the superlative songs
celebrating the joys of sex. Here one reads in the opening line: "The
Song of Songs, which is Solomon's." Elsewhere Solomon is
mentioned, however, in the third person (1:5; 3:7, 9, 11; 8:11-12).

Certain superscriptions in collections of biblical Proverbs derive from an earlier period, though still looking back upon the era of Hezekiah when wisdom flourished. Information gleaned from the book of Isaiah confirms the presence of an active group of sages at this time, prompting considerable discussion of Isaiah and wisdom. Essentially three forms of superscription occur in Proverbs: (1) "The proverbs of Solomon" (10:1); (2) "The proverbs of Solomon, son of David, king of Israel" (1:1); and (3) "These also are proverbs of Solomon which the men of Hezekiah king of Judah copied" (25:1). Perhaps these men of Hezekiah who presumably transmitted and copied proverbial collections link up with a phrase uttered by the Queen of Sheba. That expression, "Happy your men," need not be emended. David surrounded himself with his own entourage, skilled warriors with special responsibilities, and Hezekiah seems to have done the same thing. Since mastery of one's emotions is preferable to physical prowess (Proverbs 16:32), Hezekiah's men may indeed have been sages rather than warriors.

Mention of Solomon within at least one of the superscriptions (Proverbs 25:1) to the various collections of Proverbs postdates Hezekiah. Another derives from a period sufficiently removed from Solomon's monarchy to necessitate an identifying qualification ("Son of David, king of Israel" [1:1]). Only one superscription (10:1) has any claim to an earlier period than Hezekiah, and it can hardly be dated. In short, nothing within the superscriptions demands a date prior to the eighth or seventh centuries. This fact must be kept in mind when raising the larger question of compositional dates for the several proverbial collections. Positive proof of a tenth century date for certain proverbs still would not require us to ascribe Solomonic authorship to them, although making it a live option. Thus far no demonstration of a tenth century date for proverbs has appeared, even if the trend to consider the collections to derive from the period of the monarchy seems correct for all but the first (Proverbs 1—9).[6]

The Deuteronomistic historian preserves three further narratives that throw considerable light upon the tradition of Solomonic wisdom. In each of these, Solomon's dream at Gibeon (1 Kings 3:4-15), the royal judgment in a case of disputed parentage (1 Kings

3:16-28), and the king's literary activity (1 Kings 4:29-34), Deuteronomistic language and vocabulary which is typical of predominately late literary works abounds. In addition, each story makes copious use of stylistic traits and motifs typical of legend. Any attemps to peel away legendary accretions in search of historical record cannot succeed unless these fictional aspects of the stories are taken with utmost seriousness.

The account of Solomon's dream at Gibeon constitutes an old defense of that cult center. Its preservation in the Deuteronomistic history is astonishing, since exclusive worship at a central sanctuary in Jerusalem plays such an important role in that work. This special plea in Gibeon's behalf reflects the practice of incubation, by which a devotee of a particular deity slept at a sanctuary hoping to receive a visit from the god in question. The story teems with features that do not belong within wisdom texts, suggesting that the gift of wisdom is either a secondary development or that the language about wisdom is used in a general rather than a technical sense. Within wisdom literature only in Sirach do we encounter the description of Israel as God's chosen people who are so numerous they cannot be counted. What is more, dreams play no role in sapiential texts, although this particular incident may explain Sirach's ambivalence toward them.[7] On the one hand, he knows they pose a threat to individuals, but he also recognizes that God may use dreams to accomplish his will.

Actually, the putative "wisdom" language belongs to royal ceremony. The clue to such an understanding of the passage is provided by Solomon's formula of humility: "I am a little boy; I don't know how to go out or to come in" (3:7).[8] Like kings throughout the ancient Near East, Solomon confesses his dependence upon his god. Other features of this text recall Egyptian literature as well. In response to the blank check which God offered to Solomon ("Ask what I shall give you" [author's translation]), the young king requested a *hearing heart* to judge God's people, discerning good and evil.[9] When a pleased God announced the gift which he intended to grant the pious ruler, he varied the language significantly: "I give you a wise heart and unparalleled understanding" (author's translation). Naturally, Solomon received as a bonus those things on which he was discreetly silent: riches and honor.

The story about two harlots (1 Kings 3:16-28) is intricately connected with this account of God's gift to Solomon, for it demonstrates the king's hearing heart to judge God's people.[10] Even those individuals who have no social status stand boldly before the divine representative, who disseminates pure justice. The tale is a polished narrative, and begs to be analyzed in depth. Such an explication would begin with the excessive wordiness of the two women, which undoubtedly signifies their extreme nervousness in the presence of royalty. The first harlot takes great pains to rule out the possibility of a guilty third person: "We two were together in the same house, and there was no one else, just the two of us" (author's translation). Later both harlots press their claims with complete abandon, provoking the king to describe the dilemma facing him in their own words: the one says "the living child is mine, and the dead one hers" (author's translation) and the other says, "No, for your child is dead and mine is alive" (author's translation).

The story demonstrates rare psychological insight in yet another way. Solomon's verdict relies upon maternal instinct, that compassion for the fruit of the womb that few mothers could abandon. Strangely, the narrator seems compelled to explain this reality, lest simple-minded persons miss it. Nevertheless, there is curious silence with regard to the reasons prompting the original exchange of the dead boy for the living one under cloak of darkness, for one can assume that a child was no great blessing to a harlot. The story is entirely consistent, for it also explains why the mother of the live child woke up early in the morning; she was motivated by a desire to nurse the infant.

Solomon's test brought out the basest and noblest feelings within the two women. The threat of cutting the child into two halves, each to be presented to one of the harlots, evoked tender compassion from the true mother, but it also provoked bitter resentment within the woman who had accidentally smothered her own son. Here is a singular example of a king's hearing heart for judging between good and evil. Such a wise king can speak with utter confidence: "Give her the living child, and by no means kill it; she is his mother" (author's translation).

Now all Israel saw evidence that God's wisdom rested upon King Solomon. In all fairness, we must acknowledge that the basic story antedates Israel's king by quite some time, and surfaces in many different cultures. As many as twenty-two variants of the story have been located, the earliest of which is thought to come from India.[11] Like the pregnant motif of the "third day," which also occurs in this story and often elsewhere to signify a significant transition point in ancient literature,[12] this incident was popular far and wide, since it honored the ruler and assured everyone that justice lay within his or her grasp. It follows that this story has been adapted by the Israelite narrator and secondarily applied to Solomon. Hence it hardly supplies authentic material from Solomon's era.

The third narrative alludes to Solomon's skill at coining proverbs and songs, praising him as superior to all peoples of the East and of Egypt (5:9-14, Hebrew Bible, hereafter Heb.).

Four persons renowned for their wisdom are mentioned (Ethan the Ezrahite, Heman, Calcol and Darda, sons of Mahol). The number of proverbs ascribed to Solomon is three thousand; his songs are set at one thousand and five. Their subject matter includes trees, beasts, birds, reptiles, and fish. Within canonical wisdom literature we search in vain for proverbs and songs that deal with these topics. The brief miscellaneous collection of numerical proverbs in chapter 30 constitutes the single exception. In short, Solomon's literary works either were non-existent or have disappeared.

Another text throws indirect light upon traditions about Solomon. Deuteronomy 17:14-20 warns against enthroning a king who will multiply horses, wives, silver, and gold. Few scholars today doubt that Solomon sat for this portrait, one that must have appealed greatly to King Hezekiah, who by the grace of the Assyrian military machine no longer had a rival upon the throne at Samaria and, like Solomon, was free to dream great things. Since wisdom is missing from this passage reflecting the Solomonic tradition, perhaps we should discount the text altogether. On the other hand, silence with regard to the function of wisdom at the royal court may be more significant than it appears on the surface.

Scattered stories within the Hebrew Bible register suspicion about wisdom, since it can be used to accomplish rather dubious ends.[13] The old story about the crafty serpent who seduced the first woman and man to rebel against external authority demonstrates an awareness of wisdom's questionable features from ancient times. Similarly, the description of Jonadab as clever enough to devise a means for Amnon to obtain his dishonorable wishes with Tamar, his half sister, shows how widespread the knowledge of wisdom's devious ends had come to be in Israel. When one also considers the incidents involving the wise woman of Teqoa[14] and the wise mother in Abel,[15] both of whom use their craftiness to achieve at the very least questionable goals, the negative attitude toward wisdom is certainly one that made its presence felt in the Israelite community. The prominence that foreign powers gave to its sages, and the conflicts arising within the political arena, naturally strengthened this suspicion with regard to wisdom. Small wonder wisdom was not viewed as an attribute of God until quite late in the Hebrew Bible,[16] for those humans who acquired *hokmah* did not always use it to accomplish noble goals.

Now it is possible that the Deuteronomist knew this negative attitude toward wisdom and subscribed to it. If so, his failure to mention wisdom in this portrait of Solomon might indicate the legend about that king's mastery of wisdom had not yet arisen.

In sum, our examination of the biblical traditions about Solomon's wisdom discovers no shred of evidence deriving from the era of that king. Instead, every account teems with material typical of popular legend and folklore. The only possible authentic allusion, Solomon's reputation for composing proverbs and songs with a subject matter vastly different from those preserved within the canon, is so full of legend that fact cannot be separated from fiction.

Our ascent of the mountain constructed by biblical legend has led us to a vantage point from which we perceive still another peak obscured by low–lying clouds. That range of mountains has been erected by scholars reflecting upon biblical materials. For a brief moment the burning sun penetrates the clouds and illuminates one pathway that leads directly to the top. Signs along the way read "Le mirage salomonien" and "Solomon's posthumous reputation for wisdom."[17] One well-known traveler along this route refuses to mention Solomon at all in a comprehensive study of ancient oriental wisdom in its Israelite-Jewish configuration.[18] To these journeyers, the legendary mountain poses no obstacle. Wisdom and Solomon have nothing to do with one another.

For others, the reality of the mountain is beyond question. It is founded on solid fact rather than legend.[19] Accordingly, new mounds of dirt and stone are forever brought to the mountain. Let us examine this glorification of Solomon by modern exegetes.

Perhaps the least satisfactory view is that which attributes proverbs and songs to Solomon, but explains their disappearance as the result of their inferior quality. When judged against standards which later sages achieved, Solomon's attempts at composition paled by comparison. More importantly, by the time the various proverbial collections were taking final shape, the Solomonic songs and proverbs had become archaic beyond comprehension.[20] The essential flaw in this argument lies in the consequent loss of an explanation for the son of David's reputation for great wisdom. If Solomon's contribution to the literary heritage of the ancient sages possessed only momentary value and if the compositions were mediocre, why did the wise honor him as sage par excellence?

A more attractive hypothesis draws heavily upon parallels in Egypt and Mesopotmia where noun lists (onomastica) functioned as a means of ordering the vast store of knowledge achieved by students of nature.[21] The subject matter of Solomon's proverbs and songs, according to 1 Kings 4:32-33 (Heb. 5:12-13), resembles these noun lists more than the so-called Solomonic proverbs within the Bible.

> He spoke of trees, from the cedar that is in Lebanon to the hyssop that grows out of the wall; he spoke also of beasts, and of birds, and of reptiles, and of fish.

With the exception of a few numerical sayings in Proverbs 30, the proverbial teachings of the wise manifest little interest in natural phenomena. It follows that the Israelite beginnings in natural science were lost to posterity, although not as a result of their inferiority. On the contrary, Solomon adapted such noun lists to his own use, transforming them into poetic compositions. This demonstration of originality, daring, and ability explains the honor bestowed upon Israel's king, who excelled the renowned sages of the east.

While such an explanation for the disparity between the tradition in 1 Kings 4:32-33 and the actual content of canonical proverbs is inherently plausible, it rests upon several dubious assumptions. The first concerns the non-didactic character of noun lists as opposed to the moralizing tendency within biblical proverbs which allude to animals, insects, and the like. What precludes an interpretation of Solomon's proverbs and songs from the background of these sayings which draw lessons from the world of nature? Stated another way, what requires a jump from natural phenomena to noun lists? The supposed onomastica within the divine speeches recorded in the book of Job[22] function as a powerful lesson that those who think they can tell God how to govern the universe should master their own little world before trying to branch out to the remote reaches of space. Another objection centers upon the claim that Solomon's superiority over other sages arose from poetic craft. Nothing supports the view that Solomon freely rendered noun lists into poetic form. On the face of it, the text suggests that his superiority derived from the vast number of proverbs and songs, for the clear emphasis lies there rather than upon their external form. A third objection presents itself as particularly forceful: such proverbs and songs may have constituted riddles and fables which became lost over the years. Since animals, trees, and insects are essential to these literary forms, and Israel's sages undoubtedly composed enigmatic sayings, this explanation is more natural than resorting to onomastica for which there is no clear evidence within biblical wisdom. In short, why appeal to Egyptian and Mesopotamian texts for clarification of 1 Kings 4:32-33 when a better explanation can be formulated on the basis of Israelite sapiential literature.

These observations demonstrate the difficulties accompanying every attempt to view 1 Kings 4:32-33 as reliable information about King Solomon. A negative decision with regard to the historicity of this text does not preclude Solomonic literary activity, although it renders such unlikely. One could still associate Solomon with Israel's sages in another manner. He may very well have functioned as "patron of the arts," and in this capacity the full weight of royal privilege and resources may have become accessible to the sages. Solomon's bold attempt to establish a government faintly resembling the Egyptian pattern lends credibility to this hypothesis of royal patronage for wisdom, but the case is by no means established beyond reasonable doubt.

If in truth the king did take an active interest in promoting the intellectual life of his court, the era may have become significant in shaping the literary traditions of ancient Israel, as many interpreters believe.[23] Such a burst of activity may have vastly extended the scope of knowledge in tenth century Jerusalem, particularly with respect to models for conduct, a cultivation of the individual, a nursing of rhetoric, and scientific interests. Naturally, this new departure would have maintained an openness to knowledge acquired from all peoples, so that a humanistic spirit emerged and focused upon psychological insights into what it means to be truly human. Perhaps such humanism gave birth to a radically new understanding of God's activity among the people. No longer breaking into ordinary events, God's actions could now be perceived only by eyes of faith, and a distant Lord accomplishes his purpose through human agents. Hidden within this understanding of divine activity was the seed that soon sprouted and grew into full-blown skepticism.[24]

While this elevation of the Solomonic era may be on target, it remains a hypothesis for which little supportive evidence exists. For that reason alone, the phrase "Solomonic enlightenment" seems inappropriate.[25] In short, the theory of a Solomonic enlightenment claims that the old view of things, that is, pan sacralism, vanished with this era, and in its place a fresh breeze of humanism swept through the royal court. In truth, secularistic and sacral thinking existed alongside one another from the very beginning. The most that can reliably be asserted is that the emphasis may have shifted appreciably in Solomon's day, but even the literature that supposedly dates from this period bears distinctive signs of sacral thinking. Clearly, the conviction that God honors certain sacred acts thrives within the Succession Narrative (2 Samuel 9—20; 1 Kings 1—2) and the Joseph story. On the other hand, the Samson saga provides strong evidence that secularism invaded the bastion of pan sacrality long before the era of Solomon, for the earlier form of Samson's heroic exploits must surely antedate the tenth century. When this datum is added to the sacral emphases within the Succession Narrative (for example, David's consulting the Lord at crucial times, his submission before the power of a curse, obedience to a prophetic oracle, agonizing in prayer before God on behalf of his sick child, and his devoted servants' selfless act in pouring out water acquired at great peril), the weakness of the claim that the sacral interpretation of reality disappeared with the Solomonic era becomes apparent.

Even the thesis that a fresh wave of humanism and concern for the individual characterized the period overlooks harsh reality, for Solomon stopped at nothing to fill the royal coffers. His rule was almost unrivaled for tyranny in ancient Israel; oppression of subjects who were forced to perform slave labor and from whom exorbitant taxes were exacted ruled the day. While such cruelty could go hand in hand with scholarly activity of an unprecedented nature, this suppression of human beings demands that one use the word "enlightenment" cautiously if at all.

To be sure, Solomon's connections with Egypt were sealed through royal marriage, but the leap to sponsorship of sapiential activity is a major one. Supportive evidence does not necessarily come from royal liturgies within Isaiah 9 and 11, for such texts inevitably emphasize a king's exceptional wisdom. Canaanite literature as reflected in Ezekiel 28 furnishes a satisfactory background for convictions that the ruler possesses wisdom sufficient for the task committed to him. As for the presence of counselors in David's court, nothing requires an interpretation of the word yoʻeṣim (counselors) as a technical term for sages.[26] As a matter of fact, Ahithophel and Hushai function in a purely political role.

To recapitulate, biblical traditions about Solomon's great wisdom are late legends, while the fame he enjoys among biblical interpreters is equally undeserved. How did Solomon's connections with wisdom arise? One answer is that such legends grew because they were grounded in fact. The decisive factor in this view has been the disparity between biblical proverbs and the reputed character of Solomon's literary compositions. Another explanation for the legends can be given, one so simple that it conceals its cogency. The fundamental premise of the wise is the orderliness of creation, or stated another way, belief in the calculable quality of reality. Wisdom leads to life, folly to death. Wisdom secures one's being, granting wealth and happiness. The significance of this profound faith cannot be exaggerated for the entire wisdom corpus, even if it functions as a foil for Ecclesiastes.

Now the equation of wisdom and wealth in old wisdom leads naturally to the conclusion that since Solomon was the wealthiest man in Israel's history, it follows that he must have been the wisest. Legends about his prowess in wisdom constitute the faith of the wise in their universe. These legends take as their point of departure the ancient claim about royal wisdom, originally understood in a general sense. From here they move to wondrous legendary wisdom, and make of Solomon the sage par excellence. Indeed, they leave strong clues behind, particularly in the story about the Queen of Sheba's visit. Here wisdom and wealth have kissed each other; the marriage is consummated. Therefore the strange emphasis upon wealth in the legend about Solomon's wisdom does not clash with the rest of the story after all.

Once Solomon is thought of as a sage surpassing all others, he embraces all types of wisdom. Accordingly, legends grow up demonstrating his skill in drawing lessons from natural phenomena, his judicial wisdom, and his ability to discover the mysteries of life. About Solomon as sage par excellence it can be said:

> It is the glory of God to conceal things,
>   but the glory of kings is to search things out.
>
> (Proverbs 25:2)

In time the canonical principle latches onto this glorification of Solomon, attaching to his name the third division of the Hebrew Bible. Moses dispenses law, Solomon, wisdom.

THE ANCIENT NEAR EASTERN CONTEXT

A single feature of the Solomonic tradition strikes readers as strange beyond measure: the comparison of Solomon's wisdom with that of non-Israelite sages. One can hardly imagine a prophetic narrative which placed a Yahwistic prophet alongside a Baalistic one, even if Yahweh's spokesman were ranked first. This unusual feature of wisdom furnishes a clue to the international character of the sapiential tradition. We shall examine non-Israelite wisdom later on, but wish at this time to paint that phenomenon in broad strokes.

Both Egypt and Mesopotamia had a flourishing wisdom tradition, consisting of professional sages who composed extensive literary works which manifest remarkable thematic and formal coherence.[27] In Egypt those writings included instructions and reflections upon life's deeper mysteries. Such texts functioned within the royal court as a means of educating future courtiers, and in time produced a scribal profession that looked upon other vocations as inferior to their own exalted one. Similarly, Mesopotamian wisdom texts preserve valiant gropings with the problem of human suffering, but also contain numerous collections of popular proverbs.

This literature manifests an international spirit, inasmuch as it speaks about truths which present themselves to persistent inquirers regardless of the historical context. Moreover, a strong humanism pervades the tradition, although that optimism regarding human potential springs from a conviction that God has created the universe orderly. Furthermore a tinge of eudaemonism, or indulgent self-interest, persists in the sapiential world view, since the world has been programmed to reward virtue and punish vice. Naturally, this wisdom tradition had no place for special revelation beyond the secrets of the universe which were implanted there at the moment of creation.

We shall see that the sapiential tradition throughout the ancient Near East was sufficiently uniform to permit the incorporation of a section from an Egyptian instruction into the biblical book of Proverbs, and to prompt modern critics to label Mesopotamian texts a "Sumerian Job" and a "Babylonian Ecclesiastes." To be sure, significant differences exist among the three cultural contexts, but the idea of a sapiential tradition in the ancient Near East has considerable merit.

The locus of the sapiential tradition in Egypt was the pharaonic court, while Mesopotamian sages functioned primarily in a temple school. It follows that the different settings affected the character of the wisdom literature emerging from each group. Whereas Egyptian wisdom concentrated on providing instruction for successful life at the royal court, its Mesopotamian counterpart gave special consideration to assuring the good life by means of cultic practices. In Egypt a propagandistic tendency inserts itself into the literature, and in Mesopotamia expertise at interpreting signs or omens was cherished by the sages who earned their livelihood from such activity and from scribal duties which they performed for wealthy individuals.

What, then, was the setting for Israel's sapiential activity? We have seen that the Solomonic court left its mark on a tiny portion of canonical proverbs, although the allusion to the "men of Hezekiah" suggests that some sages must surely have functioned at the court in Jerusalem. The vast majority of biblical proverbs seems to have arisen in a context other than the royal court. That setting for numerous proverbs was the family, where parental instruction was very much at home. This clan ethos saw the virtual union of law and instruction, both of which carried the full authority of the patriarch. During this long period in Israel's history, careful observation of the immediate world paid significant dividends in the form of proverbs and maxims. Such sayings focused upon the agrarian enterprise, personal relationships, particularly sexual ones, self-control, and the many ways one could enrich or impoverish life. It seems likely, therefore, that most biblical proverbs arose in this family setting.

To be sure, some canonical proverbs could easily have arisen within a court setting, although references to a king hardly demand such a conclusion. On the other hand, many older proverbs could have been adapted for use in the royal court, since self-mastery was as much a desideratum in this setting as it was in the clan. It follows that a clan origin for most canonical proverbs does not necessarily exclude a subsequent function at the Jerusalemite court.

A third setting for sapiential activity manifests itself in Sirach, where one reads that a house of learning stands in readiness for those who wish to pursue the scholarly vocation. From Ben Sira's remarks, it is clear that such education was costly. Perhaps we can also conclude that the curriculum represented a convergence of sapiential and sacred traditions.[28] Whether that house of learning stood apart from the place of worship, or formed a vital part of the holy place, we cannot say with any confidence. In any case, the prominence of the school in the Hellenistic world probably stimulated the growth of a similar educational institution among the Jews.[29]

To recapitulate, Israel's sapiential tradition seems to have arisen during the period of the clan, flourishing subsequently at the royal court and in houses of learning.

The question arises, then, about the actual dates of the various literary complexes which comprise the wisdom corpus. Naturally, most canonical proverbs antedate the monarchical state, with the possible exception of the first collection (Proverbs 1—9). Although we cannot establish the dates of Job and Ecclesiastes with certainty, it seems likely that Job was composed in the sixth century and Ecclesiastes in the late third or early second. The situation is different with Sirach, for there can be no doubt that Ben Sira lived in the early second century. Since he includes a eulogy of Simon the Priest, he must have composed his work between 190 and 180 B.C.E. Wisdom of Solomon comes from an even later time, perhaps the first century.

We shall discuss the themes which characterize the wisdom tradition in connection with the individual analyses of Proverbs, Job, Ecclesiastes, Sirach, and Wisdom of Solomon. Certain themes take on increasing significance within these books: the fear of the Lord, Yahweh's self-manifestation through personified wisdom, the problem of innocent suffering, the meaning of life, the justification of God's ways, the limits of human knowledge, and the inevitability of death. Given the range of this literature, we may conclude that Israel's sages struggled with life's fundamental questions. Their way of addressing these issues, and the solutions they reached, stand as a perpetual witness to a remarkable group of people.

AN ENDLESS SEARCH

In a sense, the characteristic features of this significant class was its *pursuit* of insight, its search for the unknown. Indeed, the sages believed that God had hidden precious secrets from human eyes: God's glory was to conceal things. Over against this fact, sages juxtaposed human striving for knowledge, especially a king's attempt to fathom such mystery.

> "Whence then comes wisdom?
>   And where is the place of understanding?
> It is hid from the eyes of all living,
>   and concealed from the birds of the air.
> Abaddon and Death say,
>   'We have heard a rumor of it with our ears.' "
>
> (Job 28:20-22)

This majestic poem goes on to say that God alone has access to wisdom, and ultimately identifies religion and wisdom. Now if God has sole possession of wisdom he can dispense it at will. The few persons who beat a path to wisdom's door come by way of prayer, as "Solomon" proclaims mightily in the wisdom book by his name.

> I went about seeking how to get her for myself. . . .
> But I perceived that I would not possess wisdom unless God gave
>   her to me—
> and it was a mark of insight to know whose gift she was—
> so I appealed to the Lord and besought him,
> and with my whole heart I said:. . . .
>
> (Wisdom 8:18, 21)

The author of Tobit took issue with the sages' depiction of reality in terms of competing wills to conceal and to search out the hidden. Here the angel Raphael introduces a different contrast between God and kings. In his view, kings' secrets should remain closely guarded mysteries, whereas divine truth ought to be proclaimed far and wide. Twice the angel announces this variant to Proverbs 25:2.

> "It is good to guard the secret of a king, but gloriously to reveal the
>   works of God."
>
> (Tobit 12:7,11)

In this text two different kinds of secrets seem to be envisioned. Prudence dictates caution with regard to what kings desire to conceal from others, for the spreading of forbidden knowledge can serve no good purpose. By way of contrast, God's marvelous works should not be closely guarded secrets among a faithful few, but deserve royal heralds who will announce glad tidings throughout the universe.

These two texts deal with different realities. In one, the king clutches precious data to his chest while God allows free proclamation of his works; in the other, kings eagerly search for what God presses to his bosom. Both perceptions capture distinct features of reality with which the sages wrestled. Some truths freely surrendered to royal search, while others refused to budge an inch. Perhaps that inconsistent response to the sages' quest arose from God's desire to guard sacred mystery while divulging partial knowledge. In any event, both texts point to a reality that complicates all attempts to understand ancient wisdom: the awareness that wisdom eludes those who search for her, and the conviction that she gives herself freely to those who love her. Sirach sums up this paradox in tantalizingly enigmatic fashion:

> For wisdom is like her name,
> and is not manifest to many.
>
> (6:22)

While Proverbs 25:2 specifies kings as those upon whom the quest for hidden things falls, other texts extend that hunt to all subjects of kings. Indeed, the idea of searching for wisdom as for precious metals occurs again and again in wisdom literature. Wisdom makes herself known.

> If you seek it like silver
> and search for it as for hidden treasures.
>
> (Proverbs 2:4)

She is worth more than red coral or precious jewels; gold and silver are like sand compared to her. To acquire wisdom one should gladly give up a fortune in silver, for she will pay dividends in gold.

Still other texts change the image from precious metals to that of a bride. Wisdom is to be pursued like a beloved, for in her hands are long life and happiness.

Wisdom is radiant and unfading,
and she is easily discerned by those who love her,
and is found by those who seek her.
She hastens to make herself known to those who desire her.
He who rises early to seek her will have no difficulty,
for he will find her sitting at his gates. . . .
because she goes about seeking those worthy of her,
and she graciously appears to them in their paths,
and meets them in every thought.

(Wisdom 6:12-15, 16)

I loved her and sought her from my youth,
and I desired to take her for my bride,
and I became enamored of her beauty.

(Wisdom 8:2)

Considerable emphasis falls on wisdom's initiative. Not only does she meet her lover halfway, but she also actively invites people to search for her. Those who love her are loved in return, and whoever finds her discovers life. At first her discipline may seem unusually harsh, but in time her fetters will take on a wholly different appearance. In retrospect, lovers will consider her price a trifling sum.

Like the quest to discover the mystery of a lover, the search for wisdom never ends. In a moment of poetic flourish, Sirach compares wisdom to several kinds of trees, and invites his readers to eat their fill.

"Come to me, you who desire me,
　　and eat your fill of my produce.
For the remembrance of me is sweeter than honey,
　　and my inheritance sweeter than the honeycomb.
Those who eat me will hunger for more,
　　and those who drink me will thirst for more."

(Sirach 24:19-21)

Like a fire, a parched land, an empty womb, and Sheol, knowledge never cries out, "Enough" (Proverbs 30:15-16). Qoheleth's familiar adage, "The more one knows, the more sorrow" (Ecclesiastes 1:18, author's translation) has its corollary in "The more people know, the more they are eager to learn what remains hidden."

Perhaps this allusion to unquenchable thirst is Sirach's way of expressing *wisdom's essential hiddenness.* Although she may give herself freely to those who seek her, wisdom also withdraws until she is wholly outside human reach. Like the Creator who delighted in her presence before the creation of the world, wisdom is both present and hidden. The poet who composed the poem that has been inserted into chapter 28 of the book of Job painted a detailed picture of men searching the darkest recesses of the earth for valuable ore, only to highlight their inability to discover wisdom. Similarly, Qoheleth laments God's withholding of vital knowledge from human beings (Ecclesiastes 3:11) and defiantly challenges sages who claim success in finding wisdom (Ecclesiastes 8:16-17).

> . . . even though a wise man claims to know, he cannot find it out.
> (Ecclesiastes 8:17)

This emphasis on a royal search within wisdom literature may underlie the well-known text in which the pursuit of wisdom leads to kingship, a passage which uses a Greek device known as *sorites* (ideas are strung together like pearls on a necklace).

> The beginning of wisdom is the most sincere desire for instruction,
> and concern for instruction is love of her,
> and love of her is the keeping of her laws,
> and giving heed to her laws is assurance of immortality,
> and immortality brings one near to God;
> so the desire for wisdom leads to a kingdom.
> (Wisdom 6:17-20)

In Sirach 14:20-27 the image of a hunter who stalks his prey occurs, in addition to those of camping alongside wisdom's house and resting under her shade.

> Blessed is the man who meditates on wisdom
>   and who reasons intelligently.
> He who reflects in his mind on her ways
>   will also ponder her secrets.
> Pursue wisdom like a hunter,
>   and lie in wait on her paths.
> He who peers through her windows
>   will also listen at her doors;
> he who encamps near her house
>   will also fasten his tent peg to her walls;
> he will pitch his tent near her,

> and will lodge in an excellent lodging place;
> he will place his children under her shelter,
>   and will camp under her boughs;
> he will be sheltered by her from the heat,
>   and will dwell in the midst of her glory.

In the quest for wisdom one adopts whatever means are necessary to accomplish the goal, whether these happen to be appropriate social conduct or not. Wisdom's elusiveness is signaled by shifting images. She first appears as a wild animal; later she is described as a house and a tree, and ultimately she assumes human form.

In a word, Israel's sages envisioned themselves actively hunting for precious wisdom, and they described that search in rich imagery. These lively metaphors for the object of hot pursuit adorn wisdom texts at every stage of their composition, indicating that the search for wisdom was no passing fad.

THE OBJECT OF THE SEARCH

For what, then, did ancient sages search from dawn to dusk? Perhaps nothing suffices to answer this important question but the word "Life." Canonical sages went in pursuit of the good life in all its manifestations: health, wealth, honor, progeny, longevity, remembrance. These teachers never seemed to grow tired of promising such bounty to faithful listeners, and of threatening fools with loss of life itself. In their eyes sufficient proof existed that life's goods accompanied wisdom, so that the few seeming discrepancies did little to alter this conviction until Job and Qoheleth registered mighty protests.

We shall use several different ideas in describing the object of the search represented by Proverbs, Job, Qoheleth, and Sirach. In essence, Proverbs is a search for *knowledge,* for the aim of the many attempts to grasp reality seems to be the acquisition of sufficient understanding about nature and human beings to enable persons to live wisely and well.

The object of Job's search was not so much knowledge about how to cope with the enigmas of ordinary existence, although he certainly achieved vital information that called all previous knowledge into question, as it was a burning quest for God's *presence.*[30] Having known God's gracious presence in the past, Job could not endure a *Deus absconditus,* a hidden God. Therefore, he searched the darkest depths of despair in pursuit of his God, and eventually risked death to achieve restored communion. To Job, God was the highest good; life itself paled by comparison.

Qoheleth endeavored to find some sense in existence under the sun. He raised the ultimate question of *meaning* in a silent universe. Like Job, he could not affirm life as the supreme good, but unlike him Qoheleth did not enter into dialogue with a living Presence.[31] The shadow of death hovered nearby,[32] and chance reigned on earth. Lacking confidence in life's goodness, and hardly drawn by the presence of divine mystery, Qoheleth searched in vain for some meaning that would enable him to endure the few days of his empty existence.

In the Hellenistic environment within which Sirach found himself, he launched a vigorous search to discover a means of presenting Jewish teaching to sophisticated audiences. In doing so, he embarked upon a significant quest for *continuity.*[33] Facing two entirely different fronts, he endeavored to show that wisdom literature actually continued Israel's venerable sacred traditions, and to convince youthful Jews that Greeks were not the only ones who boasted a magnificent intellectual heritage. His goal was tantamount to survival of the Jewish faith.

To sum up, Proverbs searched for knowledge, Job for presence, Qoheleth for meaning, and Sirach for continuity. Significantly, the temporal focus differs in each instance. The eyes of those who compiled the book of Proverbs were fixed upon the *primeval age* when God established an order that enabled life to endure. Their task was to understand the true character of reality and to live in harmony with that discovery. Job's incredible suffering increased the urgency to find relief from suspicion that God had suddenly become his enemy. It follows that his concern was wholly *present.* The ache within Qoheleth's soul arose from an inability to discern any *future* at all, since death silenced both human and beast. On the other hand, Sirach glanced backwards upon a glorious *past* which he hoped to salvage for his pupils.

Invariably, Israel's seekers, whatever their goals, arrived at a closed door that resolutely refused to swing open. Behind this door lay profound mystery, but none held the key to this room except God. This is what Proverbs 25:2 professed when it declared that God's glory lies in the tendency to conceal essential reality. At times this restriction of what could be known caused considerable chafing, but in the end it gave birth to marvelous reflection concerning a gracious opening of the door by God, primarily through means of Dame Wisdom. The tension between self-reliance, on the one hand, and hope in divine mercy, on the other, bestows great pathos upon biblical wisdom. Indeed, one can even say that the relentless search oscillated between these two extremes, trust in one's ability to secure existence, and dependence upon God's mercy. Divine compassion has the final word, whether communicated by Dame Wisdom, God's gracious turning to humans, or simply affirmed as so often occurred in Sirach.

In Proverbs 7:6-27 and 24:30-34 anecdote functions as an effective teaching aid; hence the following story.

> A little girl once wandered away from home and became hopelessly lost. After trying unsuccessfully to retrace her steps, at last she gave up, and exhausted from her effort and from the growing fear that tore at her insides, she lay down beside a log and fell asleep. Meanwhile the girl's parents had missed her and had begun to search the woods nearby. Eventually the father came upon the sleeping child, but in doing so he stepped on some dry twigs that snapped explosively, awaking her. Seeing her father, the girl cried out, "Daddy, I've found you."

Israel's wise men and women searched diligently too, but in the end became the willing objects of a greater pursuit. The search became truly Royal, one in which God came in search of humans. In what follows, we shall attempt a search of our own, hoping to understand ancient wisdom. In doing so, we shall heed Sirach's counsel.

> Put your feet into her fetters,
>   and your neck into her collar.
> Put your shoulder under her and carry her,
>   and do not fret under her bonds.
> Come to her with all your soul,
>   and keep her ways with all your might.
> Search out and seek, and she will become known to you;

and when you get hold of her, do not let her go.
For at last you will find the rest she gives,
    and she will be changed into joy for you.
Then her fetters will become for you a strong protection,
    and her collar a glorious robe.
Her yoke is a golden ornament,
    and her bonds are a cord of blue.
You will wear her like a glorious robe,
    and put her on like a crown of gladness.

(Sirach 6:24-31)

CHAPTER 3

The Pursuit of Knowledge: Proverbs

According to Israel's sages, a fundamental order lay hidden within the universe; this ruling principle applied both to nature and to humans. Discovery of this "rational rule" enabled the wise to secure their existence by acting in harmony with the universal order that sustained the cosmos. Conduct, it follows, either strengthened the existing order, or contributed to the forces of chaos that continually threatened survival itself.

This decisive order permeating the universe constituted God's gift to those who bore the Creator's image. As a sign of divine favor, the principle governing the universe was subject to God's will: the Lord of the universe always spoke the final word. No *concept* of order held that sovereign will in subjection. Israel's sages recognized this significant fact, and acknowledged the ultimate veto over every attempt to control their existence by living in harmony with the principle which God had bestowed upon the universe. At the same time, they believed that God did not exercise the right of veto arbitrarily, and thus the wise confidently endeavored to discover the principle by which they should live.

The task facing ancient sages was not simply that of ferreting out every sign post which pointed to an underlying principle. Once this important clue presented itself forcefully upon human imaginations, it had to be transferred from the realm of nature to the human sphere. The chief means of accomplishing this goal was analogy.[1] Comparisons proceeded on the level of essential reality; surface differences vanished before functional similarities. Close observation of nature and the animal kingdom convinced Israel's sages that the world was truly a harmonious *universe.*

The search for proper analogies had as its single purpose the securing of life. Those who successfully achieved correct knowledge purchased long life for themselves, together with other indications of divine approval. Knowledge was therefore a means to an end, not the end itself. This fact should be kept in mind as one examines the book of Proverbs.

LITERARY ANALYSIS

Like wisdom, the term "proverb" is difficult to define. The Hebrew word *mašal,* the plural form of which identifies the book of Proverbs, points to two possible meanings: a similitude or a powerful word.[2] The first sense of *mašal* derives from the verb which means "to be like," the second, from the meaning, "to rule." The former emphasizes the analogy that lies at the heart of every proverb, while the latter stresses its paradigmatic or exemplary character. A particularly apt description captures the second of these senses: a proverb is a winged word, outliving the fleeting moment.[3]

Etymology alone cannot suffice to define proverb in ancient Israel, for the word *mašal* occurs with reference to a wide range of literary forms: similitudes, popular sayings, literary aphorisms, taunt songs, bywords, allegories, and discourses. Attempts to characterize proverbs on the basis of form and function encounter similar ambiguities. Since Israel's sages seem never to have adopted a single notion of proverb, we should be content with a broad definition. For this reason, "saying" best retains the openness of the Hebrew word *mašal.*

All proverbs, whether similitudes or paradigms, were grounded in experience. A modern writer has captured this singular feature of proverbs in an observation that approaches the proverbial itself: a proverb is a short sentence founded upon long experience, containing a truth.[4] Brevity characterizes all proverbs; they say a great deal in a few, carefully chosen words. Observation also belongs to the intrinsic character of a proverb, which announces an important discovery in "sentence" form. The weight of tradition rests behind proverbs; they do not represent the isolated view of one person, however intelligent he or she may have been. Above all, proverbs embody truth. Upon hearing a proverb for the first time, "it is as though, within the depths of human consciousness, we perceived the proverb's content to be true. . . ."[5]

An incommunicable quality distinguishes proverbs from sayings that lack paradigmatic value. Perhaps that unknown and unknowable aspect derives from the distance separating the ancient world from contemporary scholars. In one sense, the distinguishing mark of a proverb is forever lost to modern critics, and scholars are forced to impose their own understandings upon texts from bygone days. In another sense, interpreters engage in the search for analogies between then and now, confident that at the deeper levels of human existence continuity exists between people of today and those forbears who left a legacy to treasure. In reality, humankind participates in a quest for knowledge comparable to the one occupying Israelite sages.

Proverbs encapsulated truth. Now such valuable information was not private property; instead, it belonged to everyone. To be sure, a single individual was responsible for the form that a given proverb took. But the entire community profited from each discovery. A didactic quality clings to those proverbial statements that seem to be completely neutral, for every single recognition of "the way things are" signaled a step toward mastering the universe. That task was everybody's responsibility.

The primary function of proverbs seems to have been the linking of two realms and two ages. In short, the winged word transcended time and space. It joined together nature and humans by isolating a vital correspondence between the natural realm and the social order. In addition, the proverb linked past generations to the present. By this means traditional values survived the passing of time, and ethos emerged. Ethos refers to a system of cherished values, presuppositions, aspirations, linguistic usage, and so forth.

To accomplish this union which defied space and time, proverbs needed to be transparent. They had to ring true. The combined wisdom of many and wit of one entrusted proverbs with persuasive capacity. Fundamentally, proverbs relied upon their typicality for immediate cogency. They could be tested in daily experience over and over with unchanging results. Such verifiability arose from investment of cultural values. It follows that proverbs comprise the best single source for discovering cherished values in ancient Israel.[6] In these succinct sayings we shall come upon deeply rooted ways of life; indeed, we shall even go a long way toward fathoming the people's understanding of good and evil.

The transparency inherent within a given proverb was reinforced by means of poetic imagery and stylistic devices, all of which seem to have aimed at aiding memorization and enhancing enjoyment. The chief poetic feature was parallelism, although a few sayings lack it entirely. It cannot be ascertained whether these single-line proverbs antedate the bilinear proverbs, which by far outnumber the rest, or whether they actually represent a later corruption of the two-line saying.

Three types of parallelism occur with great regularity: antithetic, synonymous, and progressive.[7] Antithetic parallelism depends upon the juxtaposition of opposites:

> A false balance is an abomination to the LORD,
>   but a just weight is his delight.
>
> (Proverbs 11:1)

An important variation is the excluding proverb, often called a "better saying." For example,

> Better is a dinner of herbs where love is
>   than a fatted ox and hatred with it.
>
> (Proverbs 15:17)

sets one reality over against another in complete opposition. The contrast implied in such proverbs suggests that the oft-used descriptive term "comparative proverb" is less satisfactory than "excluding proverb," which acknowledges an antithesis.[8] The saying does not attempt to determine the better of two good things; instead, it announces that one is good and its opposite is bad.

Synonymous parallelism reinforces an astute observation by repetition of the essential point in different words.

> Hear, my son, your father's instruction,
>> and reject not your mother's teaching;
> for they are a fair garland for your head,
>> and pendants for your neck.
>
> (Proverbs 1:8-9)

This example of synonymous parallelism uses a positive and a negative, both of which mean the same thing. Naturally, shades of meaning add variety amid synonymity. Strictly speaking, the phenomenon of ascending or accumlative parallelism lacks exact synonymns or antonymns, but builds upon an earlier idea after the fashion of stair steps. For instance,

> The beginning of wisdom is this: Get wisdom,
>> and whatever you get, get insight.
>
> (Proverbs 4:7)

advances beyond the two similar notions (wisdom and insight to whatever one obtains) an entirely new idea. A variant of the progressive proverb is the following formulation, where the second line is essential for the meaning of the proverb.

> A man who bears false witness against his neighbor
>> is like a war club, or a sword, or a sharp arrow.
>
> (Proverbs 25:18)

Examples of these three basic kinds of parallelism could be multiplied indefinitely. The following proverbs illustrate the great variety that arose within the three fundamental types.

> He who closes his ear to the cry of the poor
>> will himself cry out and not be heard.
>
> (Proverbs 21:13)

> Do not rob the poor, because he is poor,
>> or crush the afflicted at the gate;
> for the LORD will plead their cause
>> and despoil of life those who despoil them.
>
> (Proverbs 22:22-23)

> Train up a child in the way he should go,
>> and when he is old he will not depart from it.
>
> (Proverbs 22:6)

> Leave the presence of a fool,
>> for there you do not meet words of knowledge.
>
> (Proverbs 14:7)

The first of these shows how a conditional clause in the first line is followed by its natural conclusion. The second example expands the proverb to twice its normal length, and the second half of the proverb gives the reason for the advice in the first half. The third illustration shows how the result of a given course of action can be presented in the second half of a proverb, while the final example demonstrates the use of second person in proverbial statements.

Two further forms deserve special recognition. The first is the numerical proverb.

> Three things are stately in their tread;
>   four are stately in their stride;
> the lion, which is mightiest among beasts
>   and does not turn back before any;
> the strutting cock, the he-goat,
>   and a king striding before his people.
>
> (Proverbs 30:29-31)

The second type is the listing of comparable phenomena without numerical heightening.

> Four things on earth are small,
>   but they are exceedingly wise;
> the ants are a people not strong,
>   yet they provide their food in the summer;
> the badgers are a people not mighty,
>   yet they make their homes in the rocks;
> the locusts have no king,
>   yet all of them march in rank;
> the lizard you can take in your hands,
>   yet it is in kings' palaces.
>
> (Proverbs 30:24-28)

Just as diversity characterizes Hebrew parallelism within proverbial literature, multiplicity of patterns adds abundant variety. At least seven different patterns have been isolated: (1) identity, equivalence, invariable association; (2) non-identity, contrast, paradox; (3) similarity, analogy, type; (4) contrary to right order, futile, absurd; (5) classification and clarification; (6) value, relative value or priority, proportion or degree; (7) consequences of human behavior or character.[9]

Variety in parallelism and patterns extends to the several collections within the book of Proverbs. Four extensive collections and five short ones can be recognized on the basis of superscriptions and content.

1.	1—9	The Proverbs of Solomon son of David, king of Israel
2.	10:1—22:16	The Proverbs of Solomon
3.	22:17—24:22	The Sayings of the wise
4.	24:23-34	More Sayings of wise men
5.	25—29	More Proverbs of Solomon transcribed by the men of Hezekiah king of Judah
6.	30:1-9	Sayings of Agur son of Jakeh from Massah
7.	30:10-33	(no superscription)
8.	31:1-9	Sayings of Lemuel king of Massa, which his mother taught him
9.	31:10-31	(no superscription)

The international character of Hebrew wisdom is reflected in three collections which are attributed to (or borrowed from) foreign sources (3, 6, 8). The instruction, from which eleven of thirty sayings in collection three derive, is Egyptian in origin, and is now known as "The Instruction of Amen-em-opet."

The first collection (1—9) differs greatly from the others, both with respect to form and content. Formally, it makes use of the short essay which links individual sayings together loosely. As a result, certain themes surface, particularly the dangers posed by an adulteress. In addition, poetic personification functions pedagogically. Dame Wisdom woos her followers, inviting them to a banquet in her house which she has built by innate expertise, and Madam Folly lurks in the night, actively seducing simpletons to their ruin. The entire collection breathes a deeply religious spirit, for the individual sayings adopt as their motto: "The fear of the Lord is the beginning of knowledge."[10] Furthermore, they consciously seek to instruct, both by exhortation and admonition. Forever holding out the promise of reward or threat of punishment, these essays endeavor to shape character much more self-consciously than is the case in the other collections.

In some instances a real proverb lies encased within a brief essay (1:10-19; 6:20-35; 9:13-18). The first essay warns against joining criminals who devise schemes to get rich at the expense of helpless individuals. It reinforces the warning by citing a proverb:

> For in vain is a net spread
> in the sight of any bird.

(1:17)

Similarly, the second exposes the risks involved in sexual debauchery:

> Can a man carry fire in his bosom
> and his clothes not be burned?
> Or can one walk upon hot coals
> and his feet not be scorched?

(6:27-28)

This short essay (6:20-35) argues that fire inevitably burns, and only fools think they can dally with another man's wife with impunity. The third "Brief Paragraph" (9:13-18) demonstrates Madam Folly's skill at citing appropriate proverbs which reinforce her smooth words of invitation to forbidden pleasures:

> "Stolen water is sweet,
> and bread eaten in secret is pleasant."

(9:17)

The initial collection of proverbs, to use the last word in its loose sense, manifests a tendency toward sophistication in poetic technique. Here one discovers direct appeals for attention, rhetorical questions, extended metaphors approaching allegory, vivid description, anecdote, and related rhetorical devices. The combination of style and content suggests that this collection derives from a different setting than the one(s) that produced the other larger collections.

The second major collection is clearly divisible into two smaller entities (10:1—15:33; 16:1—22:16). The first of these differs from the other in its preference for antithetic parallelism. Only one (19:7) of the 375 proverbs lacks the balanced distich (two halves) structure, and it uses the tristich form. So far no principle of arrangement has been discovered for these individual sayings, although here and there signs of intentional sequence present themselves. For instance, the letter *b* joins together Proverbs 11:9-12, and the Hebrew words *leb* (heart) and *ṭob* (good) connect the sayings in 15:13-17.

It naturally follows from an absence of thematic arrangement in this major collection that description of its contents must necessarily remain hopelessly general. Covering a wide range of everyday occurrences, the proverbs pass judgment on various kinds of conduct ranging from secret actions like bribery to open vilification of poor victims of society's indifference. These brief maxims offer astute observations on the folly of pride, laziness, passion, deceit, gossip, and similar vices, and they cast their ballot in favor of acknowledged virtues such as generosity, faithfulness, self-control, industry, and sobriety.

In some respects *the third collection* (22:17—23:22) resembles the first, in which considerable Egyptian influence is visible. For example, a tiny step toward the clustering of related sayings occurs in this brief collection, where paragraph units emerge rather distinctly. Second person address sets apart the material which has been taken from the Instruction of Amen-em-opet, greatly increasing the urgency of these sayings. Unlike collection two, this one rarely employs the various types of parallelism by which Israel's sages reinforced their striking insight into one small facet of reality. Most conspicuous within this third collection is a brief essay in which the awful plight of drunkards is described with immense pathos (Proverbs 23:29-35). One other feature of this section of foreign extraction is the use of exquisite metaphors; in this regard, the collection seems to indicate an advanced stage in poetic reflection beyond that found in Proverbs 10:1—22:16.

The fourth major collection (25—29) resembles the second in its fondness for antithetic parallelism, but makes lavish use of comparative statements. These similitudes cover a wide spectrum of topics, and demonstrate keen powers of perception.

> A word fitly spoken
> is like apples of gold in a setting of silver.
>
> (Proverbs 25:11)

> Like snow in summer or rain in harvest,
> so honor is not fitting for a fool.
>
> (Proverbs 26:1)

> Like a roaring lion or a charging bear
> is a wicked ruler over a poor people.
>
> (Proverbs 28:15)

The last of these comparisons introduces a favorite subject within this collection: the king. Here as nowhere else the powerful individual with whom all subjects had to reckon is acknowledged, although occasional allusions to royalty surface in other collections.

The first minor collection (24:23-34) lacks parallelism (except in 30, 32, 34), but employs both exhortation and admonition. It shows an unusual relationship with Proverbs 1—9, inasmuch as a single proverb from this extensive collection (6:10-11) has been taken over and used as the "traditionally sanctioned message" which undergirds a brief essay on laziness. Assuming the rare form of anecdote, this passage concludes with a marvelous metaphor.

> I passed by the field of a sluggard,
>> by the vineyard of a man without sense;
> and lo, it was all overgrown with thorns;
>> the ground was covered with nettles,
>> and its stone wall was broken down.
> Then I saw and considered it;
>> I looked and received instruction,
> A little sleep, a little slumber,
>> a little folding of the hands to rest,
> and poverty will come upon you like a robber,
>> and want like an armed man.
>
> (Proverbs 24:30—34)

The second incidental section (30:1-9) comprises a dialogue between a skeptic and a believer, to which has been affixed a profound prayer to be spared either extreme, poverty or riches.[11] It concludes:

> lest I be full, and deny thee,
>> and say, "Who is the LORD?"
> or lest I be poor, and steal,
>> and profane the name of my God.

The third minor collection is largely composed of numerical sayings and simple listing of related phenomena. It brings together things that resist all efforts to stifle desire for more; phenomena that defy explanation; situations in which certain persons become unbearable; insignificant things that achieve unexpected results; and proud parading on the part of animals and humans. Proverbs 31:1-9 takes the form of advice offered by a Queen Mother to her young son. The strong warning against sexual profligacy and drunkenness comes perilously close to harangue, although the intimate language points to genuine affection. In addition, the final appeal for fairness in exercising royal judgements links up with similar ideas throughout the ancient Near East. The fifth collection supplies an appropriate ending to the book of Proverbs, which sings Dame Wisdom's praises and confesses that a good wife is a gift from God. The alphabetic poem (31:10-31) extols the virtues of a capable wife. Whereas the basis of her unparalleled reputation is wholly secular, the religious note erupts toward the end:

> Charm is deceitful and beauty is vain,
>> but a woman who fears the LORD is to be praised.
>>> (Proverbs 31:30)

Efforts to divide the older Solomonic proverbs into an architectonic structure have not been altogether successful. One significant hypothesis of four sections with thematic coherence may be noted.[12] According to it, the following divisions apply:

1. 10—15   Righteousness versus Wickedness
2. 16:1—22:16   Yahweh and the King
3. 25—27   Nature and Agriculture
4. 28—29   The King or Potential Rulers

Another approach to the vexing problem of overall structure in the book of Proverbs takes its cue from the two primary forms of Egyptian proverbial wisdom. Into the category of Instruction fall 1—9; 22:17—24:22; 31:1-9. The remaining proverbs belong, in this view, to the Sentence (10:1—22:16; 24:23-34; 25—29).[13]

Within the extensive collection of Solomonic proverbs, one group gives the impression of moral neutrality, a feature that has often led to the conclusion that such purely secular sayings indicate great antiquity.[14]

> One man gives freely, yet grows all the richer;
>> another withholds what he should give, and only suffers want.
>>> (Proverbs 11:24)

From the fruit of his words a man is satisfied with good,
and the work of a man's hand comes back to him.

(Proverbs 12:14)

One man pretends to be rich, yet has nothing;
another pretends to be poor, yet has great wealth.
The ransom of a man's life is his wealth,
but a poor man has no means of redemption.

(Proverbs 13:7-8)

The poor is disliked even by his neighbor,
but the rich has many friends.

(Proverbs 14:20)

A worker's appetite works for him;
his mouth urges him on.

(Proverbs 16:26)

A man's gift makes room for him
and brings him before great men.

(Proverbs 18:16)

The poor use entreaties,
but the rich answer roughly.

(Proverbs 18:23)

"It is bad, it is bad," says the buyer;
but when he goes away, then he boasts.

(Proverbs 20:14)

The glory of young men is their strength,
but the beauty of old men is their gray hair.

(Proverbs 20:29)

Such observations about "the ways things are" scarcely pronounce judgment upon one or the other phenomenon being described. We must guard against an assumption that Israel's maxims underwent a gradual development from wholly secular proverbs to fervently religious precepts. Presumably, even the most devout sage was capable of describing reality without always feeling obligated to affix a moral. In any event, religious sayings belong to the oldest collections, and appear with great frequency.

The mere placing of these neutral observations into larger collections with didactic intent transforms the maxims in some small way, for they then take on the persuasive spirit of the whole unit. As a result of the new setting, a wry observation about the advantages rich people enjoy over the poor cannot be understood properly apart from the sages' attitude to poverty and riches. Modern interpreters face an added peril—the temptation to assess wealthy individuals in the light of later suspicion about the virtue of those upon whom fortune smiles.

The *didactic impulse* manifested itself in many different ways. Perhaps the most noticeable expression of a desire to teach was the shift from observation to exhortation or admonition, and the resulting disintegration of the proverb form. The simple addition of motivation clauses and energetic warnings signaled an unwillingness to allow the proverb to communicate its own message. The consequences of a given action come to the forefront, and direct address punctuates the discourse. In addition, value judgments reflecting this all-consuming passion pervade the steady stream of advice. We note further the introduction of an arsenal of rhetorical devices: paranomasia, assonance, alliteration, puns, repetition, rhyme, and synonymy.

Nothing in this account of the shift from sentence to instruction demands a school setting, although many scholars seem inclined to posit such a transformation in the actual context of learning.[15] All of the conscious educational techniques mentioned above lay within reach of sages who studied at their parents' feet. In short, we must be alert to danger from two different fronts. On the one hand, the temptation to date all proverbs late if they possess elaborate teaching aids; on the other hand, the assumption that only persons trained in professional schools had an ounce of literary expertise. One does not have to endorse the untenable theory of a noble savage or its corollary, the gifted *Volk*, to recognize that perceptive members of Israelite clans could have coined exquisite proverbs and persuasive instructions.[16]

It naturally follows from these observations that sufficiently sophisticated analytic tools to date the individual proverbs, or even the larger collections, with any confidence are not available. Although these sayings, by and large, reflect life as it is known from other sources, they are completely silent with regard to the great historical events that must have been taking place simultaneously with their compilation. Whoever wrote these proverbs knew that the truths they proclaimed remained unchanged regardless of the ceaseless jockeying for territorial sovereignty in the ancient world. Israel's proverbs do not contain a single reference to a recognizable historical person or event, with the exception of the editorial superscriptions which mention Solomon and Hezekiah's men. The sages searched for universal truth; they acknowledged no geographical boundaries where insight into reality was concerned.

THEMATIC ANALYSIS

At the very heart of the wise's search for knowledge lay a value judgment: life was the supreme good. The word "life" is used here in its pregnant sense—a long existence characterized by good health, an abundance of friends, a house full of children, and sufficient possessions to carry one safely through any difficulty. Of course, the sages reckoned with death as a real factor, but the book of Proverbs never utters so much as a sigh over the prospect of natural death. The lack of any anxious lament over the universal decree, "You must die," becomes all the more astonishing when we consider the fact that these wise men and women entertained no hope of life beyond the grave.

Perhaps this limitation of life to existence on this side of the tomb explains why images like "tree of life" and "fountain of life" recur with such frequency in the sayings. Indeed, Dame Wisdom is even pictured with long life in her right hand, riches and honor in her left hand. Or again, she is called a staff of life to those who grasp her, and a refuge for all who cling to her (Proverbs 3:16-18).

Another image that plays an important part in the vocabulary of Israel's sages who composed the book of Proverbs is the *path* or *way* to life.[17] The significance of this terminology depends upon the double sense with which the word for way was used: path and sovereignty. A singular example of the reliance upon this double meaning for the Hebrew word *derek* (way) is found in Proverbs 30:18-19.

> Three things are too wonderful for me;
>   four I do not understand:
> the way of an eagle in the sky,
>   the way of a serpent on a rock,
> the way of a ship on the high seas,
>   and the way of a man with a maiden.

Here the incomprehensible feature of the four movements concerns the lack of any "tracks" or telltale signs of progress.[18] The vulture splits the air without leaving any trail; the serpent slithers along a rock, leaving behind no sign of its movement; the ship parts the ocean's floor momentarily; young people cohabit and no one can ascertain that such conduct has taken place.

The notion of a path was particularly appropriate in the thinking of Israel's wise men and women, for at birth everyone had embarked on a journey which led to a full life or to premature departure. Useful road maps existed; they were the fruit of long effort. Those who relied upon their own ingenuity soon became hopelessly lost along winding foot paths. Often God overruled human itineraries, leaving helpless individuals somewhere off the beaten path. From this encounter with human finitude, sages learned an important lesson.

> A man's steps are ordered by the LORD;
>   how then can man understand his way?
>
>   (Proverbs 20:24)

Nevertheless, the wise journeyed toward their ultimate destination with sure confidence that they would reach that place safely, whereas fools would lose their way.

On this path of life two distinct groups of pilgrims walked toward different goals. They were known as *the wise and the foolish;* all people fell into one or the other category. There was no middle ground for those who participated in folly, or in wisdom, only minimally. Moreover, an ethical understanding of the two categories prevailed. The wise were righteous, and fools were wicked. This surprising conclusion arose from the operative assumption that anyone who strengthened the order upholding the universe belonged to God's forces, while those who undermined this harmony were enemies of the Creator.

Although the wise did not allow for a middle ground between wisdom and folly, they did make careful distinctions among fools. This was achieved by varying their language when characterizing fools. Eight different terms for "fool" occur within canonical Proverbs.[19]

1. *pethi*—the naive, untutored individual
2. *kᵉsil*—one who is innately stupid
3. *ᵉwil*—a person characterized by obstinacy
4. *sakal*—one who persists in folly
5. *baʿar*—a crude individual
6. *nabal*—a brutal, depraved person
7. *holel*—an irrational madman
8. *leṣ*—a foolish talker who values his opinions overmuch.

Naturally, not all of these persons were beyond help. The *pethi,* for example, presented a real challenge, inasmuch as he or she could readily be influenced for good or ill. Like an inexperienced young girl, whose vulnerability offered a rare opportunity for preying individuals, the *pethi* could easily be swayed. For the rest, the wise had nothing but comtempt. Believing them to be God's enemies, who schemed to overthrow the principle governing the world, the sages could hardly have adopted a tolerant attitude toward fools.

Now if all humans belonged to two camps, each of which was clearly distinguishable, we should be able to describe two different lifestyles. One pattern of behavior secured existence, and its opposite led to destruction. To a certain extent, any attempt to characterize life-sustaining conduct and its counterpart is hampered by the sages' tendency to speak in general categories. For instance, they enjoin *right action* and *justice,* which pleases God more than sacrifice (Proverbs 21:3), and encourage *goodness* with confidence that their meaning leaves no ambiguity. In short, these teachers take for granted a common understanding of good and evil, one that modern interpreters must construct with great care if they are to guard against erroneous conclusions.

CONDUCT WHICH SECURED EXISTENCE

Perhaps a word of caution should be registered at this point. Placing various themes in an orderly sequence inevitably gives the impression of priority. Whatever receives first treatment must surely have been most important, and the farther down the scale something appears, the less significant it must have been. No such intention prompts the order into which kinds of conduct appear in this discussion, for the nature of the book of Proverbs rules out any such attempt to place relative values upon topics which are treated in isolated sayings. We may even be misled into thinking that frequent treatment implies special fondness, whereas it may only result from accident in the process of selecting what proverbs would be preserved. Still, certain things stand out impressively as the means by which the wise secured their existence.

Obedience to parents occurs as a cherished good; no individual who walks roughshod over those who gave him life can hope to enjoy its bounty. Proper respect extends beyond childhood to later years when age alters a father and mother's appearance and behavior, and when senility creeps into family relationships. Children honor their parents by heeding advice, that is, through listening to instruction and putting it into practice in their daily conduct.

Corporal punishment reinforced obedience to parents. Israel's sages never tired of urging vigorous lashings for children and fools. It seems that they almost thought a sound thrashing accomplished wonders.

> Blows that wound cleanse away evil;
>   strokes make clean the innermost parts.
>
> (Proverbs 20:30)

Convinced that young persons who were pointed in the right direction would forever retain their bearings, the sages freely used chastisement as a means of orientation. This bodily punishment must have been particularly harsh, for warnings against *killing* children and slaves are sprinkled throughout the proverbs. Loving parents sought justification for such cruelty in the belief that discipline sprang from love. They even elevated this principle to a higher realm.

> My son, do not despise the LORD's discipline
>> or be weary of his reproof,
> for the LORD reproves him whom he loves,
>> as a father the son in whom he delights.
>
> (Proverbs 3:11-12)

But bodily punishment was wasted on fools, who obstinately clung to their folly, and intelligent persons, for whom a tongue lashing accomplished wonders. Verbal rebuke therefore functioned as an alternative mode of discipline for certain individuals, and knowing when to apply this option was a sign of intelligence.

The Hebrew word *musar* (discipline) embraced far more than simple thrashings or verbal rebuke. It also signified a whole body of teaching whose purpose was to bestow life. Naturally, such precepts and instructions had to be learned. Israelite children looked upon endless study no more enthusiastically than their Egyptian counterparts, despite promises of reward and threats of punishment. Such discipline resembled a yoke by which animals were forced to work for their master's good, but in time it transformed itself into a garland of honor or a beautiful necklace. Hence, it is not surprising that Wisdom, like God and human parents, submits individuals to an uncommon discipline (Sirach 6:23-31).

One consequence of disciplined action is *self-control*. Perhaps the most difficult task of all was mastering the tongue. This tiny member possessed remarkable power for healing, just as it could also destroy innocent victims. The sages recognized the value of eloquence, and cherished words fitly spoken. An ability to present a case well was indispensable to the sapiential enterprise. Eloquence consisted of more than artful expression; it also demanded a sense of timeliness—the ability to discern the right occasion for a given word. Even fine tones and beautiful words did not commend themselves at all times and in every circumstance.

> He who sings songs to a heavy heart
>> is like one who takes off a garment on a cold day,
>> and like vinegar on a wound.
>
> (Proverbs 25:20)

Mastery of the tongue meant one further thing—the ability to remain silent when speech would produce harmful results.

Another sign that discipline had achieved its target was the *subordination of the passions*. The honor due soldiers in the ancient world was considerable, but the sages believed self-mastery deserved more praise.

> He who is slow to anger is better than the mighty,
>   and he who rules his spirit than he who takes a city.
>
> (Proverbs 16:32)

Rampaging passions brought nothing but dishonor and destruction; small wonder Egyptian sages developed this distinctive mark of wisdom and folly into technical vocabulary. The wise were "silent ones," whereas the foolish were "passionate ones."[20] In Israel the distinction never produced surrogate designations for opposing factions, but the heated person was certainly one who camped squarely in the midst of fools. Those who kept their passions in check, even when anger seethed within, soon learned the definite advantages residing in calculated, rational action.

A good wife assisted in the endeavor to gain control over one's passions. Perhaps more than any other divine gift, a faithful companion filled a man's days with sheer ecstasy.

> House and wealth are inherited from fathers,
>   but a prudent wife is from the LORD.
>
> (Proverbs 19:14)

> He who finds a wife finds a good thing,
>   and obtains favor from the LORD.
>
> (Proverbs 18:22)

Unfortunate in marriage, a man wandered about aimlessly and sighed.

Besides these things which secured existence in the ancient world, about which the sages readily conversed, other values, though equally cherished, occur in the sayings less frequently. In some instances, they almost have to be deduced from the way something is expressed. For example, a good name is actually mentioned far less often than it forms the unspoken presupposition of what is being proclaimed.

A different problem relates to the way certain givens are used, particularly wisdom, kindness, and truth. Here virtues appear whose worth none would question in theory, but in practice the wicked trampled upon them all. Whoever hoped to find life beat a path to wisdom's door. Possessing her, they learned kind treatment of friends *and enemies*. Modern interpreters may quibble about the selfish motive for refusing to repay evil deeds in the same coin, but the pragmatic ethical basis for all sapiential ethics should be kept in mind constantly. Behind such pragmatism stood God's will.

> Truthful lips endure for ever,
> but a lying tongue is but for a moment.
>
> (Proverbs 12:19)

> Lying lips are an abomination to the LORD,
> but those who act faithfully are his delight.
>
> (Proverbs 12:22)

Generosity also caused a smile to form upon the divine countenance, especially when alms fell into pockets of poor men and women.

> He who oppresses a poor man insults his Maker,
> but he who is kind to the needy honors him.
>
> (Proverbs 14:31)

So far we have examined important means by which sages achieved life, without noting that even good things sometimes participate in ambiguity. Wealth is one such sign of favor that carries concealed within its train the possibility of great spiritual deprivation. This is exactly what the author of Proverbs 30:7-9 saw with exceptional clarity, and because of this insight, asked to be spared excessive riches lest he forget that creaturely existence is one characterized by dependence upon the Creator at every moment.

This ever-present ambiguity extended to other things besides possessions, and gave rise to the notion of propriety.[21] The deed had to be matched with the occasion. To answer a fool according to his folly only dignified his response, but not to respond to him strengthened the folly itself. As a result of these two possible interpretations of silence, sages had to choose which answer addressed the actual situation. Even silence possessed a measure of ambiguity, particularly when it arose from lack of courage.

Israel's teachers believed that inner resolve on their part was matched by external forces which assisted them in the struggle for life. They viewed the accumulated wisdom tradition as a social force which enhanced their own efforts significantly:

> discretion will watch over you;
>> understanding will guard you;
> delivering you from the way of evil,
>> from men of perverted speech.

(Proverbs 2:11-12)

Elsewhere they developed the notion of wisdom as a guard who watched over the sages while they slept. With this idea they arrived remarkably close to the modern concept of culture or "ethos," that powerful network of sanctions that all individuals unconsciously assimilate just as naturally as they eat and breathe. This acknowledgement that individual effort plugged into a power which depended upon communal achievement places the sages' notion of self-reliance in an altogether new light. It follows that we should balance individualism with group influence when trying to characterize wisdom.

CONDUCT WHICH LEADS TO DESTRUCTION

The vivid descriptions of *"the adulteress"* within the first major collection of Proverbs leave no doubt about the arch villain in that author's view. Indeed, the previously cited allusion to prudence and understanding as guards who watch over obedient children concludes with the promise that these two qualities will also give protection from the seductive words of the loose woman. This text goes on to point out that she travels a direct path to death, so that anyone who falls victim to her blandishments abandons the path to life. By means of such language, the teacher confronted hot blooded young men with stark reality: anyone who fools around with an adulteress, regardless of the smooth talk with which she presents her case, has by that very decision opted for death. To her, the act comes as naturally as eating.

This is the way of an adulteress:
   she eats, and wipes her mouth,
   and says, "I have done no wrong."[22]

(Proverbs 30:20)

But her husband takes quite a different view, and no amount of money will satisfy his lust for revenge.

For jealousy makes a man furious,
   and he will not spare when he takes revenge.
He will accept no compensation,
   nor be appeased though you multiply gifts.

(Proverbs 6:34-35)

The husband's wrath is not the only factor to be reckoned with once the adulteress' enticements have caught their prey. Shame, loss of wealth, starvation, and dreaded disease befall him as well. In the end his pitiful lot will evoke a painful concession that he should have listened to his teachers' advice.

That valuable counsel took many forms: direct appeal, extended metaphor, and autobiographical narrative, to name only three. An exquisite short essay on fidelity likens adultery to drinking from a stranger's cistern, and letting one's own springs flow into the streets. This text uses several metaphors for a wife—cistern, fountain, a lovely doe, a graceful hind—and pictures her as a protective garment wrapped around her husband. The image of clothing then becomes a leitmotif which returns to the original idea of marital fidelity. Why should you be *wrapped up* in the love of an adulteress, the teacher asks, until you reach your destination, *wrapped* in a funeral shroud (Proverbs 5:15-23)?

Another essay in autobiographical style resembles this one in its descriptive power (Proverbs 7:6-27). The narrative purports to describe what a teacher has observed from his window, although it takes great liberty by exposing the imagined conversation that the author thinks must have taken place between the adulteress and her foolish young man. The time is, of course, twilight, when dark deeds multiply. Dressed like a harlot, the eager wife accosts a youth, who has already taken a step in the direction of her corner, and assures him that her husband has gone on a journey and has sufficient funds to keep him away for some time. Her appeal combines beauty and seductive speech; the foolish lad cannot reject her promise of a whole night devoted to love-play, for the fantasy of drowning himself in pleasure overwhelms him. So he takes her hand, and she leads him to his death like an ox to the slaughter-house.

> All at once he follows her,
>> as an ox goes to the slaughter,
> or as a stag is caught fast
>> till an arrow pierces its entrails;
>> as a bird rushes into a snare;
> he does not know that it will cost him his life.
>
> (Proverbs 7:22-23)

While the greatest danger confronting young men was undoubtedly another man's wife, prostitutes also lured them into wayward paths. Proverbs 6:26 seems to imply that sexual relations with a harlot are a peccadillo when compared with adultery, although the point may simply be that a prostitute's price is a pittance when set over against what a married woman demands for her favors. In the small collection that shows striking affinities with The Instruction of Amenemopet, we find the following observation about a *married* prostitute.

> For a harlot is a deep pit;
>> an adventuress is a narrow well.
> She lies in wait like a robber
>> and increases the faithless among men.
>
> (Proverbs 23:27-28)

Apparently, Israel's sages did not feel constrained, like their Mesopotamian counterparts, to warn against marrying a prostitute whose husbands are legion.[23]

It is difficult to determine which posed a greater threat to the pursuit of life's nectar: *drunkenness or laziness.* At least, the sayings treat both with considerable vigor. To be sure, wine enhanced life when used wisely.[24] But like so many good things, excessive use of wine and strong drink brought ruin without delay. One saying goes so far as to claim that anyone who loves wine and oil, the symbols for pleasurable living, will never grow rich (Proverbs 21:17). Such austerity must have struck a solitary note in a society which placed a premium on life's good things. Be that as it may, the following picture of drunkards' wretched plight rings true.

> Who has woe? Who has sorrow?
>> Who has strife? Who has complaining?
> Who has wounds without cause?
>> Who has redness of eyes?
> Those who tarry long over wine,
>> those who go to try mixed wine.
> Do not look at wine when it is red,
>> when it sparkles in the cup
>> and goes down smoothly.
> At the last it bites like a serpent,
>> and stings like an adder.
> Your eyes will see strange things,
>> and your mind utter perverse things.
> You will be like one who lies down in the midst of the sea,
>> like one who lies on the top of a mast.
> "They struck me," you will say, "but I was not hurt;
>> they beat me, but I did not feel it.
> When shall I awake?
>> I will seek another drink."
>
> (Proverbs 23:29-35)

Numerous sayings denounce sluggards and describe the dismal lot which befalls lazy persons. Matchless imagery compares a sluggard tossing upon his bed with a door's turning upon its hinges. Sometimes an element of ridicule intrudes, as in the observation that a sluggard is too lazy to lift a spoon to his mouth. The flimsy excuses that he offers for inactivity present themselves as ludicrous, for example, when he stays in the house for fear a lion might lurk on the outside. The consequences of such laziness lacked the slightest tinge of humor—since the sluggard had failed to plow his fields and plant a crop, starvation would raid his pantry. One saying almost personifies poverty and want.

> A little sleep, a little slumber,
>> a little folding of the hands to rest,
> and poverty will come upon you like a vagabond,
>> and want like an armed man.
>
> (Proverbs 6:10-11)

The point may have been that poverty will overpower its hapless victim, rather than taking him by surprise. In any event, Israel's sages tried their utmost to reduce the possibility that any sluggard could interpret his miserable fare as wholly unexpected.

Alongside these three (the adulteress, drunkenness, and laziness), *gossip* and other misuse of the tongue worked to bring destruction and to undermine society itself. So universal was this evil that one saying almost equates talkativeness and sin:

> When words are many, transgression is not lacking,
>   but he who restrains his lips is prudent.
>
> (Proverbs 10:19)

Given the strong attraction privileged information concerning forbidden conduct possesses, one is not surprised to read:

> The words of a whisperer are like delicious morsels;
>   they go down into the inner parts of the body.
>
> (Proverbs 18:8)

Some individuals reinforced their insidious vocabulary with appropriate body language:

> winks with his eye, scrapes with his feet,
>   points with his finger.
>
> (Proverbs 6:13)

For such persons, violence was food and drink.

Those who became adept at body language transformed their entire being into an organ of speech—one that succeeded in communicating wickedness from head to toe.

> There are six things which the LORD hates,
>   seven which are an abomination to him:
> haughty eyes, a lying tongue,
>   and hands that shed innocent blood,
> a heart that devises wicked plans,
>   feet that make haste to run to evil,
> a false witness who breathes out lies,
>   and a man who sows discord among brothers.
>
> (Proverbs 6:16-19)

Here as elsewhere (Proverbs 8:13) the subversive power of the tongue gets equal billing to actual physical violence. In this instance the enormity of abusive and lying words lingered in the author's imagination so powerfully that the saying returns to this theme after completing a clever "essay" about various parts of the body.

These *four kinds of threats to existence—adultery, drunken debauchery, laziness, and gossip*—were by no means the only dangers that lured young people and adults away from the path to life. But the numerous other temptations elicited less picturesque attacks. In most cases, the teachers simply name the villain: folly, pride, greed, presumption, and so forth. Often a theological refutation of such behavior is offered. False scales are an abomination to God; mockery of the poor is an affront to their Creator; pride is detestable to the Lord.

One kind of evil must have caused immense suffering through no fault of the victim, if the proverbs are to be taken at face value. I refer to the oft-mentioned *nagging wife*, who made existence a living hell.

> to restrain her is to restrain the wind
> or to grasp oil in his right hand.
>
> (Proverbs 27:16)

In short, both at home and in the open streets mighty foes poised in readiness to attack innocent prey, eager to drag still one more victim into their lair.

THEOLOGICAL SYNTHESIS

To combat such foes, self-reliance hardly sufficed. Instead, one donned the armor forged by the entire wisdom tradition (Proverbs 28:26). Whether that suit of armor fashioned wholly by human hands could withstand the poisonous arrows whistling from every direction was a debatable point. At least one teacher advised against dependence upon one's own understanding (presumably however much it was informed by the wisdom tradition) in favor of complete trust in the Lord (Proverbs 3:5). At a much later time this tension between self-reliance and trust in God crops up in the teaching of a single individual.

> Whatever you are doing, rely on yourself,
> for this too is a way of keeping the commandments.
>
> (Sirach 32:23, NEB)

> But also trust your own judgment.
> for it is your most reliable counsellor.
>
> (Sirach 37:13, NEB)

In both instances, these strong affirmations of self-reliance within Sirach give way to a religious impulse: trust the Lord, and above all pray to the Most High.

The struggle to assert the sufficiency of human effort, on the one hand, and to defend a conviction that divine aid was essential, on the other hand, turned Israelite wisdom into an exciting contest. We shall soon discover that these competing comprehensions of reality ultimately transformed the essential character of wisdom. For now, let us take a close look at this theologization of wisdom within the book of Proverbs.

To begin with, it is essential to reject the common assumption that old wisdom, as it is usually called, lacked religious content altogether. Anyone who accepts the hypothesis of an earlier secular wisdom must reckon with the fact that a conscious editing process has infused later piety into the old wisdom texts so thoroughly that the additions can only be removed by sheer conjecture. Or the person who opts for secular wisdom must be compelled grudgingly to admit that it never in fact existed. The truth residing within this attempt to isolate secular wisdom is that a definite editing of earlier sayings has taken place, one in which deeply felt religious sentiments were consciously allowed to interpret older texts. However, this editing process must surely have found a kindred base upon which to work. It follows that wisdom contained a religious element from the beginning. That ingredient must have focused upon the limits imposed upon human beings by the Creator.

> No wisdom, no understanding, no counsel,
> can avail against the Lord.
> The horse is made ready for the day of battle,
> but the victory belongs to the Lord.
>
> (Proverbs 21:30-31)

> The plans of the mind belong to man,
> but the answer of the tongue is from the Lord.
>
> (Proverbs 16:1)

As one attempts to trace the evolution of wisdom thinking in ancient Israel, he or she should not posit a movement from pure secularism to theological reflection. But how else can one tackle this vexing problem? One way is to distinguish three fundamental stages in that phenomenon called wisdom: clan, court, and theological wisdom. These three distinct types of thinking differ with regard to the goal envisioned, the stance, and the method adopted to achieve that purpose.

Clan wisdom aimed toward the accomplishing of a single goal: the mastering of life. As a means of achieving this valuable ambition, sages combined their talents in order to understand nature and human relationships. That is, they developed nature and practical wisdom. The former consisted of the study of natural phenomena and the compilation of lists in which comparable actions were placed alongside one another. The fruits of such labor now exist in the numerical proverbs and enumeration of kindred things that have been collected, for the most part, in Proverbs 30. Possibly, such texts lie behind other passages in the larger corpus of wisdom literature, particularly the divine speeches in Job, as well as Sirach 43. Practical, or experiential, wisdom was an elementary ordering of life in all its dimensions. It entailed close study of human behavior in every conceivable situation, from which certain basic principles for successful conduct were formulated. Such lessons assumed proverbial form—brief, pregnant, paradigmatic.

The chief disseminator of such succinct aids to successful living was the father. Presumably, he was assisted in this task by the mother. The two terms, father and mother, occur with sufficient regularity to warrant the conclusion that a family setting was the original context within which clan wisdom spread. Emphasis upon character formation belongs naturally to this intimate circle, as do also strong admonitions to industry, sobriety, and control of the tongue. Here sharp divisions serve to remove any possibility for error where good and evil, truth and falsehood, wisdom and folly are concerned. The hortatory stance arose as an appropriate means of reinforcing parental authority for sayings which in themselves lacked motivations and warnings to undergird their cogency. It is likely that at this early stage legal formulations and sapiential instruction greatly resembled one another, especially in style.[25]

Although the vast majority of canonical proverbs seem to have arisen within a clan setting, a few of them may derive from the *royal court*.[26] There is no reason for the tradition to arise associating Hezekiah with wisdom unless a historical basis for such thinking existed, although legends do seem to cling to this king (Isaiah 36—39) just as they do to Solomon, whom Hezekiah sought to resemble. To be sure, no single proverb demands a court setting, for persons who resided far away from palaces could reckon with royal power and the mystery of a king's personality. Conversely, members of a court could easily have reflected on the concerns described under clan wisdom above.

Court wisdom had a limited clientele; it was restricted to a select group of potential rulers and advisors to persons in power. Such activity that enabled the government to survive endless attack from without and ruthless insiders who hungered for power had to be unflinchingly realistic [27] and at times unscrupulous. The adjective "secular" characterizes this kind of wisdom. The chief means of communicating court wisdom was didactic. Here the teachers seem much more conscious of pedagogical technique; thus they attach motive clauses and reasons to their sayings. In addition, they use rhetorical questions freely, and often rely upon exhortation and admonition.

Their basic interests reflect the situation of the court: proper table manners, eloquence, propriety, humility before superiors, fidelity, and so forth. Of course, court wisdom instructs future court personnel about ways to behave around kings, and warns against presumption with respect to kings' dispositions. This kind of wisdom stresses the king's responsibility for ensuring justice, and recognizes that his throne is founded on righteousness. Perhaps the royal court gave special urgency to the universal problem of passion, inasmuch as temptations to adultery may have increased the nearer one came to the royal court. Advice about business investments and truthful witness had its place at the court. It is not known whether eloquence included the art of entertaining nobility; certainly this interest in lively dialogue comes to prominence in late wisdom. The "Contest of Darius' Guards" preserved in 1 Esdras 3:1—5:3 bears eloquent testimony to such entertainment. Nor can we be absolutely certain that riddles and impossible questions belonged at the royal court, although biblical legend and a tradition within Josephus' *Antiquities* make it highly likely that these sages sometimes busied themselves with life's enigmas.[28]

The third type of wisdom differs fundamentally from these two predecessors. *Theological wisdom* [29] spreads its net widely, hoping to catch as many subjects as possible. Its goal is to provide education for everyone, regardless of his or her social standing or vocational intention. The primary means of reaching this target are dialogue and admonition, a direct appeal that rests upon religious foundations. Argument accompanies exhortations or warnings, and themes are developed in brief essays. Underlying the whole system of instruction is a religious dogmatism concerning proper conduct before God and humans. To a certain extent, even God is caught up in this system, especially in the notion of exact reward and retribution.[30] Conscious didactic concern gives rise to numerous stylistic "niceties" and eventually produces a powerful means of relating God to creatures without relying upon direct revelation to prophets, priests, or poets.

Possibly the most distinctive feature in theological wisdom is the notion concerning proper *fear for the Lord*. This idea changes over a period of time, so that its use differs considerably in Job and Ecclesiastes from that in Proverbs. [31] For now, we are concerned only with the usage in the book of Proverbs. Here the fear of the Lord amounts to religion as we understand it today. By fear of the Lord these sages called attention to religious devotion in the richest sense of the phrase. It meant, purely and simply, that which every human being owes the Creator. That is why the editor who wrote the motto for the first collection of Proverbs can affirm that religious devotion constitutes the beginning and fundamental principle of all knowledge. Without a vital relationship with God, no one could possibly attain sufficient wisdom to merit the adjective "wise."

Initially, the phrase "fear of the Lord" seems to have amounted to religious devotion or proper awe in the face of divine mystery, but as time passed the idea became considerably broader. In the older collections within Proverbs, particularly those designated Solomonic, the term has this narrow sense of religious duty. The initial collection uses the phrase "fear of the Lord" in such a way as almost to suggest *the laws and statutes* which God had made known to Israel. To be sure, the sages who edited and compiled these discourses never quite identify the old idea, "fear of the Lord," with covenantal obligations, but one senses that these teachers would have claimed Sirach as an authentic heir to their specific tradition. In him the implicit assumptions underlying Proverbs 1—9 become entirely explicit. Fear of the Lord consists of the ancient covenantal obligations, and no genuine conflict exists between wisdom and sacred history.

The second feature of theological wisdom is by far the liveliest theme in Proverbs; that is the *personification of wisdom and folly*. This remarkable development in theological reflection arose from frequent talk about limits imposed upon human knowledge and ability, as well as from the recognition that men's and women's fates lay in their own hands. The silence of heaven was a terrible burden; so was the lack of certainty about the vast accumulation of knowledge. Did it, or did it not, accord with the will of God? In short, frail humans acknowledged a need for contact with the universal Lord, particularly as the idea of exact reward and retribution for good and evil gradually eroded. Personified wisdom achieved that purpose for these teachers.[32]

It naturally follows that prophetic influence intrudes where Dame Wisdom is concerned, for inspired utterance had been equated with prophecy from time immemorial. Thus we are not surprised to hear Dame Wisdom berating those who spurn her invitation; even her language is drawn from prophetic indictment (Proverbs 1:20-33). Here a spurned woman complains that no one heeded when she stretched out her hand in invitation, so now she will laugh when calamity strikes. Futhermore, she will withdraw so that no one can find her to intercede during the time of punishment. This dreadful moment is described with language faintly resembling futility curses—the fruit and surfeit of their labor will hardly be something for enjoyment.[33] We should note the scene for Dame Wisdom's activity: she proclaims her message in the crowded marketplace, daring to compete with one and all for the attention of the people. At one point this remarkable woman goes beyond what any prophet would have said. She promises life to those who listen to her. An Amos, for example, could speak in God's name: "Seek me and live" (5:4). But it is unthinkable that he would have spoken this way in his own name.

Some of these same themes characterize Proverbs 8, but this passage introduces some wholly new concepts. The location for her proclamation is the same, that is, the busy places where people carry out their daily activities. Dame Wisdom emphasizes the reliability of her teaching and promises that it is priceless. In addition, she boasts considerable authority—kings and governors, princes and rulers, derive their nobility from her. All this is just what one expects Dame Wisdom to say, right down to the brief description of things she despises: pride, presumption, evil courses, subversive talk. But she does not end her speech with characterizations of her present task or invitation. Instead, she reflects upon the beginning when she played in God's presence prior to the creation of the world.[34]

Wisdom was the first of God's creative works; she was fashioned long before earth and sea came to be and before the mountains and hills settled into their place. She stood beside God and watched as he constructed the heavens, girdled the ocean with the horizon, fixed the clouds, prescribed limits for the sea, and knit earth's foundation together. Playing before God, Wisdom was daily his delight, a little child bringing great pleasure. Once the earth was created she changed her playground and began to delight in men and women. Therefore, she issues her invitation to life, and pronounces blessings upon those who find her.

Once upon earth Dame Wisdom does some fashioning of her own (Proverbs 9:1). Then she invites simpletons and fools to dine in her house which had seven pillars. Her maidens assure these unlikely prospects for wisdom that all is not hopeless in their case. A few sips of her spiced wine and several morsels of her food, together with resolve to abandon folly, will accomplish wonders.

For now, we shall postpone discussion of the rich development in the sages' understanding of Dame Wisdom, particularly as they describe her in Job 28, Sirach 24, Wisdom 7—8. However, one further word needs to be said about an interesting variation in Proverbs. Just as wisdom is pictured as a woman, so folly is also portrayed in human form. Lady Stupidity is set over against Dame Wisdom, each competing for the lives of individuals.

> A foolish woman is noisy;
>> she is wanton and knows no shame.
> She sits at the door of her house,
>> she takes a seat on the high places of the town,
> calling to those who pass by,
>> who are going straight on their way,
> "Whoever is simple, let him turn in here!"
>> And to him who is without sense she says,
> "Stolen water is sweet,
>> and bread eaten in secret is pleasant."
> But he does not know that the dead are there,
>> that her guests are in the depths of Sheol.
>
> (Proverbs 9:13-18)

Here, as also in Genesis 3, knowledge is closely associated with forbidden fruit.[35] Of course, no mention of knowledge occurs in this harsh caricature of Lady Wisdom, but she must surely be understood as the opponent who boasts a better kind of knowledge than Dame Wisdom can offer. For some strange reason, later sages do not develop this highly interesting character of a Seductress. Such reluctance to speak further about Lady Stupidity surely arose from the attractiveness of fertility goddesses in the ancient world.

So far in this discussion nothing has been said about the source for this personification of Wisdom and Folly. Perhaps the Hebrew plural form *hokmot* offers a clue that a Canaanite goddess by that name existed,[36] but convincing proof for this hypothesis is lacking. On the other hand, considerable evidence for an Egyptian provenance for this portrayal of Wisdom can hardly be denied.[37] The similarities between Dame Wisdom and the Egyptian notion of *Ma'at* are striking, particularly with regard to the cosmological speculation (existence before creation, the darling of God) but also with respect to the wooing of individuals and possession of life in her hand. To be sure, Israel's psalmists and poets expressed themselves at times by means of personified virtues. From pictures of righteousness and truth kissing each other, or prudence and understanding watching over someone, it is a tiny step to personified Wisdom. But the further jump to cosmological speculation probably came as the result of outside influence.

Regardless of the provenance for this personification, the picture of Dame Wisdom possessed remarkable didactic power. Besides vividness, the portrait had sex appeal which must have captured young men's fantasies immediately. The highly erotic language associated with Dame Wisdom certainly justifies this understanding of the image. Most importantly, the idea enabled sages to talk about a heavenly messenger without unduly compromising their conviction that they themselves controlled their fate. By means of Dame Wisdom, these teachers were able to say that God does more than conceal truth at the moment of creation. Through her, he communicates life-giving knowledge in the living present.

This amazing development within canonical Proverbs means that the sages understood the tension between their own quest for knowledge and wisdom's readiness to be found, which implied in their thinking that God really desired to communicate life-giving knowledge despite a propensity toward concealing precious data. Thus they wrestled increasingly with a fundamental problem: am I for myself, or is someone else for me? That is, must I secure my existence through my own ingenuity and right conduct, or does the Creator bestow favor upon me because my own achievements do not suffice? This question became an existential one for the author of the book of Job.

CHAPTER 4

The Search for Divine Presence: Job

The book of Job comprises a poetic dialogue which has been inserted into a narrative framework.[1] As a result of this strange marriage of incompatible literary strata, tension between the prose and poetry mounts. The differences are so pronounced that many scholars refuse to interpret the dialogue by means of clues provided within the story.[2] Unfortunately, the poetry requires an introduction of some kind; otherwise it begins *in medias res* and readers are left to supply a proper beginning which would illuminate the subsequent dialogue. The epilogue, on the other hand, can be dispensed with altogether, since the poem ends appropriately with Job's acquisition of first hand knowledge about God by means of the divine self-manifestation for which Job risked everything, and the prologue has arrived at a satisfactory solution of the problem under discussion without the happy ending.

THE NARRATIVE

The theme underlying the epic substratum[3] of the didactic narrative concerns the search for a single instance of *disinterested righteousness*. The adversary (*the* Satan) formulates the problem in his initial conversation with God: For *naught* does Job serve God?" The cynical charge that Job's piety depended upon favorable external circumstances struck at the heart of ancient religion. The radical denial of genuine religious devotion was met by an equally adamant claim on God's part that his servant Job rose above selfish interests where faith was concerned. The suffering which befell God's servant provided the means by which the two opposing convictions could be adjudicated. It follows that innocent suffering functions as a *secondary* theme of the story,[4] inasmuch as Job demonstrated the *proper manner of responding to undeserved suffering.*

The prologue (1:1—2:10b) consists of *five scenes* in which action alternates between earth and heaven. The opening scene (1:1-5) sets the stage in the distant past when legendary heroes roamed the earth. The folktale beginning introduces a semi-nomadic sheikh named Job who enjoyed preeminence in the land of Transjordanian Uz, just as King Solomon is reputed to have surpassed the wisdom of the Easterners and Egyptians. Job's exceptional qualities have four foci; he was "blameless and upright, one who feared God and turned away from evil." Naturally, his family circle was complete. He had seven sons and three daughters, who enjoyed one another's company on festive occasions, which seem to have arisen frequently.[5] He also had impressive holdings: seven thousand sheep, three thousand camels, five hundred yoke of oxen and an equal number of she-asses, and of course, innumerable servants. Only one thing marred this idyllic existence; Job seemed overly anxious that his *sons* may inadvertently have sinned against God. So the suspicious father took proper precautions to ward off an angry deity.

While Job's children gathered together for the purpose of eating and drinking, a heavenly assembly of God's *sons* also took place (1:6-12).[6] Into their presence came the adversary; the Hebrew *gam* (also) almost identifies the Satan as an intruder.[7] An inquiring God learns that this figure has been traveling hither and yon to see whether a single individual worshiped God with purity of heart. The Satan's occupation had left him an utter cynic, resulting in the following creed: "Touch Job's possessions and he will curse you openly." Curiously, the Satan's eyes had not fallen upon Job during his investigations of human conduct, so that God had felt obliged to call attention to his faithful servant and to inform the adversary about Job's fourfold virtue. In doing so, God differs appreciably from that earthly father Job, who thought the worst about his own sons. (The sins of his daughters are not mentioned.) Instead, God could not imagine Job's departing from genuine piety. That trust was soon to undergo the ultimate test, for God consented to allow the Satan to strip Job of all worldy possessions. In a single stroke the protective hedge would vanish completely, and Job would prove one of these heavenly figures to be a liar. To accomplish this worthy end, Job's life had to be spared. At this point, God manages to preserve Job's health as well.

The next scene occurs back on earth where God's bounty flowed freely (1:13-21). The description of the Satan's activity achieves unusual dramatic power, particularly through repetition of certain phrases. A reference to the sons and daughters eating and drinking offers a *false sense of security,* which is soon shown for what it is when that allusion recurs in a report that knocks Job to his knees and elicits the profound confession: "Naked I came forth from my mother's womb, and naked I shall return there; the Lord gave and the Lord took, blessed be the name of the Lord."[8] Between those two references to sons and daughters who went about enjoying life's goodness two refrains drone away, shattering Job's protective hedge bit by bit. The first is the messenger's comment, "I alone escaped to tell you," and the second is the transitional remark, "While this one was speaking, another came and reported." The substance of these messages concerns four decisive blows, two from earthly powers and two from heavenly forces. The Sabeans stole Job's oxen and asses; divine fire consumed the sheep; Chaldeans made off with the camels; and a mighty wind felled a house upon Job's children. Naturally, Job's many servants perished in a vain attempt to save the cattle, and only the bearers of horror remained. Confronted with such news, Job gave full vent to his grief, but earned God's approbation. Lest the point be missed, the narrator enters the story momentarily and underlines Job's integrity: "In all this Job did not sin nor attribute fault to God."

The fourth scene (2:1-6) returns to heaven, where another assembling of God's children occurred. Again the Satan presented himself before God, who repeated the earlier inquiry concerning the intruder's activity. This time God reminded the Satan that Job has held securely to his integrity "although you moved me against him to swallow him *without cause.*" This allusion to the absence of any reason for destroying Job's "hedge" recalls the Satan's initial question, "Does Job fear God for naught, that is, without cause?" and amounts to a triumphant shout. Still, the adversary refused to concede that he has misjudged humanity; instead, he cited what sounds like an old proverb: "Skin for skin: all a man has he will give for his life."[9] Accordingly, the Satan urged God to smite Job's skin and bones, confident that the afflicted one would curse God to his face. The divine confidence in Job equals the tempter's faith in his own creed, and once again God's servant falls into compassionless hands. This time, too, a qualification occurs, and the Satan is entrusted with the ironical task of *watching over* Job's life. The same verb was also used to connote the protection which God's statutes provided from the notorious loose woman in Proverbs.

The second, third, and fourth scenes began with a single Hebrew verb; that consistency explodes in the fifth scene (2:7-10b) in order to focus upon the Satan's hasty departure from God's presence. The narrative wastes no time in recounting the consequences of the awful declaration, "Behold, he is in your hands." Stricken with grievous sores from head to toe, God's trusted servant sat on an ash heap and scraped the infected skin with sherds. His wife exacerbated his misery by imploring Job to curse God and die. Whereas God had complimented Job for holding on to his integrity, she reprimanded her husband for doing so without cause, one might add. Maintaining his integrity in the face of this deepest cut of all, Job endeavored to instruct this woman who had uttered folly at the precise moment when her husband deserved a perceptive spouse. The lesson he taught was simple but profound at the same time: "Shall we receive good from God and not accept evil?" At this decisive point the *narrator intrudes* for a second time, preempting any rejoinder from Job's companion. Instead, we are told again that "in all this Job did not sin with his lips." The final three verses in chapter two make the necessary transition from this remarkable story to the poetry where the hero dares to challenge God just as

Job's wife had wanted him to do. They introduce the three friends who came to comfort Job in his misery.

The epilogue (42:7-17) tidies up the story by degrees, placing God's servant once again within a protective wall and securing his existence until death came to gather a contented Job to his ancestors. Naturally, Job's friends stood in need of his intercession, for Job himself had maintained his integrity to the end. This negative judgment on Eliphaz, Bildad, and Zophar must arise from another story which has not survived, since we cannot imagine that what they said in the poetry would have been dismissed as lies. In any event, twice God praises Job for speaking the truth about the Lord, presumably the necessity of receiving both good and evil from him. Job's restoration followed his intercessory prayer; friends and relatives dined with Job as before and bestowed gifts upon him. In the end he had twice as much property as before, and the same number of children as previously. The three daughters came in for special notice, since their beauty surpassed that of all other women, and they were the recipients of a generous inheritance from their father. In this idyllic scene of God's favorite servant surrounded by four generations, only one jarring note is sounded: the reminder that the Lord brought all the misfortunes that necessitated comforting words from Job's companions. The reader has already been informed by God that such provocation came without *cause*.

Whoever pauses to assess this narrative from a theological perspective discerns that discordant sounds produced by a seemingly amoral deity are balanced by melodious chords occasioned by God's unshakable faith in Job's integrity. To be sure, the prologue depicts a God who permits wanton destruction of innocent victims just to prove a point. Job's sons and daughters fell in their youthful innocence, as did countless servants, and nowhere does God seem to take these "Joban possessions" into consideration as differing essentially from camels, sheep, oxen, and asses. In addition, the Lord of the prologue fulminates over Job's friends' inaccurate understanding of God and requires cultic means of atonement. Above all, this guilty Lord ties all loose ends together neatly, totally oblivious to the misery he has caused.[10]

On the other hand, the prologue addresses the fundamental

questions of human existence: does disinterested piety exist, and what explains innocent suffering? The story affirms pure religion, labeling the magical assumption that pervades most religion[11] the lie that it is, and lays undeserved suffering upon God's majestic shoulders. No attempt to explain either enigma is made; the story seems content to affirm disinterested righteousness and to acknowledge instances in which a positive correlation between sin and punishment is lacking.

The tension between profound questions and naive theology prevents one from dismissing the story as trite. Precisely because evil is somehow bound up with God the matter of disinterested piety assumes vital significance. Given the painful reality that some persons suffer without reason, the narrative asks, can that undeserved misery find a corollary in devotion that refuses to count the cost? Without such integrity, how could faith survive the unfathomable ways of the Lord? The poetic dialogue probes the depths to which an innocent sufferer was driven by an arbitrary deity who hedged Job round about with violence and provoked an authentic curse on the lips that had remained sinless in the story.

THE POETIC DIALOGUE

Job's powerful lament begins and ends with a *curse*—but not upon God. To be sure, the initial curse which Job pronounced against the day of his birth (chap. 3) calls God's wisdom and goodness into question, although indirectly. This curse upon day and night achieves unusual poetic quality, particularly in such metaphors as eyelids of dawn. Job wishes to erase the day of his birth from the calendar; how he envies those skilled in magic, for if he possessed their power he could blot out all memory of that fateful day on which he was born. Alternatively, he reckons that he would have been fortunate if he had perished at birth or been exposed to die. Having been permitted to live, and consequently to endure untold misery, he now seeks death eagerly, inasmuch as God has *hedged him round about* with adversity.

The final curse (chaps. 29—31) represents Job's endeavor to achieve God's declaration of innocence, for such vindication has not come from the three friends. Despising the present, Job reminisces about the good old days when signs of divine favor abounded. In those days he dwelt securely, his children by his side, and presided over assemblies at the city gate like a beloved elder statesman. All who knew him had cause to rejoice; he served as eyes for the blind, feet for the lame, and a father to orphans. Because of him, widows' hearts lept for joy. Job's present misery saw brigands mocking him, but worst of all, God cruelly pursued the one whose harp had been tuned for a dirge. Unable to make any sense of God's behavior, Job's confusion mounts because of belief in punishment for evil and conviction that God sees everything. Since Job knows that he is innocent, he can only believe God culpable. Therefore, he pronounces a self-imprecation, an oath of innocence,[12] and challenges God to prove otherwise. In short, Job asks that his life serve as a witness to his innocence, with the understanding that false testimony is punishable by death. Perhaps Job's knowledge that lying accusation carried the same penalty strengthened his plea that God write out the crimes for which he is being punished.

Between Job's two curses a dialogue with three friends takes place. It consists of *three cycles of speeches,* the last of which is in mutilated form.[13] Job enjoys favored status literarily, for he responds to each of the three friends. In some respects the comforters speak in unison, so that it is difficult to characterize the individual viewpoints held by Eliphaz, Bildad, and Zophar. In addition, the various responses frequently ignore the addresses they purport to answer, giving the impression that Job and friends talk past one another.

Two assertions lie at the center of Eliphaz' speeches (chaps. 4—5, 15, 22). The first is stated both negatively and positively; however it is formulated, the point stands in tension with the second claim. Since no innocent person has ever perished, wicked individuals will die, for their destruction is certain. The other assertion concerns the nature of God: human virtue is no asset to him who refuses to concede that mortals can be more righteous than God. Now if right conduct does not benefit God, why does he punish wickedness, which presumably does not harm him either? Recognizing this problem, Eliphaz claims that Job is being punished because of *excessive* wickedness. Elevation of God at human expense prompts Eliphaz to view virtue as powerless to nullify the consequences of being born of woman. His argument runs from the greater to the lesser: if God cannot trust heavenly beings, how much less must he trust those who dwell in houses that can be torn down? The literal sense of this metaphor must have cut Job to the heart, despite Eliphaz' overtures toward kindness. Perhaps he understood this allusion to Job's fallen children as beneficial, for Eliphaz thought God wounded and healed in disciplinary action.

Both points which Eliphaz forced upon Job were fully endorsed by Bildad, who makes no real advance in the argument except to provide matchless imagery for the destruction of the wicked (chaps. 8, 18, 25). For example, he likens divine punishment to the extinguishing of a lamp and a plant's destruction, pictures a hunter's powerful trap, and envisions disease and death as divine agents. It follows that such ample aids for punishment completely blot out evil, destroying its offspring without mercy. On the other hand, Bildad is certain that none born of woman can be innocent. Even heavenly bodies lack purity in God's sight; how much more man the maggot and mortal man the worm. Such convictions should have led Bildad to answer his own question, "Does God pervert justice?" with a resounding "yes." How can one talk about justice when humans are by nature guilty?

Zophar concentrates fully on the fate of the wicked, which he describes with considerable enthusiasm (chaps. 11, 20, 27:11-23). The wicked flourish temporarily, but their food soon turns to poison within the body. They then become God's enemies whom he attacks mightily, demolishing their houses, destroying their sons, and handing over wicked persons' possessions to the righteous. Oblivious to Job's suffering, Zophar insists that God exacts less than Job deserves. It naturally follows that he thinks Job's claims regarding innocence stray far from the truth. All is not lost, however, for repentance alters one's fate appreciably. Therefore Zophar appeals to Job to turn from his evil ways.

Job comes perilously close to the view that human conduct does not affect God in the slightest degree, but differs sharply from his friends with regard to the fate of the wicked (chaps. 6, 9, 12, 16, 19, 21, 23, 26, 27). He asks how his supposed sin injured the watcher of men, as if he thought God's majesty insulated him from all adverse effects of evil. Nevertheless, Job is absolutely sure that God destroys the innocent and sinners alike, for no other explanation made sense of his own suffering. Indeed, he even maintains that God maliciously mocks those who have fallen victim to undeserved misery, and implies that a conspiracy exists between God and the forces of evil. From beginning to end Job refuses to yield an inch in this conviction that God has made a grievous error in Job's case; this certainty of his own innocence leads him to interpret God's conduct as malice. God, it follows, has become Job's personal antagonist.

The sheer imbalance of power between him and God thrusts Job forward to new horizons of thought: is it conceivable that someone will come forward to arbitrate our dispute? At first the idea merely looms upon the horizon as the remotest of possibilities, but eventually it recurs as if the thought has now entered the realm of the credible. Ultimately, Job stands firmly upon a conviction that his vindicator exists on high and will call God to task for his unfair treatment of Job. Thus he wishes that his words could be inscribed upon a rock as a permanent witness, which the umpire could use to win Job's declaration of innocence. If only Job can find God, he knows his vindication will follow, for no sinner can stand in the divine presence.

The bitter realization that virtue has not reaped its appropriate rewards in his own experience brings with it a readiness to question morality itself. "Why be good," Job asks, "if God reckons one to be wicked?" The most sacred convictions of the devout crumble one by one, and Job dares to parody familiar givens of faith. The comforting thought that God watches over men and women (Psalm 8) fails to console Job, who longs for a moment's relaxation of that watchful eye. He dares to accuse God of creating him solely for the purpose of catching him in an evil act, which would justify subsequent punishment.

At times Job thinks his own suffering will be as pointless as Abel's, and utters a poignant appeal that earth refuse to cover his blood. Behind this wish is the notion that innocent blood cried to heaven until the wrong was vindicated. At other times Job seems certain that he is being tested in a furnace of affliction, just as metal is purified by fire, and that he will come forth as pure gold. Of course Job also recognizes the frailty of life and the hard lot of humankind, but he knows that his own misery cannot be explained solely by the appeal to finitude. To be sure, Job sings about God's grandeur just as readily as his three friends do,[14] but knowledge that mortals touch only the fringes of God's power brings no relief. Absolute power turned malicious threatened Job's very existence.

Job's physical suffering paled in comparison with his mental agony over this unfathomable face of God, which no longer smiles upon him but now contorts itself angrily before him. It seems to Job that this God actively destroys all hope, wearing it away like the slow erosion of rocks brought about by flowing water. Job perceives an element of unfairness in the natural order of things which grants sure expectation that a tree will put forth new growth after it has been cut down, provided sufficient water reaches the stump, but denies similar hope to humans. Memory of previous relationship with God evokes an astonishing declaration: God will remember me when it is too late, and he will long for his faithful servant. On one occasion Job recalls the reciprocity that characterized their relationship (whenever he called upon God, he answered), contrasting that memory with the present when God seems bent on disgorging his former friend. One critic puts it this way: "But here is a new tone which has never been sounded before—God as the direct enemy of men, delighting in torturing them, hovering over them like what we might call the caricature of a devil, gnashing his teeth, 'sharpening his eyes' . . . and splitting open Job's intestines."[15]

Job's lament unfolds a curious situation which bristles with irony. On the one hand, he endeavors to escape God's constant vigilance, while, on the other hand, he longs to find God who conceals himself from his former friend. Job cannot believe God capable of such personal antagonism, although his eyes tell him that such misfortune can only come from God. Death alone will afford relief from the "Hound of Heaven," so he earnestly begs God to look away for a brief moment into which the messenger of death can insert itself. The realization that death cancels any opportunity to vindicate himself gives Job renewed resolve to find God at any cost, for only by doing so can he obtain the divine declaration of innocence. That is why Job complains bitterly that he cannot discover God, and thereby states his case before the heavenly court.

> "Oh, that I knew where I might find him,
>   that I might come even to his seat!
> I would lay my case before him
>   and fill my mouth with arguments.
>
> "Behold, I go forward, but he is not there;
>   and backward, but I cannot perceive him;
> on the left hand I seek him, but I cannot behold him;
>   I turn to the right hand, but I cannot see him."
>
> (Job 23:3-4, 8-9)

The two faces of God mainfest themselves in two distinct speeches from the tempest,[16] each one of which reduces Job to silence. The first speech extols the mysteries of nature, while the second indirectly acknowledges the force of Job's attack upon God. Both speeches remove Job from the center of the picture, destroying his illusion that he occupies the central position in the universe.[17] The explusion of Job from the thrust of the speech is accompanied by a similar ignoring of the charges he has laid against the deity. As a result, the divine speeches seem completely irrelevant failing as they do to provide any answers to the problem of innocent suffering and divine injustice.[18]

The first speech resembles a majestic harangue, for God mockingly asks Job where he was during the creation of the world, and challenges him to govern nature's powerful forces and to tame those creatures who dwelt beyond the regions of human habitation.[19] The examples serve to demonstrate the sheer stupidity in Job's Titanism, but an element of humor softens the rebuke. God asks Job whether he can summon lightning, eliciting from it a submissive response "At your command!" or whether he can force the great whale to plead with him for mercy. The absence of any reference to humans in the entire speech is calculated to teach Job the valuable lesson that the universe can survive without him. In truth he cannot perform midwife service at the birth of the sea, dispense dew and rain, send the sources of light on their respective journeys, provide food for wild animals, or control the instincts of creatures like hawks and vultures. Lacking the ability to perform a single act which God isolates for his consideration, Job reluctantly admits that he cannot rule the universe. In the face of such a blustering deity, who would not be speechless?

The second divine speech addresses Job's complaint somewhat more directly and comes very close to an admission that God found the task of ruling the world a difficult one. This time God rebukes Job for justifying himself at God's expense, inasmuch as Job's vindication could only come as the result of God's pleading "Guilty" to the charge of perverting justice. In self-defense God challenges Job to conquer pride within those who thought too highly of themselves and to overthrow the wicked. Only when Job's might succeeds in vanquishing overt and covert evil will God admit that the lowly creature's right hand can save him. The detailed description of the king of the beasts, in this case a crocodile,[20] reminds Job just how ludicrous his verbal attacks upon God have been.

For a second time Job attempts a proper response now that his search for God has ended in dialogue, but the shift in subject matter leaves him unprepared to do anything except acknowledge God's power, which had never been questioned. What follows can only puzzle readers who have been led to believe Job's earlier relationship with God throbbed with vitality. Now Job claims that all previous knowledge stemmed from secondary report, whereas the present moment corrects partial knowledge through immediate sight. Earlier he had spoken things which he did not fully understand, for which Job despises himself and repents in dust and ashes. No reading of this final speech by Job removes the perplexing features,[21] nor explains why he feels obliged to repent over incomplete knowledge. Where has Job's integrity gone?

> Then Job answered the LORD:
> "I know that thou canst do all things,
>   and that no purpose of thine can be thwarted.
> 'Who is this that hides counsel without knowledge?'
> Therefore I have uttered what I did not understand,
>   things too wonderful for me,
>   which I did not know.
> 'Hear, and I will speak;
>   I will question you, and you declare to me.'

I had heard of thee by the hearing of the ear,
     but now my eye sees thee;
therefore I despise myself,
     and repent in dust and ashes."

(42:1-6)

Between Job's negative confession (31) and God's response (38—41) another speech (32—37) attempts to provide a more adequate answer to Job than the three friends had managed. The speaker, an Israelite named Elihu, is introduced in a prose section (37:1-6) which emphasizes his intense anger at Job for making himself more righteous than God and at the friends because they failed to give a convincing refutation of Job. The intrusive character of this speech is reflected in God's silence concerning this brash young man who thinks he has the final word on every question. Similarly, Job ignores him altogether, for he has already grown tired of human words.

Since Elihu's speech represents an addition to the debate, it utilizes the content of the previous arguments. This youth may have thought that he had a furrow to plow, but his fundamental line of reasoning borrowed heavily from others. Essentially, Elihu emphasized God's majesty, which removed him from human criticism, and his justice. Since God is greater than mortals, no one can condemn him. After all, sin touches humans only, and is a matter of small consequence to God. On the other hand, Elihu insists that God pays everybody exactly what they earn, although he uses suffering to instruct people in the way they should walk, and overlooks sin to allow time for repentance. From such firm convictions it naturally follows that Job is a sinner and a rebel. Therefore he stands no chance of winning his case in the heavenly court, even if he were able to find the Almighty. Instead, he must rely upon the angelic mediator's intercession, together with his own repentance and confession of sin. Naturally, this leaves no place for pointing an accusing finger at God.[22]

The tempest which brought God to Job swept all rumor concerning the deity far away. In wisdom's case no such correction of secondary knowledge takes place, and she remains known only to God. Such is the thesis of the exquisite poem concerning wisdom's inaccessibility (chap. 28) which has somehow found its way into the debate between Job and his friends. The poem paints a detailed picture of human efforts to discover precious metals and rare gems within the innermost recesses of the earth, contrasting this dangerous activity with the peaceful growth of grain far above. In this search for valuable minerals human ingenuity overcomes every obstacle, achieving resounding success. No victorious shout accompanies the quest for wisdom, whose price far exceeds that of gold and silver. Desperately seeking a clue about her whereabouts, mortals question the abyss and the sea, only to be told that wisdom does not reside with them. The closest humans come to her is a report from Abaddon and Death that they know wisdom by rumor. God alone has access to her, but he distills wisdom to humans in religion and piety. True wisdom, the poem asserts, consists in the fear of the Lord.

The poetic section has been described using such words as debate and argument, although one expects a lament from Job and comforting assurances from his three friends. The reason good intentions quickly faded arises from the disparity in starting points. Job's insistence that God was at fault could hardly be reconciled with the friends' conviction that he could not trample upon justice. They rested their case upon the general truth that God rewards virtue and punishes vice, whereas Job based his argument on the particular instance which he knew best, his own situation. Naturally, each position had much to commend it, which explains the copious arguments in defense of the general truth and the specific instance. The two sides struggled to produce authoritative warrants for their claims.[23]

The three friends appealed to at least *eight different kinds of authority* in their vain attempt to justify God's ways. They argued from universally accepted truth, for example, when claiming that the triumph of the wicked is short-lived, or when reinforcing that position with an argument from concensus.

"Can papyrus grow where there is no marsh?"

(8:11)

But a stupid man will get understanding,
when a wild ass's colt is born a man.

(11:12)

Personal experience prompted them to say, "I have seen" such and such, while careful inquiry led to certainty regarding some matters.

> "Lo, this we have searched out; it is true.
> Hear, and know it for your good."
>
> (5:27)

Access to tradition, particularly paternal legacies, afforded still another means of acquiring authoritative information.

The three friends did not stop with these easily verified warrants for their argument, but pressed forward into dimensions which were not subject to validation. Eliphaz mentions a terrifying theophany that made his hair stand up, and insists that God spoke a decisive word to him on that memorable occasion.

> "Now a word was brought to me stealthily,
> my ear received the whisper of it.
> Amid thoughts from visions of the night,
> when deep sleep falls on men,
> dread came upon me, and trembling,
> which made all my bones shake.
> A spirit glided past my face;
> the hair of my flesh stood up.
> It stood still,
> but I could not discern its appearance.
> A form was before my eyes;
> there was silence, then I heard a voice:
> 'Can mortal man be righteous before God?
> Can a man be pure before his Maker?"
>
> (4:12–17)

The question, "Can mortal man be more righteous than God?" indicates that the deity perceived the real issue being debated and endeavored to incline the scales in a particular direction. Elsewhere Eliphaz refers to God's spirit which whispers within the ear as sufficient directive, and mockingly inquires whether Job has stood within God's secret council. Zophar, too, thinks God actively declares his word and expounds wisdom's secrets. Finally, both Bildad and Eliphaz rely upon age as an accurate indication of intelligence.

> Both the gray-haired and the aged are among us,
> older than your father.
>
> (15:10)

The warrants for Job's argument do not differ appreciably from those employed by his friends to refute him. He appealed to universally acknowledged fact, for example, when insisting that an ass does not bray when its belly is full, and he did not shrink from the bold claim, "This I know!"[24] when it corresponded to general truth such as the impossibility of winning a case against God. Job also used the sages' customary language with reference to personal validation of information ("I have seen, heard, and understood") and mentioned nature wisdom as a significant source of truth, for cattle, birds, creatures, and fish bear witness to God's heavy hand. In addition, Job recommended the acquisition of information from travelers abroad, who can tell what occurs on wider perimeters of human experience. He did not hesitate to challenge one important sign of wisdom, inasmuch as he had not lived nearly so long as his friends had. Therefore, Job conceded that age gives wisdom, but noted that God turns people into idiots, which may be a polite way of accusing the friends of senility. Above all, Job insisted that personal experience possessed the power to call dogma into question. In his view every theory, however pious, was subject to personal confirmation or disconfirmation.

> "Lo, my eye has seen all this,
>   my ear has heard and understood it.
> What you know, I also know;
>   I am not inferior to you."

(13:1–2)

Elihu agreed with Job about the positive correlation of wisdom with age, since he, too, lacked seniority. The warrants for his argument comprise a happy union of personal conviction and divine inspiration. Confident that God instilled his spirit in him at birth, Elihu also claimed that God kept that inspiration up to date by means of dreams and visions. As if such ready access to God were not sufficient grounds for his rebuke, the angry Buzite even relied upon universal truth, for instance, when insisting that one who hates justice could in no way hold the reins, and alluded to nature wisdom, although disparaging what can be learned from beasts and birds.

God's careful avoidance of such warrants for his speech is

entirely in character. Everything contributes to his majesty, which needs no justification for action. Even the Hebrew syntax underlines this fact, for the questions function as strong declarations. "Were you present when I established the foundations of the world?" really means "You were not present on that auspicious occasion." Perhaps Job's grasp of this fundamental truth partly explains his ready acquiesence to God's might, for he finally realized the futility of arguing with one who rose above the law.

A HARP TUNED FOR A DIRGE

Job's spiritual crisis evokes a similar one within modern readers, who find it exceedingly difficult to sustain an objective attitude to the book.[25] In this pitiful victim of divine indifference they sense a finely tuned instrument being forced to emit unaccustomed sounds. For no reason of his own, Job's praise has changed to lament, and weeping fills the hours which drag themselves toward dawn's portals. At some time during the dark night of the soul this obedient servant launches an offensive against God. What led to his bold enterprise?

The first step toward answering this question requires one's recognizing the exemplary character of Job, who must surely stand for "everyone" in ancient Israel. In him there is a particular example of the universal situation enveloping humanity. For that reason his cries seem to arise in the depths of our being, and his longing for God who withdraws farther and farther away strikes a familiar chord in us. This means that Job's exemplary character extends to the present, transcending time and space, for his suffering resembles our own.

Now the thesis which Job exemplified is that the spiritual crisis in his life was no private affair, but represented a decisive stage in Israel's dealings with her God. The belief in divine justice threatened to collapse because of the burdens placed upon it by historical events. The older simplistic understanding of divine providence hardly reckoned with powerful empires led by deities other than the Lord, nor did it take sufficiently into account the status of individuals. To be sure, the convenient explanation for suffering—that adversity arose as punishment for sin—sufficed for a brief interval, but eventually produced a mighty outcry.[26]

That protest surfaced in various literary strata of the Old Testament, as if it had reached the nooks and crannies of daily reflection. The patriarch Abraham became its spokesman for a brief moment, and formulated the basic issue in a passionate question: "Shall not the Judge of all the earth do right?" (Genesis 18:25).[27] Wholesale slaughter of cities no longer seemed appropriate activity for a moral deity, and Abraham dared to suggest that the leavening presence of a few righteous persons ought to count for something in God's eyes. Similarly, Jonah sulked outside Nineveh's walls because God had blatantly ignored justice's requirements, and Jeremiah complained bitterly that God could not be trusted. The same suspicion overwhelmed Gideon, who called attention to a gaping disparity between belief and reality, and Habakkuk, who observed sufficient evidence to justify belief in divine blindness. The unknown author of Psalm 73 illumined the problem posed by the prosperity of the wicked in a manner that detailed his own internal struggle to survive among the faithful. Together these voices and hundreds like them raised a mighty wail in the name of justice.

Guardians of the theory that virtue is rewarded and vice punished in exact measure championed God's justice, sparing no effort in their zeal to secure cherished belief. As a consequence of this intense search for appropriate responses to the hue and cry of spiritual rebels, several explanations for suffering presented themselves with varying degrees of adequacy.[28] The essential conviction that adversity arose as divine retribution for sin took on various colorations, two of which undermined the fundamental theory. Suffering often was God's means of disciplining wayward or foolish children; it functioned to test the quality of faith; or it fell into the category of an illusion which would quickly disappear like a dream. Adversity, according to some critics, belonged to the human condition, and thus was inevitable. Therefore attaching moral blame to those whom misfortune had struck could only be viewed as a grievous error. Others acknowledged a mysterious element within suffering, and humbly abandoned the attempt to explain it. Still others preferred to see an arbitrary feature at the center of the phenomenon, divorcing suffering from moral considerations completely. One daring poet, Deutero-Isaiah, discerned a redemptive capacity within adversity, insisting that others benefited from undeserved suffering which was freely endured.

Now haphazard misfortune and vicarious suffering fall outside a theory of exact retribution; the one demeans God, and the other exalts humans. We have seen the same sort of tension within the attacks upon God's justice, for God's appeal to Jonah rests upon a passionate belief that mercy should transcend justice's strict requirements, and Psalm 73 takes comfort in the touch of God's hand despite the continued prosperity of the wicked. A readiness to take personal experience into account seems to have adopted permanent residence in both groups, hence the whole truth dwelt at neither extreme. The same judgment applies to Job and his detractors, for truth and error intermingle freely as they do in real life.

Despite this intrinsic flexibility, the conflict between proponents of these two viewpoints achieved incredible harshness. Close friends stooped to personal vilification when it became clear that neither Job nor his companions would relinquish cherished beliefs. Youth threw off restraint, claiming superior insight to gray-haired ones and implying that those who disagreed with him were fools. A distraught wife felt constrained to encourage her miserable husband to precipitate the death sentence, and one is left to wonder about her motive for suggesting an unusual form of euthanasia. Such taking leave of one's senses extended to heaven, where God deigned to show a face which inspired terror in an obedient servant who had hitherto rested in the shadow of solicitous care. As a result of this new face, innocent sons and daughters fell victim to fatal blows wielded, with God's express permission, by a member of the heavenly court.

Job's friends cherished religious conviction more than a vital relationship with the living God, for they believed in a rational deity who was enslaved by a greater principle: justice. According to them, two principles ruled the universe, and the first was not God.[29] In such a theological system, the deity was reduced to the category of *reaction*. Suffering invariably exposed guilt, and grievous misfortune signified heinous offense. Nothing justified human visions of grandeur, for decisions by men and women, however selfless and wise, made little if any difference with God, whose ways were unfathomable. Vast regions of space separated creatures from their Creator, and essential differences as well kept them at safe distance. The Lord of the Universe had more important things to do than attending puny earthlings. His unflinching commitment to justice assured restoration for properly repentant individuals, but ruled out all questioning of God's integrity even when that reputation was purchased at the expense of a great man's honor.

Job's miserable condition soon extinguished the philosophical question, "Why does God *permit* me to suffer?" and set afire the bold formulation, "Why does God *make* me suffer these injustices?"[30] The shift from suffering to God as the real problem reveals the depths of Job's agony. Torn by the discrepancy between past memory and present reality, Job strove mightily to reconcile the two faces of God. The present fury directed against him made no sense in the light of clear recollection of divine favor in bygone days. A single question burned itself into Job's anguished spirit: "Is God for me or against me?" Intuition told him that nobody could force a claim upon God, but reason insisted that virtuous individuals laid up dividends which a just God dispensed fairly. Unless this latter belief accorded with reality, Job's complaint that he had been wronged lacked force. Paradoxically, his attack on God destroyed the ground on which he stood. Nothing in Job's present experience gave the slightest reason to believe that God acted justly.

Perhaps Job could have endured God's fury if it had not been followed by his withdrawal, which shut off all dialogue.[31] An eclipse of God took place at the precise moment of Job's pressing need for answers. Faced with silence from his former dialogue partner, and confronted with empty words from human substitutes, the distraught father adopted extreme measures of provocation. The bold charges against God aimed at a single goal: to evoke God's response at any cost. Confident that a sinner dared not take a stand before God, Job aspired to personal vindication by overcoming divine silence.

THE ROOT OF THE MATTER

Placing the book of Job within the context of a spiritual crisis in ancient Israel is only the first step in the demanding task of interpretation and appropriation. Like all great literary works, this one rewards readers who come to it from vastly different starting points. What follows will attempt to indicate the rich variety of viewpoints that exists today with regard to Job.

Perhaps the only area in which something resembling consensus has formed concerns the *sui generis* nature of the work, despite comparable discussions in Mesopotamian literature. Nothing that has survived from the ancient world achieves such sublimity of thought and expression, a combination which explains the singular influence of this work to the present day. Poets, artists, philosophers, psychologists, and playwrights are drawn to Job like bees to fresh blossoms' nectar, and each one who wrestles with the book captures new insights that had previously eluded readers.

Occasionally, such new readings of Job filter down to the populace and provoke lively discussion of existential issues from people who possess little theological sophistication but who care deeply about life's essential questions. Archibald MacLeish's Broadway play, *J.B.*, introduced religious thinking into the lives of countless thousands who found his brand of humanism attractive indeed.[32] This modernization of Job conveys the spirit of the original with remarkable accuracy and power, although *J.B.*'s God lacks the ambiguity—and passion—of the biblical work. For this reason alone, *J.B.* fails to recreate the scandal that pervades Job: the tension within God between love and justice. *J.B.*'s God does not really matter, for he simply *is*; Job's God is both more majestic and more terrifying.

The uncanny ability to capture the spirit of the canonical work without doing justice to its ambiguity is also true of Carl Jung, whose *Answer to Job* represents a powerful emotive statement concerning injustice in high places.[33] Naivete with respect to ordinary historical critical issues detracts from the many fresh insights throughout this book, so that its cumulative effect scarcely reaches the heights achieved by the biblical masterpiece. Nevertheless, Jung's protest against divine disregard for human questions and his insistence that God respond more fully by embracing the human problem touch base with the concerns expressed by the source of his inspiration, however differently that author formulated them.

Naturally, other works deriving their inspiration from Job deserve some acknowledgment in this context. In most instances these examples surrender to the modern spirit so fully that they distort the sense of the original in one way or another. Goethe's *Faust* borrows the idea of a wager with the devil and creates a situation which permits him to discuss life's futility arising from the problem of evil. Classical Greek ideas and romantic philosophy suppress whatever Hebraic features may have informed the work, and the necessity for a happy ending mars this masterful discussion of the two souls residing within the human breast. A similar surrender to contemporary political philosophy or to the ideals of the counter culture has rendered recent attempts to appropriate Job less than satisfactory, despite much that is worthwhile.[34]

Literary analysis of Job confronts difficulty at the outset. What genre best describes the book? Answers vary, partly because scholars cannot agree whether to disregard the prose tale or not. If one takes the book as it stands, the most appropriate category would seem to be debate or dispute, particularly as this genre occurs in Mesopotamian wisdom. This form consists of a mythological introduction and conclusion, a dispute proper, and a theophany in which God resolves the debate. On the other hand, disregarding the prose framework, two solutions to the problem of genre commend themselves: dialogue and lament. Of these two choices, the first takes account of the fact that Job's speeches are matched by comparable ones from several individuals, so that they form a dialogue concerning human response to suffering and the character of God. Still, the dialogue opens with Job's curse and closes with his submission, so that a genre which concentrates on Job's singular position must not be ruled out in principle. That being so, the category lament naturally comes to mind. Of course, one can further refine such attemps to isolate the peculiar genre that best characterizes Job. The book may thus be viewed as a paradigm of an answered lament, which implies that it served as a model to teach people how to respond during suffering.

Resemblances between laments within the Psalter have not escaped notice, for many of Job's speeches register the same complaints that occupied the authors of individual psalms. These similarities are so striking at times that they have generated discussion of Job's dependence upon the Israelite cult, particularly with respect to repentance, confession, and forgiveness. In addition, the theophany has seemed to corroborate such thinking, since God's self-manifestation within the cult played a significant role in Israelite religion. On the other hand, complaints do not necessarily point to the cult, for laments occurred widely in daily life, just as repentance and restoration did. The same goes for theophanies, which took place wherever God chose to lift the curtain concealing his holiness from human eyes.

Further cause for caution in this endeavor to relate the book of Job closely with the cult arises from the careful avoidance of anything that would identify Job as an Israelite. To be sure, this tendency derived from the sages, who had acquired international tastes. For this reason, the search for historical allusions within Job is not likely to produce positive results, for Job's experience does not signify the main events of Israel's history. However, resemblances between Job and certain canonical works, specifically Deutero-Isaiah[35] and the hymnic passages in Amos,[36] attest to a desire to link Job more closely with Israel's religious thought. In their own way, these two literary entities were just as radical as Job, for the doxologies of Amos praise God despite a death sentence, and the prophet of deliverance views vicarious suffering in a redemptive light.

Such affinities between Job and other canonical works complicate matters when it comes to determining the ethos within which this powerful discussion of innocent suffering and divine character arose. Prophetic elements, psalmic features, legal language, and wisdom occur. Thus far silence has prevailed with regard to striking references to a trial before the heavenly tribunal. This explicit language permeates Job's speeches, and suggests that the debate is more properly a legal dispute.[37] The difficulty with this attractive hypothesis is that Job longs for the opportunity to confront his accuser in court, but despairs of doing so. His final imprecatory oath certainly belongs to a legal dispute, but ritualistic and cultic associations seem to prevail. The divine speeches make a mockery of human notions concerning a trial, as also do baseless accusations by Job's three friends and Elihu.

Despite these elements from various literary strands, the dominant one is surely wisdom. That judgment does not depend wholly upon analogy with Mesopotamian wisdom literature, but finds reinforcement from closer to home. The theophany preserves choice examples of nature wisdom, while the entire book owes its inspiration and much of its language to the sapiential tradition. We need not assume that the poem on wisdom's inaccessibility derives from the same hand that wrote the dialogue, but we ought to congratulate the unknown person who inserted this unusual poem, for it certainly catches the spirit of the greater literary entity. True wisdom, like God, defies human reason.

The partial nature of all answers to ultimate questions can find no more eloquent testimony than the book of Job. Who speaks for the author? Since Job is given free reins to respond after each of his friends, it has been claimed that the scales tilt in his favor. That sort of reasoning cannot suffice if we consider the Elihu speeches, to which Job proffers no reply. Surely we must not suppose that the poet intended for Elihu to be his or her mouthpiece. By the nature of the case, God supplied the definitive word, which crushed Job's Titanism like a caterpillar under the wheels of a steamroller. But does God speak for the poet? Certainly Job's friends do not speak for God, since they succeeded only in earning God's scorn—if the narrative ending can be heeded.

In determining the poet's sentiments, the reader must ask whether the ancients appreciated spiritual rebels any more than institutionalized religion does today. The answer to that question may not be quite so significant after all, for the wisdom tradition was itself a witness to a different understanding of reality from the one that characterized Israel's religious community. Nor should one overlook the remarkable tolerance with prophetic, legal, and narrative texts. At times it appears that God welcomes a good debate, so eager is he for dialogue. In the light of numerous instances of rebellion against God in the Hebrew Scriptures, together with accounts in which the Lord of the Universe entered into discussion with troubled souls, Job was not automatically labeled a rebel without cause. Ancient readers must surely have responded positively to his cry, and therefore could have heard the poet's voice in Job.[38]

This judgment does not lead to denigration of Job's friends, (but see 42:7-9) for these men endeavored to lead Job on the path to repentance. While their conviction that God ruled the universe fairly brought immense spiritual consternation to Job, we must not forget that they suffered considerable abuse from their friend. In addition, who can say that adherence to religious conviction in the face of contradictory evidence is wholly wrong? Only shallow faith would result if the dimension of mystery departed, and we clung only to what could be verified. In a way, Job's friends are partly victimized by the literary genre in which they appear, but they also exceed proper bounds when praise of God comes at the expense of human beings. Surely no sage wished such sentiments to be mistaken for his own.

To a certain degree, modesty would have prevented the poet from putting his own words in God's mouth. To be sure, the divine speeches communicate effectively for the poet, but his sympathies lie with Job rather than with his attacker. At the same time, the poet's own feelings surface in God's painful concession that the human realm posed acute problems to his rule, if that is really the meaning of the challenge to conquer pride and wicked conduct among humans. Therefore Job's final remark should not be understood ironically. Neither Job nor the poet, in my view, showed contempt for the kind of God who parades before his wild creatures and recalls the taming of nature. Such a God must surely have inspired awe—would it have been God if his appearance accomplished less?

What, then, has Job learned from this first-hand encounter with God? Perhaps the first thing he discovered concerned the mistaken reason for Job's quest. The consuming passion for vindication suddenly presented itself as ludicrous once the courageous rebel stood in God's presence. By maintaining complete silence on this singular issue which had brought Job to a confrontation with his maker, God taught his servant the error in assuming that the universe operated according to a principle of rationality. Once that putative principle of order collapsed before divine freedom, the need for personal vindication vanished as well,[39] since God's anger and favor show no positive correspondence with human acts of villainy or virtue. Job's personal experience had taught him that last bit of information, but he had also clung tenaciously to an assumption of order. Faced with a stark reminder of divine freedom,[40] Job finally gave up this comforting claim, which had hardly brought solace in his case.

Job's loss may have been accompanied by significant gain—the ability to cherish God's presence for naught, to quote the Satan's language. But God seems not to have encouraged Job along these lines, perhaps because presumption with regard to personal relationship can be equally as wrong as presuming that God bows before a principle of human justice. That is why Job's sole recourse was to melt away before divine mystery. Nevertheless, enforced silence in the presence of one who has just spoken, even in rebuke, surpasses speechless indifference from on high. Unlike a fortunate Job, Qoheleth never so much as provoked a personal reprimand from the silent heavens.

CHAPTER 5

The Chasing After Meaning: Ecclesiastes

With Qoheleth the ultimate goal of wisdom became considerably more ambitious than it was in Proverbs or Job. The sages who composed canonical proverbs undertook a modest task—the discovery of life-securing knowledge by which they could demonstrate fidelity to the divine will as it penetrated the universe itself. For the unknown author of Job, the single purpose that enabled the innocent sufferer to endure incredible agony was the hope of recovering an earlier relationship with a God who had withdrawn into inpenetrable silence. Both quests were accompanied by faith in the universe and its Creator, even if in Job's case the basis for such trust had crumbled. In addition, both Proverbs and Job are products of a wisdom ethos that placed great confidence in the human intellect. The author of Qoheleth lacked trust in either God or knowledge. For him nothing proved that God looked upon his creation with favor, and the entire wisdom enterprise had become bankrupt. The astonishing thing is that such skepticism did not prevent Qoheleth from asking the question of questions: does life have any meaning at all?

The understanding of wisdom as a search is singularly appropriate for Qoheleth. Twice the name Qoheleth occurs within the body of the book; in each case the author speaks self-consciously about his goal as a sage. In both instances he uses two words for searching, as if to say that his entire life had constituted a quest for meaning. Moreover, the first text (1:12-18) has Qoheleth identify himself as king over Israel in Jerusalem, a literary fiction that justifies the adjective *royal*. Here two verbs for searching occur (*daras* and *tur*) as the focus of firm resolve. Qoheleth's determination to seek out and explore everything that happens under heaven was achieved through means of wisdom. While *daras* suggests ordinary searching, *tur* connotes extraordinary measures more appropriate to spying. Together the verbs imply that Qoheleth left no stone unturned in his relentless search for a single meaningful act on earth.[1]

The final verdict of this quest pronounces judgment upon God: "It is a sorry business which God has given humankind to occupy itself with."* Small wonder Qoheleth announces the results of his search in a refrain that the entire book echoes: "Then I saw everything that is done under the sun, and lo everything is empty and a striving after the wind." For him divine gifts evoked no ecstatic shout, inasmuch as one's lot could not be altered. The crooked could not be straightened, and what was lacking could not be counted. Indeed, superior knowledge comprised no real asset, for increased sorrow invariably accompanied expanding insight.

The other text (7:23-29) juxtaposes Qoheleth's vision of achieving wisdom and the stark reality of its inaccessibility. No amount of desire to become wise sufficed, since the goal remained far away and very deep, beyond human acquisition. Although Qoheleth determined to know, explore, and search out wisdom and the sum of things, he found one good man in a thousand and no woman among all these. In this context the verb which suggests spying is coupled with a customary expression for seeking (*baqas*), and both are reinforced by the oft-recurring verb for finding (*masa'*). Unfortunately, Qoheleth was able to find out nothing positive. From such unhappy discoveries he drew a painful conclusion: "God has made mankind upright, but they have sought out many contrivancies." The implication is that collectively they

---

* Translations of Ecclesiastes are the author's, unless otherwise indicated.

have found ways to corrupt things, a view which stands in tension with the earlier denial that those who dwell under the sun could change their pre-determined lot—unless we should attribute perverse intentions to God. Does Qoheleth imply that God fixed all fates in such a way that perversion naturally followed?

The author of the first epilogue within the book remained true to Qoheleth when trying to characterize his mentor's activity (12:9-11). After calling his teacher a wise man who taught the people, this admirer describes Qoheleth as one who deliberately searched for and arranged numerous proverbs. The sense of the rare verb (*'azen*) is uncertain, but it must mean something like weigh or ponder. The second verb (*ḥeqer*) is identical with that used in Proverbs 25:2 with reference to a king's glory in searching out things that are hidden. As if this allusion to seeking were insufficient, the student proceeds to reinforce the idea. Qoheleth sought (*baqaš*) to find (*maṣa'*) pleasing words, and faithfully wrote truth. In short, both Qoheleth and his epilogist used verbs connoting search whenever the title Qoheleth occurred.

MAJOR THESES

At the end of this search, what discoveries enriched Qoheleth's knowledge? An attempt will be made to clarify Qoheleth's thinking by examining five major convictions: (1) death cancels everything; (2) wisdom cannot achieve its goal; (3) God is unknowable; (4) the world is crooked; and (5) pleasure commends itself. All five of these theses flow from a loss of trust in the goodness of God, the presupposition of earlier wisdom. Even Job had secretly harbored a powerful faith that God really intended good things for devout people, despite the serious rupture in the universe at the moment. But Qoheleth could muster no confidence in God's disposition to reward virtue and punish vice. In his view, Job's exceptional experience of innocent suffering had become the rule, and the death angel[2] made no distinctions among creatures. Naturally, Qoheleth thus struck at the heart of the tradition in which he had been nurtured. Between him and old wisdom stretched a great abyss which was too deep for either to cross.[3]

A. Death Cancels Everything

The chasm separating Qoheleth from his predecessors could hardly be wider than in 2:17 ("So I hated life because the work that is done under the sun is burdensome to me; for everything is empty and a chasing after wind"). Life, the highest good to earlier sages, has now become an object of loathing. This shocking discovery registers Qoheleth's conclusion to a series of experiments concerning possible meanings of life. Pretending to be King Solomon, whose wisdom surpassed that of eastern kings and whose power was limitless, Qoheleth tested the various answers to life's meaning: pleasure, work, wealth, renown, wisdom. In the end he judged them all to be worthless since death cancels any advantage which might have accrued to the sage. Ultimately, all of these so-called meanings, for which humans strive relentlessly, amount to nothing. The two images emphasize the insubstantial quality of such rewards for striving. The first (*hebel*) refers to breath, which is real but fleeting, while the second (*reuth ruaḥ*) alludes to chasing after wind (or feeding upon air).

In denying absolute value to feasting, toil, possessions, fame, and knowledge Qoheleth conceded that they do possess fleeting significance. Still, pleasure vanishes quickly, while time eventually erodes human achievements and obliterates all memory of great men and women. Knowledge, too, bestows only relative advantage, enabling people to see the fate that encounters them. Unfortunately, a common end unfolds for the wise and the fool. Moreover, that death often benefits surviving fools who inherit the fruit of a sage's toil. Such reflection thrust Qoheleth forward into radical denial of life's goodness. After a lifetime of toil, no profit remains, and the sum of things resembles one mighty act of breathing.

In this regard humans merely participated in a futile exercise that characterized the universe as well. While generations come and go, the world endures time's passing. But ceaseless movement of the cosmos succeeds only in going around in a circle. Streams flow to the sea, the sun pants toward its goal, and the wind blows endlessly—yet things remain unchanged. The sum of all activity, human or natural, was one huge zero, the greatest emptiness.

It follows that Qoheleth preferred the day of death to the

moment of birth, since human illusions burst before the harsh reality that removes all distinctions among people. Sheer honesty compels Qoheleth to declare that it is "better to go to the house of mourning than to frequent the house of feasting, since it is the end of everyone, and the living should reflect upon it." Thus he concluded that sadness was better than laughter, inasmuch as a heart is gladdened by a sorrowful countenance. Precisely what he means by this declaration escapes us, unless he refers to the proverb that understood harsh discipline as a necessary stimulus for eventual happiness. In any case, he notes that the wise gravitate toward houses of sorrow while fools throng banquet halls.

In one sense death commended itself to one and all: it brought rest from all labor. The image of death as rest functions powerfully in Qoheleth's thought. Consideration of the sorry lot experienced by those who lacked power to fend for themselves among corrupt companions moved him to startling observations: the dead were more fortunate than the living, and better than both were those who have not been born. In this context the twofold reference to an absence of comforters indicates how close Qoheleth came to throwing off his disinterested cloak. The chiastic linking (*abb'a'*) of rampant oppression and evil under the sun (4:1, 3) demonstrates the unusual impact social injustice achieved on this teacher.

Not all cruelty originated with humans. In 6:1-6 Qoheleth moved from considering divine injustice to questioning the advantages of living when compared with the peace surrounding an aborted birth. This extreme judgment was not put forth without qualification; to ignore the circumstances prompting the strange conclusion would lead to gross misunderstandings. Qoheleth objects to instances in which wealth and longevity have not been accompanied by power to profit from them, however fleetingly, so that a stranger devoured the fruit of another man's labor. In such instances a stillborn child was luckier than the miserable wretch who toiled in vain, for it found rest.

These two texts (4:1-3; 6:1-6) look upon death as entirely welcome under certain circumstances. The first generalizes from common misery, and the second refers to a specific instance. Since wickedness thrives unchecked, death—nay, non-existence—is better than life. The powerlessness of poor victims of society is thus taken for granted; devoid of hope, they face an intolerable existence. Sometimes the unfortunate individuals are those who seem to enjoy divine favor, for all life's good things surround them. For some unexplained reason, certain persons live in luxury's lap without a moment's fulfillment of desire. When that happens, Qoheleth observes, an aborted birth is more fortunate.

For others whose experience has been different, Qoheleth concedes the natural desire to live as long as possible. Thus he advises against conduct that would shorten one's days; this warning to avoid extreme virtue or vice endorses a sort of middle way, the path of least resistance.[4] Perhaps Qoheleth would have urged others to greet death with open arms if they could have discovered the right time to do so. Unfortunately, such conduct remained without meaning so long as death's proper time lay in mystery. To be sure, the debilitating effects of inevitable decay (12:1-8) hardly commend themselves to anyone. In effect, the deterioration of body and mind slowly drains away every ounce of dignity a person has accumulated in a life time, leaving utter emptiness. Unlike a newborn babe, this human shell has used up its potential once and for all. The shattering bowl can only presage release for one whose existence death finally cancels.

Even when Qoheleth seems to endorse life as intrinsically better then death, he may speak ironically. The crucial text (8:16—9:6) bristles with polemic against the wisdom establishment. In this instance Qoheleth boldly rejects claims that sages can find out what God is doing. Although human deeds, good or evil, reside in God's mighty hand, no one can determine whether God's disposition toward human beings is love or hate. With absolute certainty one thing looms before them: a single fate befalls righteous and unrighteous, clean and unclean, sacrificer and non-sacrificer, good and bad, swearer and the one who disdains oaths. No wonder human hearts are filled with evil and madness, which death alone stills.

At this point Qoheleth pauses to declare that the living have hope, "for the living know that they will die, but the dead know nothing, and have no more reward, since their memory is forgotten" (9:5). In addition, "their love, their hatred, their passion have already perished, and they no longer have a portion in anything that is accomplished on earth" (9:6). To demonstrate his point, Qoheleth quotes a familiar aphorism: "A living dog is better than a dead lion" (9:4b, RSV). Whatever this saying means in context, it surely does not imply that knowledge that one is going to die constitutes real hope. Instead of giving hope to the living, such insight furnishes a stark reminder that all human achievement is futile. At least those who have entered the land of darkness have sloughed off every vestige of passion and do not participate any longer in human madness.

Futhermore, death carries its victims on a journey from which none returns. Just as persons came into this world naked, so they return without anything which they accumulated in the intervening years. Both people and beasts share the same fate—they return to dust. Qoheleth shrinks from the impact of this observation only far enough to qualify it with a rhetorical question: "Who knows whether human breath ascends and animals' breath descends?" (3:21). Elsewhere he leaves no doubt about his own answer to this question. A god who tests human beings to show them that they are but beasts cannot be expected to separate the two in death. At that decisive moment chance reigns:

> The race is not to the swift, nor the battle to the strong, nor bread to the wise, nor riches to the intelligent, nor favor to the men of skill; but time and chance happen to them all.
>
> (9:11, RSV)

The divine hunter's snare falls without warning, and silence ensues.

For a fleeting moment Qoheleth flirts with the remote possibility that death occasions a remarkable distinction between humans and beasts. Whereas dust returns to the earth, human breath ascends to God who gave it. Surely this text (12:7) furnishes solid evidence for abiding hope. On the contrary, for Qoheleth proceeds to declare the meaning of the matchless allegory concerning old age and death: "The emptiness of emptiness, says Qoheleth, everything is empty" (12:8). Such a conclusion would be meaningless if the allusion to breath's return to God contained the slightest foundation upon which to build any hope. For Qoheleth the divine support of life has entirely vanished. In his view the final word is death's chilling summons.

The natural conclusion to the twin concepts that death offers *rest* for the weary and that the living have no *real* advantage over the dead must surely be an enthusiastic endorsement of suicide. The puzzling inconsequence of Qoheleth's thought concerns the lack of any positive attitude toward speedy termination of life. Unlike those who composed comparable works in Egypt and Mesopotamia, Qoheleth refused to view suicide as a way of resolving the immense existential anxiety in which he moved and breathed. Its lure would seem irresistible for one who hates life and who falls into despair's vise-like grip. As we shall soon see, another powerful answer presented itself and etched its features indelibly into Qoheleth's heart.

B. Wisdom Cannot Achieve Its Goal

Death's shadow was not the only cause for Qoheleth's *ennui*. Another source of his negative observations about life was the recognition that wisdom could not secure existence. Earlier sages had endorsed wisdom with confidence that knowledge assured life's good things. In their view, one could know "what was good for women and men," and, knowing it, he could achieve the desired end. Such optimism failed to persuade Qoheleth that individuals could control their future. Instead, he insisted that wisdom could not achieve its goal.

To be sure, some insight surrendered to persistent inquiry, but that tiny bit of knowledge only complicated reality. Far from bestowing tranquility upon those who successfully acquired a degree of wisdom, this information resulted in troubled minds and exhausted bodies. Open eyes beheld grievous injustice, both human and divine, and sought in vain for redress from wrong. In such a world, ignorance was surely a way to insulate individuals from suffering because of grievous injustices on every hand.

Random insights hardly sufficed for Qoheleth, who aspired to total knowledge. His vocabulary soars over the expanse of the universe; phrases like "under the sun," "under heaven," "everything," "the sum of things" and so forth abound. Here is a thinker who wanted to accomplish more than the mere cumulation of facts about separate entities. Indeed, Qoheleth wished to penetrate to the underlying meaning of all knowledge. In the end, he lacked the key that would unlock the vault within which ultimate purpose lay untouched.

That closed door was not God's way of preventing humans from discovering that the world was their greatest enemy. On the contrary, the universe was created orderly, since everything was appropriate in its time. Qoheleth did not wholeheartedly accept the priestly writer's enthusiasm concerning the goodness of creation, but altered the language significantly. Whereas the first creation account repeatedly declares that "God saw that it was good," Qoheleth qualifies that declaration.

> He has made everything beautiful in its time,
>   he has also placed ignorance in their heart,
> yet so that one cannot find out the work God does from first to last.
>   (3:11)

Here one encounters theologically neutral vocabulary instead of the weighty priestly writer's terms for "create" and "good." In addition, Qoheleth attributes a gift of dubious value to God. That difficult word has been translated "ignorance" although "eternity" is also possible. In either case, this divine gift does individuals no good, since they cannot discover it at all.[5]

Like unused wisdom, a gift that defies discovery amounts to heartless teasing. Elsewhere Qoheleth mentions a tragic instance in which a poor wise man's knowledge went to waste because no one remembered him when the city was threatened by a powerful king (9:13-16). If only someone within the besieged city had recalled the poor sage, he would have delivered the unfortunate people.[6] Since his knowledge about warfare lay dormant when survival depended upon its awakening, calamity struck a forgetful population. Even when men and women remember God's gift, it remains untouched and thus inconsequential. In fact, such a gift actually generated anxiety, for it created a longing for full knowledge or for eternity.

This desire to achieve complete knowledge has a single purpose: to control the future. It follows that inability to find out God's activity at any point signals doom for all efforts at securing one's existence. To be sure, Qoheleth seems to acknowledge wisdom's capacity to grant life to its owner in one instance (7:12), but the context places such optimism under a heavy cloud. As so often happens in Qoheleth's thought, traditional wisdom is cited for the purpose of demonstrating its inadequacy. How can wisdom bestow life, he asks, when no one can alter what God has already shaped? Futhermore, nobody can discover anything concerning the future (7:13-14). If the twisted reality God has fashioned inevitably persists, and the future lies under a veil of ignorance, then wisdom cannot give life to those who strive for earthly security.

In dealing with the inability to control the future Qoheleth registers his own certainty through his choice of syntax; rhetorical questions function as powerful statements (7:13; 6:12; 8:7; 10:14). No one can straighten what God has made crooked! No one knows what is good during one's empty life which he passes like a shadow, and nobody can tell him what will occur afterwards on earth! No one can predict the future! Such linguistic forms scarcely yield evidence that Qoheleth's mind fluctuated with regard to securing the future by wisdom.

Wherever the topic of an uncertain future surfaces, it invariably gives no comfort to those who endeavored to transform the wisdom enterprise into a "science of the times."[7] While we cannot be sure such a background evoked Qoheleth's sharp rebuke in 8:17, it seems likely. Sages may claim to possess knowledge of the times, but their many boasts are empty lies. That much Qoheleth knows for certain. Like the contingencies of birth and death, over which individuals have no power, the future lies in God's hand. Nobody knows what will be, for who can inform him about the future (8:7)? Ceaseless toil alone cannot enable one to find out what God is doing (8:17). Although a definite time for everyone exists, none can ascertain that fateful moment. As a result, all people blunder blindly into the net like fish, and are captured like helpless birds when the trap falls (9:12).

The reason for the miserable plight of God's creatures lies in the nature of wisdom, which is beyond reach. Qoheleth's description of wisdom as a deep abyss reveals an astonishing lack of faith in human goodness. Members of the masculine minority have precious little grounds for pointing an accusing finger at women, since only one in one thousand separates the two genders where virtue is concerned (7:23-29). Elsewhere Qoheleth denies that anyone succeeds in doing right all the time, so that ultimately all who once were upright *(yašar)* now veer from their true destination. Unable to penetrate into the depths and to retrieve the secret that unlocks one's fate, we conjure up emergency aids.

If we cannot determine our future, however much we try, God's disposition toward us becomes a matter of life and death. Happily, Qoheleth thought that God was generous beyond comprehension. The only problem was that the gifts seemed to follow no identifiable pattern, so that an element of arbitrariness prevailed. Men and women possessed no control over the goods which God dispensed in his own time and manner. Not even morality purchased the best gifts, and often good people waited in vain for signs of divine favor while rich rewards speedily greeted evil acts. In short, the trouble with gifts was that God retained control over them. In a sense God forced men and women to rely upon him for everything. Where, then, does human mastery of existence through wisdom find a toe hold?

The inevitable consequence of such thinking would seem to be some form of determinism. Since God's works cannot be altered, and none can discover what the Creator is doing now or intends to do in the future, the nerve of life atrophies. The temptation is to throw up one's hands in despair, rather than to tackle life's enigmas with confidence. In such unhappy circumstances the perfectly natural reaction is to reject the possibility of knowing the meaning of anything (8:1).

Now if one asks what has transpired within wisdom thinking at this point, a single response resounds through the halls of learning. The urge to master life has suddenly rammed against a solid wall; the earlier assumption that wisdom could secure life has collapsed for Qoheleth. Once upon a time individuals could identify themselves as devout ones *(ṣaddiqim)*, inasmuch as they belonged to a particular group by virtue of their essential character. Goodness was a status, and people could recognize to which camp they belonged. Such assurance no longer existed, and nobody knew whether God smiled or frowned on him or her.

C. God Is Unknowable

Of course, the mystery surrounding God need not arouse consternation, for the One who fills heaven and earth is by nature invisible. Still, Israel's sages had managed to say much about this mysterious deity whose wondrous name concealed more than it divulged. Qoheleth acknowledged God's mystery, likening it to the amazing power that forms an embryo within the womb of a pregnant woman. Instead of deriving comfort from this unknown and unknowable divine essence, Qoheleth complained that God's activity was just as hidden as his nature. The miracle of life occurs and no one knows how such transformation takes place; likewise God moves within the universe without leaving enough clues to permit men and women to recognize divine presence at any time (11:5).

Contemporary thinkers find Qoheleth's theism somewhat puzzling, for it would seem more natural to abandon belief in God altogether. Not for a single moment did he entertain the possibility of atheism. For Qoheleth God was a given which not even the skeptic could doubt. How perilously close he comes to depicting God as the force behind all things! Indeed, Qoheleth speaks as if God were indifferent power before which we must cower in fear, and often equates God's will with whatever happens.

In one sense God approaches the personal—he acts with malice toward his creatures. On one occasion Qoheleth actually describes God as testing men and women to show them that they are beasts (3:18). In the conclusion based on the majestic poem about an appropriate time for everything he implies that God conceals the knowledge that would enable people to take advantage of this gift (3:1-11).[8]

Such an understanding of God left no place for personal relationship, however desirable it may have been to persons whose God was extolled for fidelity to a covenant. Although earlier sages had never adopted this kind of language from prophets and priests, neither had they presented God as indifferent to human conduct. In

Qoheleth's mind it was impossible to tell whether God looked upon humans with interest or with disdain. As a result, Qoheleth never addresses God in dialogue, either in prayer or lament. Whereas psalmists frequently complained about the same inequities that disturbed Qoheleth, they directed their attacks to God. They did so because of a vital personal relationship with the champion of widows and orphans. Like Job, these bold defenders of justice believed that God wished to repair the rupture that had endangered a vibrant personal relationship.

Lacking any such experience with God, Qoheleth advocated prudence before absolute power. The best procedure was to avoid the limelight, but if people must approach sacred territory they should do it cautiously. Economy of speech was better than extended talk, for the more individuals speak the more likely they are to incur divine wrath. Besides, a great distance separates worshipers and deity. Does Qoheleth mean that God cannot hear the words, and that they are so much wasted breath? On the other hand, Qoheleth warns against taking vows if one is not absolutely certain they will be carried out. The danger posed by an angry deity implies that God hears vows and later checks to make certain they have been kept. Apparently, the messenger from God is the death angel, who can hardly be expected to excuse foolish impulses (5:1-6).[9]

With this passage we have arrived at one of the most vexing problems in Qoheleth's thought. Did he believe God would judge the sinner and punish wickedness? To be sure, a few texts assert the traditional understanding of retribution. On the other hand, the overwhelming impact of the book points in the opposite direction. In one remarkable case Qoheleth argues that every official owes allegiance to another, so that injustice occasions no real anxiety. The inevitable conclusion of such reasoning places the responsibility for abuse of power upon God, the ultimate Ruler. It follows that the deity alone can be blamed for the cruel realities that surround us daily (5:7-9). In one sense Qoheleth embraced the expectation of divine judgment: God would bring every living thing into the waiting arms of death. Nevertheless, Qoheleth differed from traditional views in denying that God was likely to make moral distinctions at that time.

The careful reader will have noted that Qoheleth seems to know far more about God than his theology of divine mystery allows. In truth, he frequently makes assertions about God's will and activity despite the protestations about God's hiddenness. In some instances these observations come rather close to the modern notion of fate, and in others they reflect an equation of God with whatever happens. Occasionally, such comments almost endorse humor with respect to God.

Perhaps the most conspicuous declarations concerning God's will have to do with the gift bestowed upon humans indiscriminately. That gift can be labeled "sorry business" (1:13), but it can also be called the single answer to the endless quest for meaning (2:24-26; 3:13). Eating, drinking, and enjoying life constitute God's gift to those who make the most of their youth. In one surprising text Qoheleth encourages such behavior and justifies it with the claim that God has already approved the action (9:7). Such a defense of festive living seems to presuppose that God endorses whatever happens, since he has ultimate power. Obviously, nothing could happen that did not meet with divine approval.

Twice Qoheleth speaks of God in highly ambiguous language (3:15; Heb. 5:19 [5:20]). The first instance pictures God chasing prior events as if to ensure that nothing new occurs under the sun. Here God seems preoccupied with past, present, and future—so much so that wickedness thrived on earth. The other text may allude to God's way of reducing the troubled hearts of men and women, so that joy alone impresses itself upon the memory. Alternatively, it may accuse God of afflicting them with thoughts of unachieved joy. The latter of these interpretations accords with Qoheleth's understanding better than the former. Both texts therefore approach the ludicrous. God's ceaseless activity is just as meaningless and vexing as human striving. No wonder Qoheleth took the further step toward nihilism: the universe itself cannot be trusted.

D. The World Is Crooked

Qoheleth's predecessors made two fundamental assumptions about the nature of reality: God was moral, and the world was trustworthy. Neither presupposition survived Qoheleth's critical scrutiny. Natural movement led to no purposeful goal (1:4-9), since nothing unexpected ever intruded upon the scene. No episodic moments when nature smiled upon good men and women brightened the horizon, and no goal beyond the sunset awaited saint and sinner. Instead, the breezes went on their daily rounds, and rivers flowed into the sea, but nothing about this circular movement suggested that an underlying purpose could be found.

Within the existential boundaries of birth and death fell many meaningful eventualities, provided that one could discover the right time for each. No such fortune befell mortals, who watched helplessly as these great events transpired in their own time.

> a time to be born, and a time to die;
> a time to plant, and a time to pluck up what is planted;
> a time to kill, and a time to heal;
> a time to break down, and a time to build up;
> a time to weep, and a time to laugh;
> a time to mourn, and a time to dance;
> a time to cast away stones, and a time to gather stones together;
> a time to embrace, and a time to refrain from embracing;
> a time to seek, and a time to lose;
> a time to keep, and a time to cast away;
> a time to rend, and a time to sew;
> a time to keep silence, and a time to speak;
> a time to love, and a time to hate;
> a time for war, and a time for peace.
>
> (3:2-8, RSV)

Inasmuch as no one could match a moment with the appropriate deed, a certain degree of chance inevitably followed. Earlier wisdom was founded upon the conviction that one could indeed discern the right deed for the occasion.

In such a universe suffering is hardly eased by soothing thoughts that it was deserved or that it will eventually be removed by a forgiving deity. Instead, innocent victims weep uncontrollably and nobody comes to their aid. The hopelessness of the human condition prompts Qoheleth to repeat himself when thinking about the absence of comforters. The mighty cry of oppressed individuals resounds through the heavens, but no comforting response breaks the silence of eternity.

To be sure, humans share the responsibility for perverting the world. Not a single individual does good always and escapes sin's clutches (7:20). Given Qoheleth's view about the inability to know the correct time for any act, how could it be otherwise? That is why he becomes more excited about the end of an event than its beginning; how differently it would have been if he could have faced the future with confidence that he possessed the decisive key to appropriate conduct.

Because everyone lacks important knowledge about admissible and inadmissible deeds at any given moment, society suffers from lack of vision. The social upheaval which accompanied major shifts in power had left its mark upon the community within which Qoheleth found himself, but he refuses to view his own situation as qualitatively different from all others. In this regard, Qoheleth resembles the book of Job, which also generalizes from personal experience. But Qoheleth lacks the comforting faith that resolves all inequities in the epilogue of Job just as he lacks the disquieting memory of better days. For Qoheleth, a depressing sameness envelops former days and those yet to unfold before his eyes.

E. Pleasure Commends Itself

Precisely because the world refuses to encourage goodness by dispensing rewards to those who deserve them, pleasure commends itself as the only real means of salvaging a small portion of life. Invariably, Qoheleth links the two themes of vanity and enjoyment. In doing so he calls attention to the fact that such attempts at pleasurable living constitute grasping for a straw. The enjoyment of fine foods, clothing, and women was only a kind of lifeboat ethics. This conclusion can hardly be avoided, since Qoheleth claims that he made a test of pleasure and dismissed it as empty. That is why the contexts within which his so-called positive advice appears render the message somewhat hollow.

For example, Qoheleth sprinkles these bits of advice with a heavy dose of extract from bitter herbs. The reminder that enjoyment depends upon God's pleasure was Qoheleth's way of saying that not everyone can take advantage of his free advice. The power to enjoy life belonged to the category of divine gift. As such it lay outside one's grasp and made mockery of those who furtively reached for pleasure when God chose not to grant it. For this reason, Qoheleth passed judgment on life within the shadow of such pleasure. This, too, he mused, is vanity (2:1-3, 24) during the brief span of time allotted everyone (5:18-19; 9:7). Even youth succumbs before the severity of this judgment, for it also is empty (11:9-10).

At times Qoheleth seems almost to identify toil with the pleasures of the appetite it makes available. One could even say that he understood work as one of life's genuine pleasures. On the other hand, gainful employment enabled individuals to purchase the means of pleasure, and for this reason toil belongs within the contexts which enjoin the pursuit of sensual gratification. Ironically, Qoheleth notes that excessive profits from toil only lead to sleepless nights, and that increased riches vanish because of the additional claim upon available funds made by a coterie of servants.

These encouragements to live with gusto occur throughout the book of Ecclesiastes and are evenly divided between the two sections which treat the theoretical foundations for Qoheleth's thought and the practical conclusions which he draws. No clear distinction in terms of subject matter is discernible, insofar as I can see, in either half of the book, for the admonition possesses a remarkable repetitiveness where genuine enthusiasm should have created some examples of poetic flourish. For that reason I cannot subscribe to the theory that Qoheleth's enthusiasm knows no bounds when calling others to share in the pleasures life holds.[10]

Perhaps the fullest explication of what he has in mind by this counsel appears in the sequel to Qoheleth's wry observation that in some cases the dead possess definite advantages over the living. Here he specifies the good things which he envisions: eating in circumstances where joy prevails; drinking wine when the heart is free from care, since God has already approved such action; wearing fine clothes unceasingly; using ointment generously; and enjoying the warmth supplied by the woman you love. All of this sounds marvelous, until one pays attention to the somber undertones: enjoy these things throughout your empty days which he has granted you under the sun all the days of your vain life! Furthermore, all this pleasure reaches its destiny in Sheol to which you are going (9:7-10). One cannot escape the suspicion that Qoheleth wants to assure those who grasp for pleasure that emptiness will reign regardless of their successful use of life's opium, until death seizes its prey.

When we examine the things which Qoheleth approves, however half-heartedly, we see how self-interest dominates his thought. The old query, "What is good for man and woman?" is understood in a thoroughly selfish manner. Curiously, the experiment which convinced him that pleasure also fell into the category of vanity was hardly adequate, for he insisted that his rational faculties governed the entire test (2:1-3). Of course he can be faulted for refusing to let go, but we must remember that Qoheleth was, after all, a sage. The self-interest which stands out so noticeably in Qoheleth's total experiment, and which the personal pronouns punctuate dramatically, prevents him from using to best advantage the important insight that life without companions is hazardous (4:9-12). For a fleeting moment he recognizes the advantages of teaming up with another person for mutual protection from the terrain, brigands, or frigid winds. Even here, however, Qoheleth is scarcely thinking about alleviating someone else's suffering.

The prophetic conscience is entirely lacking here, and *moral impotence* reigns.[11] Qoheleth may see the same kind of injustice that Israel's prophets inveighed against, but he does not seem constrained to do battle against those who perpetrate the villainy. Instead, he advises against struggling with someone who possesses superior strength and sees no value in verbal harangue. How differently Job weighed the situation, and how valiantly he waged battle against the Almighty![12]

So far nothing has been said about Qoheleth's further qualification of his positive advice that seems to reverse all values (7:2-3). Grief and mourning are adjudged to be better than festive living. Even if Qoheleth's better sayings cannot properly be termed "excluding proverbs," nevertheless this passage certainly places the other admonitions to pleasure under a dark cloud.

To sum up, Qoheleth's positive counsel has little cause for exhilaration. The advice invariably occurs within contexts which emphasize life's vanity and attendant inequities, as well as those which stress God's control over human ability to enjoy life. Qoheleth's concept of divine gift is an expression for human limitation rather than an extolling of a generous God. The sources of pleasure—woman, wine, food, clothes, ointment, toil, and youth—are empty like life itself. In the end none accompanies the dead to Sheol. In spite of the limited satisfaction such pleasure affords, it does amount to something. Like breath which cannot be seen but makes life possible, such enjoyment renders existence endurable. Still, that life-endowing breath returns to its source and leaves a corpse, and the pleasant moments disappear without a trace. Fleeting satisfaction may be conjured up through an active memory, but even that means of storing up youthful pleasure soars aloft when the death angel raises its wings and departs with its reluctant burden on a journey into nothingness.

LITERARY CHARACTERISTICS

A. Form

The essential literary form by which Qoheleth chose to communicate his message owes its origin to ancient Egyptian instructions. Often called *royal testament,* this device readily lent itself to a literary work that purported to register King Solomon's understanding of reality. In general the pharaohs or their viziers collected their insights for the benefit of young aspiring rulers, whom they hoped to steer successfully along paths of wisdom. Such advice appeared in autobiographical form, inasmuch as it constituted the king's legacy for his successors.

In addition, the book preserves a number of proverbs, many of which Qoheleth quoted for the purpose of refuting.[13] Others, however, represent school wisdom that he used in his own formulation of sapiential instruction. The entirety of these proverbs and instructions may actually comprise Qoheleth's lectures to students,[14] some of whom may have composed the epilogues which render his unusual views a trifle more acceptable to those who endorsed traditional wisdom.

Two poems which Qoheleth either composed or borrowed from some other source and the final allegory about the decay which accompanies old age have already been mentioned. These exquisite poems concerning the cycles of natural events and the time which exists for everything resemble some extant Egyptian texts, but could easily have been written by Qoheleth himself.[15] The same is true for the description of the deterioration which presages death, except that in this case an Egyptian instruction opens with a comparable poem.[16]

Qoheleth advises remembrance of one's cistern/grave, not Creator.[17] This unusual word recalls his "positive" advice to "enjoy the woman you love" and negative warning about approaching death. Such remembrance stood in stark contrast to the much lamented threat of forgetfulness in Sheol and offered an appropriate introduction to the waning years which occasion entrance into that land.

> before the sun and the light and the moon and the stars are darkened and the clouds return after the rain; in the day when the keepers of the house tremble, and the strong men are bent, and the grinders cease because they are few, and those that look through the windows are dimmed, and the doors on the street are shut; when the sound of the grinding is low, and one rises up at the voice of a bird, and all the daughters of song are brought low; they are afraid also of what is high, and terrors are in the way; the almond tree blossoms, the grasshopper drags itself along and desire fails; because man goes to his eternal home, and the mourners go about the streets.
>
> (12:2-5, RSV)

B. Structure

The diversity in literary form and content prevents certainty with regard to internal structure. Older divisions of the book into a theoretical foundation (1—6) and practical conclusions (7—12) have lately given way to sections which are determined by refrains. Perhaps the most attractive of these hypotheses is that which envisions two fundamental units (1:12—6:9; 6:10—11:6) enclosed by an introductory and concluding poem (1:2-11; 11:7—12:8).[18] The two main sections employ different refrains. Whereas the first uses "(emptiness and) chasing after wind," the second has "cannot find out" or "who can find out?" and "do not know" or "no knowledge." These refrains occur with regularity in the two sections, as if to mark off smaller units as well. In addition, a single refrain introduces and concludes the work: "Emptiness, emptiness, says Qoheleth, all is empty" (1:2; 12:8). This verse functions as a motto for the whole book.

Qoheleth's fondness for repetition leads to remarkable recurrence of preferred vocabulary. His favorite expressions include: under the sun, under heaven, no profit, one fate, portion, gift of God, toil, the whole. Furthermore, he uses several expressions as transition markers: "then I turned and saw, or gave myself up to," "I applied my mind to understand;" "this also is emptiness and chasing after wind." Rhetorical questions abound within the book, as if in defiance of school wisdom's assumptions that much can be known.

C. Unity

Although the present text of Ecclesiastes has achieved a certain unity of theme and perspective, strong evidence of supplementary glosses exists. Besides those attempts to salvage the traditional view of retribution (3:17; 7:18; 8:12-13; 11:9b), at least two epilogues are readily discerned (12:9-12; 12:13-14). The epilogues testify to the difficulty such thought encountered, and inaugurate the first of many attempts to tone down Qoheleth's theology.[19] His words are adjudged to be true, although hard to take, and readers are warned to fear God and keep his commandments, for he will judge every secret, whether good or bad.

D. Authorship

The literary fiction of Solomonic authorship does not persist throughout the work, but disappears after the section on the royal experiment. Elsewhere Qoheleth writes from the standpoint of one who lacks power to correct human oppression and reflects about kings from the position of a subject. Even the claim of Solomonic origin seems to have been taken lightly, for the author indicates an appalling lack of vital information about the Davidic monarchy. Although only David preceded Solomon on the throne at Jerusalem, Qoheleth boasts that he excelled all those who went before him. Furthermore, he gives more information about his genealogy than necessary if he actually were Solomon.[20]

The language of the book resembles the latest Hebrew in the canon; in some respects it comes closest to Mishnaic Hebrew.[21] The preference for participles, use of the relative *šᵉ*, and occasional Aramaic words point to the late third century as the most probable date for the book.[22] Although the evidence is debatable, the provenance for this work in Jerusalem has much to commend it. Actually, the tools which are sufficiently reliable to answer the question of authorship and date except in general terms are lacking.

The unusual title Qoheleth[23] is just as enigmatic as the book itself. In the opening verse the word functions as a proper name, and the identification with Solomon is provided; but 12:8 speaks of *the Qoheleth* as if the word were a common noun with the definite article. In the Septuagint of 7:27 Qoheleth is also a common noun, although the Hebrew can be understood as a proper name. Elsewhere the word can be translated either way. In any event, the title refers to an office or function, which explains the feminine ending and accompanying verbal form. The similarity with *soperet* (scribe) is readily apparent, even if the actual office to which Qoheleth refers escapes us.

On the basis of various forms of the root *qhl,* the most obvious explanation for the task designated by Qoheleth has something to do with assembling people for some specific purpose. This meaning has given rise to the Greek title Ecclesiastes, the churchman. In light of Qoheleth's teachings, such a translation seems entirely inappropriate. One could understand Qoheleth as a teacher who assembled his pupils for instruction, an interpretation which would do justice to the title without turning him into an ecclesiastical figure.

Of course the title may derive from the literary fiction of Solomonic authorship rather than from an official function of the author. If so, at least two possibilities present themselves: it may refer to Solomon as a *gatherer of women,*[24] or it may suggest a teacher's attempt to tally the sum of things. The former interpretation may derive support from the strange allusion to "one in a thousand," which registers the opinion that King Solomon's thousand wives left much to be desired. Anyone who gathered wives as freely as Solomon did certainly deserves a title like "the assembler."

The second alternative takes its cue from the strange expression in 7:27 ("Said Qoheleth, one to one to find the sum"). Could this unusual phrase contain a hidden clue about the use to which the author put the title Qoheleth? If this reference to adding up the sum of things represents the teacher's task of discovering the profit (or lack of it) in living, the title Qoheleth becomes intelligible. The teacher gathers together the total of individual experiences in the hope of finding some meaning in life. A remarkable irony intrudes at this point: the mathematical compilation achieved its purpose, and the gatherer announced his profit as a worthless zero. Attractive though this hypothesis may be, it depends upon an extension of the root *qhl* to things in addition to humans. Elsewhere only people stand as the object of this verb. In light of the author's equation of animals and humans in God's sight, such an extension of *qhl* cannot be ruled out in principle.

Another title for the teacher occurs in 12:9, which mentions one shepherd. The royal background for this metaphor seems undeniable[25]; as a result, this reference must derive from the attempt to attribute these skeptical teachings to Solomon. Even apart from the Egyptian affinities, this literary fiction functions to underscore the negative impact of the book. If one who had absolute power and unlimited riches pronounced life empty, who are we to argue with him? The rabbinic claim that Solomon wrote this book in his dotage only heightens its message, for senility and the ultimate broken pitcher fells the most avid enthusiast who vainly assembles his own version of life's bounty.

CHAPTER 6

The Quest for Survival: Sirach

The sages who composed Proverbs, Job, and Ecclesiastes scrupulously avoided the slightest allusion to Israel's sacred history as it unfolds within the rest of the Hebrew Bible. An openness to the world on the part of these teachers expressed itself in borrowings from realms beyond Palestine, thereby appreciably enriching canonical wisdom with regard to form and content. At the same time, those whose allegiance fell outside the sapiential enterprise believed strong resistance to anything which lacked universality greatly impoverished Jewish wisdom by excluding an important dimension of daily life. The theophany within the book of Job bears eloquent testimony to an awareness that the experience of the living God belonged to the essence of any authentic search for knowledge. Sirach advanced beyond this cautious acknowledgment to bold proclamation that true wisdom was hidden in the Mosaic law. The consequences of this conviction were far reaching; in a word, they achieved a significant transition within wisdom.[1]

INTEGRATION OF SACRED HISTORY INTO WISDOM

Sirach's integration of sacred history into sapiential discourse was no afterthought, as one might conclude from the fact that the praise of past heroes and eulogy of a contemporary priest appear toward the end of the book (44:1—50:21). Actually, the entire work is sprinkled with explicit references and recognizable allusions to biblical persons and events, while the distinctive piety of the sages has succumbed to the powerful influence of Yahwism as it manifests itself outside canonical wisdom literature.

The boldest move in this direction is the *actual quotation of scripture.* In the light of the wholly unpromising theological context of the early second century B.C.E., the choice of that text approximates a judgment doxology:[2]

> Let us fall into the hands of the Lord,
>   but not into the hands of men;
> for as his majesty is,
>   so also is his mercy.

(2:18)

The reference is to David's decision to risk divine punishment rather than human vindictiveness, since God's mercy is great (2 Samuel 24:14). Similarly, the allusion to the Noachic covenant (17:12) underlines the Lord's compassion for the human race after the flood threatened to wipe it out, and many references to God's mercy for repentant individuals (e.g., 17:29) recall promises within prophetic and legal material.[3]

By far the most *allusions* derive from Pentateuchal traditions concerning the Primeval History (Genesis 1—11) and the Patriarchal Narratives. These include Adam (33:10; 40:1) and Eve (25:24), Lot (16:8), Sodom and Gomorrah (39:23), the fallen angels (16:7), Jacob's descendants (23:12), the flood (40:10), the tree of knowledge (38:5), the image of God (17:3), and the creation account (39:16, 23). Other biblical allusions derive from the larger canon: the six hundred thousand Israelites who perished in the wilderness (16:9-10), the divine epithet "Holy One" (4:14), the law of Moses (24:23), Zion (36:13-15), and the tree that sweetened water (38:5). Two of the last three occur within larger sections which mention components from several sacred traditions: creation by means of a heavenly mist, the pillar of cloud which symbolized God's dwelling place, Jacob and Israel, the holy Tabernacle, Jerusalem, the special people of God (24:1-12), divine signs and miracles, the reciting of God's wonders, tribes of Jacob, their inheritance, people called by God's name, Israel, God's first-born, the city of God's sanctuary, prophecies spoken in God's name, and Aaron's blessing (36:1-17).

Although Qoheleth had cautioned against hasty vows, Sirach went far beyond such sound advice to admonish active participation in the sacrificial rituals current in his day.[4] In his view, priests should be supported financially as scripture commands, specifically by means of

> the first fruits, the guilt offering, the gift of the shoulders,
> > the sacrifice of sanctification, and the first fruits of the holy
> > > things.
>
> (7:31; cf. 14:11)

Elsewhere Sirach indicates that he had been influenced by a trend toward spiritualizing cultic requirements, for he noted that deeds of kindness and almsgiving constitute flour and praise offerings, and the renunciation of evil is an atonement offering, while keeping the law is a thank offering (35:1-3). Still, Sirach refused to go the next step and view actual sacrifices as dispensable. Instead, he urged the complete performance of sacrifices which God had commanded, for the Most High is pleased by first fruits, tithes, and generous gifts of fat (35:4-11).

The fervent prayer in chapter 36:1-17 implies that Sirach also nourished strong eschatological hopes that God would manifest his power once again in political events, restoring the chosen race to its former glory. That anticipation seems also to underly the frequent warnings that God will judge wickedness at the hour of death, transforming that occasion into sufficient horror to offset all memory of pleasures gained through devious means. Since radical changes can take place between dawn and dusk, when the Lord wills it, the faithful need not be alarmed by apparent prosperity of the wicked (18:24-26).

If one asks what principle dictated the choice of canonical material which Sirach integrated into his teachings, the answer must surely be the *tension between wrath and mercy*. Even the cultic references belong to this realm of discourse, for the sacrificial system represented God's means of dealing with evil in such a way that mercy would triumph. Nevertheless, God's mercy was dependent upon human forgiveness; divine healing came only after men and women conquered their rage toward one another (28:1-7).

Within the praise of heroes belonging to Israel's history (chaps. 44—50), pride of position falls to priestly figures—Moses, Aaron, and Phineas. As a result, the eulogies of Aaron and Simon represent the high point of this account, as the poetic flourish certainly suggests. Modern interpreters marvel at Sirach's jaundiced view of prophets as miracle workers, and wonder how anyone could have ignored the really noble moments in Israel's past, but present standards of judgment must not preclude this teacher's right to select his own representatives from Israel's picture gallery. Beginning with Enoch's repentance and concluding with Simon's pronunciation of the sacred name Yahweh on the Day of Atonement, a great host of men[5] labored to make a name for themselves and to establish the covenant with God forever. It is noteworthy that the Hebrew canon dictated the actual progression of this praise of famous men. Sirach began with the Pentateuch, moved through the former prophets, then mentioned the latter prophets, and finally touched upon three heroes of the restoration. As an afterthought, he returned to his starting point, Enoch, and recalled Joseph, Shem, Seth, and Adam.

The piety characterizing these canonical works has thoroughly infused Sirach's thinking. As a result the tone shifts markedly from earlier sapiential teaching. Emphasis falls upon God's compassion, which almost seems to be an obsession with Sirach. Insisting that delay in punishment for sin arose from God's desire to give men and women time to repent, Sirach rejected the sinner's audacious claim that God could not see through darkness which concealed adulterous acts.

> His fear is confined to the eyes of men,
>   and he does not realize that the eyes of the Lord
>   are ten thousand times brighter than the sun;
> they look upon all the ways of men,
>   and perceive even the hidden places.

(23:19)

Such individuals were culpable first and foremost because they broke the law which God declared through Moses (23:23).

Elsewhere Sirach associates godless persons with violation of the law, as if the norm for conduct consists of divine statutes. Accordingly, persons deserving contempt were those who failed to keep commandments, rather than foolish sluggards who had provoked earlier sages' ire.

Naturally, Sirach recommended the study of the law (39:1) and urged meditation upon the commandments. In his opinion, the wise never despised the law, which was fully as reliable as the sacred dice used in connection with a divine oracle. It followed that the commandments were complete, needing no further supplement. Therefore, all efforts to develop a science of interpreting dreams, visions, and omens were deemed superfluous if not outright perfidy. Sirach joined Qoheleth in advising people to reflect upon death and to let that imminent threat spur them on to enjoyment of life's innocent pleasures, but he also urged such somber thoughts on death as a motive for keeping the commandments. His reasoning is clear: since you must die, let your life be exemplary in order that death may be accompanied by God's smile.

Occasionally, Sirach brought together his thinking about piety and wisdom; in doing so, he subordinated wisdom to the law and to the fear of God.[6] For example, he described worship as the outward expression of wisdom, and admonished sages to rely upon godfearers who kept the commandments. To be sure, he also encouraged self-reliance as one's most dependable counselor, but hastened to place such self-trust under a greater obligation, the necessity to pray for divine guidance (37:12-15). In one striking statement Sirach urged fighting for truth in full confidence that God would join the skirmish to assure victory. Such thinking accords with traditional interpretations of God as the champion of the poor, but earlier sages had never spoken of God as a co-combatant. Although Sirach advised sages to act as fathers to orphans, he warned against indiscriminate giving. In his opinion, those who lavished their goods upon others had to make intelligent choices, eliminating all persons who did not fear God.

The truth within the claim that with Sirach "the teacher has become a worshiper" comes closest to surfacing in the contexts which treat the subject of the fear of God.[7] Certain statements lend considerable support to the thesis that the book's central theme is not wisdom but the fear of God. For instance, Sirach remarked:

> "Better is the god-fearing man who lacks intelligence,
>   than the highly prudent man who transgresses the law"
>
> (19:24)

and he insisted that nothing was superior to the fear of the Lord or sweeter than keeping the commandments (23:27).

> How great is he who has gained wisdom!
>   But there is no one superior to him who fears the Lord.
> The fear of the Lord surpasses everything;
>   to whom shall be likened the one who holds it fast?
>
> (25:10-11)

Elsewhere Sirach identified all wisdom with the fear of the Lord and fulfilling the law (19:20).

Perhaps the strongest statement subordinating wisdom occurs in 1:1-20, which introduces readers to the two themes which recur throughout Sirach's discourses, namely wisdom and the fear of God. Like the comparable prologue in Proverbs, this one calls wisdom's first principle the fear of the Lord. But Sirach went much further, even to the extent of saying that wisdom's garland and root can be found in the fear of the Lord. That is why in another context he was able to write that fear of God alone justified a sense of accomplishment.

> The rich, and the eminent, and the poor—
>   their glory is the fear of the Lord.
>
> (10:22)

Against this elevation of the fear of God it has been argued that Sirach's tongue was loosened when extolling wisdom, particularly in the majestic hymn to wisdom (chap. 24).[8] The criterion of eloquence can only point in another direction, for Sirach's tongue was looser still in praising Aaron and Simon. The exquisite details concerning priestly duties and privileges, the glowing account of their demeanor during the daily ritual, and the excitement such thoughts engendered show clearly the precise point at which Sirach's heart beat excitedly. The high priest Simon

. . . was like the morning star appearing through the clouds
or the moon at the full;
like the sun shining on the temple of the Most High
or the light of the rainbow on the gleaming clouds;
like a rose in spring or lilies by a fountain of water;
. . . .
like an olive-tree laden with fruit
or a cypress with its top in the clouds.

(50:6-8, 10 NEB)

What, then, did Sirach say about wisdom and discipline, the two
themes which his grandson who translated the Hebrew work into
Greek singled out as noteworthy? On the one hand, Sirach
endorsed traditions which described wisdom as a cosmic entity
wholly inaccessible to men and women, while, on the other hand, he
maintained that human effort succeeded in grasping wisdom. The
two understandings are brought together ingeniously in 24:1-23,
which identifies this primordial wisdom with the Mosaic torah. This
marvelous account of wisdom's search for a permanent dwelling
place reaches back into a variety of traditional matter (creation by
the divine word; the creative mist which engendered life in a desert
oasis; the pillar of cloud that accompanied the Israelites in the
wilderness; the sacred tent in Jerusalem; Israel as God's special
possession). The identification of this heavenly wisdom with a
written document meant that she was now available to all who
thirsted for knowledge. That is why Sirach could promise those who
worked in wisdom that they would not go astray. Elsewhere he
claimed that wisdom resulted from keeping the commandments or
was acquired by keeping oneself pure. Anyone who mastered the
law achieved wisdom as well (15:1), and students discovered
genuine satisfaction in the law.

How different this view of the sages' intellectual sphere was
from earlier understandings, where study of nature and human
experience seemed to suffice. Nothing could be farther from the old
view of free inquiry than Sirach's warning against probing into
things which were too difficult or defied all attempts to answer.
Activity that once seemed to constitute the natural domain of sages
is here called meddling into God's secrets, and the intellectual

enterprise is directed towards understanding divine revelation (3:21-24). It is therefore not surprising that Sirach advised against following difficult paths or swimming against the current.

On the other hand, the secondary theme of discipline forced Sirach to qualify this warning against heroic endeavor, for wisdom first manifests itself as a grievous yoke until the individual has demonstrated willingness to be molded in the proper manner. Then the fetters fall away and wisdom presents herself as a beautiful bride, who brings life to her beloved. Sirach adopted the imagery of sowing seeds as a convenient way to highlight the labor that must go into the acquisition of wisdom, but also to focus attention upon the joyous experience accompanying the harvesting of crops.

> My son, from your youth up choose instruction,
>   and until you are old you will keep finding wisdom.
> Come to her like one who plows and sows,
>   and wait for her good harvest.
> For in her service you will toil a little while,
>   and soon you will eat of her produce.
> She seems very harsh to the uninstructed;
>   a weakling will not remain with her.
> She will weigh him down like a heavy testing stone,
>   and he will not be slow to cast her off.
>
> (6:18-21; cf. 4:11-19)

To be sure, Sirach retained earlier authentic emphases of sages, as when he encouraged the study of ancient maxims.

> Do not slight the discourse of the sages,
>   but busy yourself with their maxims;
> because from them you will gain instruction
>   and learn how to serve great men.
> Do not disregard the discourse of the aged,
>   for they themselves learned from their fathers;
> because from them you will gain understanding
>   and learn how to give an answer in time of need.
>
> (8:8-9)

Of course his own mastery of older maxims can scarcely be denied, for his teachings are filled with counsel similar to that contained in Proverbs.

Nevertheless, a distinctive difference quickly meets the eye.

Sirach perceived the *ambiguity* within things much more clearly than the earlier sages seem to have done. For example, wealth no longer indicated divine favor.

> Riches are good if they are free from sin,
>   and poverty is evil in the opinion of the ungodly.
>
> (13:24)

The rich man performed a miracle if he remained free of its taint (31:8-9), while poverty offered a unique opportunity to demonstrate virtue (20:21), or it enforced goodness for lack of an opportunity to do otherwise. Extreme need also made life so miserable that death was welcome relief. Silence arose from ignorance or lack of courage, as well as from recognition that no response at all was timely. The ideal of a large family was less important than integrity, for children were not always a blessing (16:1-3). The birth of a daughter was a loss, but not every woman provoked Sirach's scorn. To fools education resembled fetters and handcuffs, while the wise viewed it as a golden ornament or a bracelet. Modesty commends itself in some circumstances and is out of place at other times. Almsgiving is proper action in given instances, but withholding a gift is right in others. The same ambiguity characterizes "going security" for someone. Such kindness is meritorious, but its consequences often impoverish. Hence, care must be taken lest a good deed ruin compassionate individuals through the loss of all their possessions.

Earlier teachers had recognized limits to all knowledge, but Sirach even distinguished between the proper use of the intellect and a cleverness that produced expertise at performing evil.

> All wisdom is the fear of the Lord,
>   and in all wisdom there is the fulfilment of the law.
> But the knowledge of wickedness is not wisdom,
>   nor is there prudence where sinners take counsel.
> There is a cleverness which is abominable,
>   but there is a fool who merely lacks wisdom.
> Better is the God-fearing man who lacks intelligence,
>   than the highly prudent man who transgresses the law.
> There is a cleverness which is scrupulous but unjust,
>   and there are people who distort kindness to gain a verdict.
>
> (19:20, 22-25)

Just as Sirach believed a rich man was nearly incapable of virtue, he also thought merchants stood little chance of resisting greed.

> A merchant can hardly keep from wrongdoing,
>   and a tradesman will not be declared innocent of sin.

(26:29)

> As a stake is driven firmly into a fissure between stones,
>   so sin is wedged in between selling and buying.

(27:2)

Human ingenuity, like craftiness, could be enlisted in the service of evil. Sometimes an appropriate use of intelligence interfered with God's punishment of sinners, as when physicians successfully prescribed medicines for an individual. Sirach recognized a fundamental problem where the healing profession was concerned. On the one hand, the vital knowledge of medicines constituted a proper use of human intelligence, and therefore represented an important step toward mastering the world. On the other hand, according to traditional teaching, sickness was one means God had chosen to punish iniquity and any act which shortened or ameliorated the punishment placed physicians at cross purposes with God. Unable to resolve the tension between these convictions, Sirach opted for the medical profession since he knew it was essential for the well-being of society, but he also insisted that physicians should pray for assistance from the genuine source of healing. In the end, however, Sirach reaffirmed the old view that sickness was a form of divine punishment, and urged sinners to summon a physician when they fell into God's hands (38:1-15).

LITERARY ANALYSIS

In the case of Proverbs, Job, and Qoheleth neither the authors nor the time of composition are known. With Sirach, things are different. His name, the approximate date, and the general location of his scholarly activity are known.[9] His name was Jesus Eleasar son of Sirach, and he completed his work around 180 B.C.E. in Jerusalem. From the prologue, which was composed by Sirach's grandson in

Alexandria some time after 132 B.C.E., we learn that the original language of the book was Hebrew, and that the grandson had completed a translation into Greek. It follows from these facts that Simon II was the high priest whose performance of the holy ritual within the temple made such an impact upon his contemporary, Sirach.

The struggle against Hellenism had less intensity in Sirach's day than it did a decade and a half later, when the Maccabean revolt broke out in Medina. The next fifty years or so are well documented, for they produced such works as Daniel, 1 and 2 Maccabees, and Wisdom of Solomon. Since Sirach's teachings reflect the earlier situation, they demonstrate a readiness to borrow Greek expressions and ideas, so long as they were subjected to a thorough Hebraizing.

In one sense Sirach was completely Hellenized; his pride of authorship. At the conclusion of the majestic hymn to wisdom (24:1-29), he ventured to compare his teachings with prophecy, and contemplated future generations using his own inspired work alongside prophetic utterances. Such teaching was more than an ego trip for Sirach, who labored to benefit those who sought wisdom. That is why he compared his discipline to a canal that brought water to a garden. Perhaps his final product far exceeded the scope he had originally contemplated, for Sirach seems to indicate that he took up his writing implements for a second effort, as if carried along by a mighty flood (24:30-34).

In yet another context Sirach acknowledged the fact that he was a latecomer, like a gleaner following grape pickers, but insisted that his tardiness did not prevent him from achieving just as much as his predecessors. Still, Sirach conceded that his remarkable success was due to God's blessing. As if to explain why God looked upon him with favor, the teacher emphasized once more that the true motive for his labors was the desire to instruct others. In this instance he even named dignitaries and assembly leaders as those for whom he wrote (33:16-18).

On one occasion this teacher gave his name and identified his place of activity.

Instruction in understanding and knowledge
    I have written in this book,
Jesus the son of Sirach, son of Eleazar, of Jerusalem,
    who out of his heart poured forth wisdom.
Blessed is he who concerns himself with these things,
    and he who lays them to heart will become wise,
For if he does them, he will be strong for all things,
    for the light of the Lord is his path.

(50:27-29)

The book closes with a long defense of Sirach's wisdom and piety, which leads ultimately to an attempt at recruiting students for his house of learning (51:13-30). Sirach claims to have sought wisdom from his youth and to have kept himself pure as well. As a reward for his diligence God gave him eloquence with which to praise the Lord. Having settled the matter of his character, Sirach then urged all who lacked instruction to dwell in his school, where their thirst would be slaked forthwith. Perhaps he realized the attraction other centers of learning offered, for he scolded his hearers for thinking they must travel some distance to find discipline. Anticipating an objection that the cost of study in his house of learning was high, Sirach appealed to the profit motive by reminding prospective students that their modest investment would yield huge dividends.

This latecomer in God's vineyard mastered many literary forms which his predecessors had employed. Like the author of the first major section in Proverbs, Sirach used the didactic essay to great advantage. A single saying no longer sufficed to encapsulate the message Sirach hoped to communicate concerning any given subject. Instead, exposition became the normal mode of discourse. In the oldest collections of proverbs, the teachers had been satisfied with stimulating others to think through the implications of a given proverb, even at the risk of misinterpretation. Sirach resembles interpreters who rely upon others for the original material which they endeavor to illuminate by means of their highly trained critical faculties. Rarely did he permit a proverb to appear without any interpretation. Occasionally he did set one saying alongside another to provide contrasting descriptions, for example, of poverty and wealth; in the same manner that the earliest sages had done (13:3; cf. 20:5-6; 11:11-13).

The topics which Sirach chose to discuss are wide-ranging, although some subjects occur several times and give the impression of special fondness on the teacher's part. Like others before him, Sirach reflected often upon the danger posed by evil women. At times he permitted this ancient tradition about foreign women to discolor his attitude toward all women, especially when declaring that a man's wickedness is better than a woman's goodness and when announcing that the birth of a daughter was a loss. Elsewhere Sirach implied that he thought females occasioned too much worry over their virginity, and suspected that girls opened their quiver for any arrow and drank from the nearest spring like a thirsty traveler. Nevertheless, this sage cannot be labeled a complete misogynist, for he also had indirect (!) words of highest praise for good women.

> Happy is the husband of a good wife;
>   the number of his days will be doubled.
>
> (26:1)

Lacking such a wife, Sirach observed, a man walks around and sighs for a home.

Sirach was almost equally fascinated with the subject of death, which he treated with considerable depth and occasional humor, particularly when alluding to an inscription on a tombstone which read: "Mine today, and yours tomorrow." Although acknowledging that all human beings stand under the same sentence, "You shall die," Sirach recognized that individuals experienced the anticipation of that dreaded event differently. Death in its proper time belongs to the natural process, just as trees shed their leaves and put on new ones. Accordingly, such bowing out in order to make way for new generations should occasion no tears of remorse. As Sirach saw it, mourning for the dead should be carefully controlled, lest such morbid thoughts lessen one's enjoyment of life's innocent pleasures. For some people, especially those whose vigor has departed, death came as solace; for others, who still possessed power to drink life's sweetest nectar, an early death brought nothing but regret.

Other *topics* which Sirach took up cover a broad spectrum, inevitably combining wisdom and piety. Among others, they include enjoyment of life's good things (14:11-19), occupations (38:24—39:11), medicines (38:1-15), discipline (30:1-13), table manners (32:1-13), duty to parents (3:1-16), poverty and riches (4:1-10), drunkenness (31:25-31), dreams (34:1-8), and passions (6:2-4). The necessity to *encourage* enjoyment must surely arise from a changed attitude among the sages, for the good life had earlier demonstrated God's favor, thus requiring no justification. It is also possible that Sirach's admonition to honor parents rather than making fun of old people signals a decisive shift in values resulting from the conflict between the generations brought on by Hellenism. In any event, Sirach's attempt at humor suggests that the issue had not yet taken on the gravity that it later manifested.

> Do not disdain a man when he is old,
>   for some of us are growing old.
>
>   (8:6)

In several instances this inclination toward exposition of a given topic led Sirach to use *refrains* as a means of emphasizing continuity of subject matter. In one block of material three different refrains occur, each of which is used three times (2:7-18). The first, "You who fear the Lord," addresses persons who have begun to question God's justice as it had been proclaimed in the doctrine of exact reward and retribution. Sirach encouraged a "wait and see" attitude, and directed the skeptics' attention to past history.

> Consider the ancient generations and see:
>   who ever trusted in the Lord and was put to shame?
> Or who ever persevered in the fear of the Lord and was forsaken?
>   Or who ever called upon him and was overlooked?
>
>   (2:10)

Any delay in retribution was readily explained by God's compassion and mercy. At the same time, the Lord's majesty must be taken into consideration. Therefore, Sirach pronounced three woes upon all who had abandoned faith in the hour of trial, for they will be defenseless when God's time of reckoning breaks. Returning to the initial refrain, although in slightly different form ("Those who fear the Lord"), Sirach contrasted those subjects of a curse with fortunate faithful ones who adhered to God's ways, immersed themselves in the law, and humbly placed themselves in God's hands. The final quotation of scripture suggests that Sirach was not willing to let his teaching validate itself by logical consistency. Instead, he appealed to the ultimate warrant for this defense of God's justice.

Another unit uses the refrain "Be ashamed" eight times, and "Do not be ashamed" twice, followed by five instances of "for fear she may" (cf. NEB). The section closes with an attempt to link the two topics under discussion, woman and shame (41:14—42:14). In this interesting section Sirach named numerous acts that should evoke a strong sense of shame, for example, fornication, bad table manners, following up charity with a lecture, and betraying a secret. Then he mentioned things for which one should not feel shame: the law of the Most High, using accurate weights and measures, disciplining one's children, correcting the foolish, like greybeards who commit fornication, and so forth. The heavy concentration on sexual sins and disciplining children prompted Sirach to consider the anxiety generated by a willful daughter. In his opinion, fathers never escaped cause for worry over their daughters for fear they fail to marry, or fall out of favor with their husband, or lose their virginity, or commit adultery, or be unable to have children. Such a headstrong daughter succeeded only in shaming her father, according to Sirach.

> for from garments comes the moth,
>   and from a woman comes woman's wickedness.
> Better is the wickedness of a man than a woman who does good;
>   and it is a woman who brings shame and disgrace.
>
> (42:13-14)

Once again the teacher has appealed to a warrant for his message, but this time a popular proverb undergirds his words.

Some refrains adopt an entirely different principle of alternation. In 7:22-24 three questions occur, each of which is followed by a word of advice.

Do you have cattle? Look after them;
if they are profitable to you, keep them.
Do you have children? Discipline them,
and make them obedient from their youth.
Do you have daughters? Be concerned for their chastity,
and do not show yourself too indulgent with them.

This passage may be compared to 10:19.

What race is worthy of honor? The human race.
What race is worthy of honor? Those who fear the Lord.
What race is unworthy of honor? The human race.
What race is unworthy of honor? Those who transgress the
commandments.

Another pattern resembles an *aba'b'* versification scheme (19:13-17). Here "Question a friend" alternates with "Question a neighbor," and both refrains occur twice.

Not all Sirach's refrains exemplify this principle of alternation. Many of them simply depend upon repetition of a single phrase. For example, 6:14-16 uses "a faithful friend" three times, without juxtaposition with another refrain at all. Here the value of a good friend is emphasized as a sort of second thought after a highly cynical statement concerning personal relationships.

Keep yourself far from your enemies,
and be on guard toward your friends.

(6:13)

Similarly, 22:11-12 uses the word weep three times, although in different expressions, and mourning once. By this means Sirach compared mourning for fools and the dead, observing that fools occasioned more bitter tears since their darkness endured for a lifetime. Finally, in 14:1-2, "Blessed is the man" occurs twice, in each case followed by two grounds for his happiness, while 40:18-27 has nine uses of "better still" (cf. NEB).

The book of Proverbs also provided the prototype for another literary form which Sirach added to the sages' repertoire, namely *prayer*. The simple request in Proverbs 30:7-9 for a balance between poverty and wealth greatly resembles Sirach's modest appeal in 22:27—23:6, which happily uses a refrain twice ("Lord, Father, and

Ruler of my life"). The images in Sirach are exceedingly powerful, particularly those accompanying the first use of the refrain.

> O that a guard were set over my mouth.
> and a seal of prudence upon my lips.
>
> (22:27a)

> O that whips were set over my thoughts.
>
> (23:2a)

The second occurrence of the slightly different refrain ("Lord, Father and *God* of my life") is accompanied by less graphic language, and the request reaches out to embrace as much as possible. It asks for protection from desire, passion, gluttony, and lust, which seem to flow from one's eyes as freely as tears. Elsewhere Sirach mentioned a greedy eye:

> What has been created more greedy than the eye?
> Therefore it sheds tears from every face.
>
> (31:13 b-c)

The restraint exercised in this prayer is eased in the other one to be examined, allowing Sirach to utter fervent nationalistic feelings (36:1-17). In this respect the reader stands before a new stage in sapiential thinking, one in which the earlier universalism surrendered to particularistic concerns. To be sure, ancient teachers had spoken of fools with similar scorn, but Sirach made distinctions solely on the basis of nationality. That is how he could ultimately express a loathing for three nations—the Idumeans, Philistines and Samaritans (50:25-26). From the sentiment exposed within this great prayer, it becomes clear that oppression of dispersed Israelites had dulled their capacity to recite God's saving deeds, and unfulfilled prophecies threatened to drown all hopes in a sea of despair. Confidence that God intended better things for his people prompted Sirach to invoke divine action.

> Show signs anew, and work further wonders;
>   make thy hand and thy right arm glorious.
> Rouse thy anger and pour out thy wrath;
>   destroy the adversary and wipe out the enemy.
> Hasten the day, and remember the appointed time,
>   and let people recount thy mighty deeds.
>
> (36:6-8)

Gather all the tribes of Jacob,
and give them their inheritance, as at the beginning.

(36:11)

Fill Zion with the celebration of thy wondrous deeds,
and thy temple with thy glory.

(36:14)

Like Job who thought the Creator would eventually long for his handiwork, Sirach appealed to the fact that God created Israel as cause for continued interest. In addition, he reminded God that in his name prophets had announced an imminent restoration of the chosen people. But the ultimate grounds for his prayer rested elsewhere than a belief in creation and revelation. They nestled in the priestly blessing articulated in Numbers 6:23-26.

The thanksgiving hymn in 51:1-12 reiterates many themes known to us from similar psalms: rescue from death, deliverance from slander, remembrance of God's mercy, cry for help, granting of prayer, promise to praise God, and so forth. The initial epithets for God, "Lord and King," strike an unusual chord in wisdom literature, where royal language with reference to God is carefully avoided. Since the psalm of deliverance mentions slander in the king's presence, it is likely that Sirach used an old hymn or built upon earlier models without bothering to alter the facts to fit the situation in his own day when no king resided in Jerusalem.

Whereas Proverbs provided justification for Sirach's widespread use of didactic essays and occasional bending of the knees in prayer, the book of Job paved the way for *"hymnic" praise*. Three didactic compositions within Sirach's teaching demonstrate his remarkable capacity for combining sapiential insights and pious inclinations (16:24—17:14; 39:12-35; 42:15—43:33).[10] The last of these erupts into a mighty crescendo of praise, a sentiment that had allowed itself to remain dormant in the other two compositions.

Sirach 16:24—17:14 comprises a meditation upon the facts as they are proclaimed in the creation account of Genesis. The language gives the impression of rational reflection, particularly the references to exact and accurate knowledge, but also the teacher's appeal for attention and responsive listening. The poem speaks about an order in creation and a comparable principle by which men and women must live, specifically, the life-giving law. The argument seems to run as follows: the natural order has been assured by divine decree, and human conduct is subject to the same kind of lordly command. Since the individual heavenly bodies and forces do not transgress against one another or their Maker, humans should abide by the Noachic and Mosaic covenants which function to render life in community possible. In the case of men and women, a certain amount of power over animals is granted, and the right to make independent judgments belongs to those who bear God's image and have achieved knowledge about good and evil. But Sirach did not stop here; instead, he claimed that God actually spoke to lowly creatures at Sinai, thereby communicating the divine will for human conduct.[11] Naturally, one who has shown so much interest in those who rule on earth keeps constant watch over their hearts, listening for songs of praise.

Not everyone acknowledged an orderliness in the cosmos or among humans. As a result, these skeptics denied the appropriateness of natural catastrophes in a universe that was governed by a benevolent ruler. The refrain, "No one can say, 'What is this?' or 'Why is that?' " occurs twice; such questioning of an inherent order is dismissed in the second didactic composition as nonsense (39:12-35). The composition consists of an appeal for a hearing and for participation in singing God's praise (39:12-15), the hymn proper (39:16-31), and a concluding declaration that all God's works are very good (39:32-34) which leads into an invitation for everyone to praise the name of the Lord (39:35). Sirach subscribed to the Priestly Writer's positive evaluation of all things:

> "All things are the works of the Lord, for they are very good,
> and whatever he commands will be done in his time."
>
> (39:16)

But the concession that a time lapse exists between the divine command and its implementation suggests that the question, "Why is that?" was indeed appropriate. Admitting as much, Sirach promised that an answer would come at the right time. Although no one can thwart God's power, evil persons managed to rebel against their Maker, who sees all their deeds. Just as humans belong to two distinct camps, so do the elements which God created. Good things were prepared for the devout, and evil things for sinners. Or rather, the same things manifest themselves as beneficial to good people and destructive for sinners. In addition, certain things were created as agents of retribution from the beginning; among these are destructive winds, fire and hail, famine and deadly disease, beasts of prey, scorpions and vipers, and the avenging sword. In short, the hymn suggests that in its time everything will be revealed for what it is, depending upon the dispositions of human beings. It follows that faith enabled one to distinguish between real and apparent evil. Sirach believed this so deeply that he offered a personal written testimony that

> The works of the Lord are all good,
>   and he will supply every need in its hour.
>
> (39:33)

Therefore, Sirach concluded,

> And no one can say, "This is worse than that,"
>   for all things will prove good in their season.
>
> (39:34)

Elsewhere Sirach broached the idea of opposites or complementary pairs and defended God's right to shape human beings as he chose (33:7-15). Distinctions among days of the month lie within God's prerogative, Sirach claimed, so that through divine decree holy days became more important than ordinary ones. People, too, fell into two groups, despite a common origin, for they were like clay in a potter's hands.

> Good is the opposite of evil,
>   and life the opposite of death;
>   so the sinner is the opposite of the godly.
> Look upon all the works of the Most High;
>   they likewise are in pairs, one the opposite of the other.
>
> (33:14-15)

In his zeal to defend God's right to make arbitrary decisions, Sirach ignored here the element of human choice, which he took for granted elsewhere (15:11-20).

Sirach 42:15—43:33 can be appropriately classified as a hymn, whereas the two previously discussed texts belong to the category of didactic composition. To be sure, certain affinities with the other texts stand out, particularly the emphasis upon pairs which supplement each other (42:24-25), God's all seeing eye (42:20), and the orderliness of creation (42:21-22; 43:10). But the mood differs markedly, despite the occasional awareness that not everyone shared the hymn's enthusiasm (42:18, 20, 23-25). This majestic attempt to describe God's glory which fills creation pauses to single out for special consideration the sun, moon, stars, and rainbow. Such masterpieces point beyond themselves to their Creator who issues a command that speeds the sun on its course, who bends his bow in the sky, and who decrees that the innumerable stars stand at attention in their appointed places. The hymn also mentions such wonders as snow, thunder, lightning, earthquake, clouds, hail-stones, winds, frost, ice, drought, and dew.

Occasionally, Sirach became a poet, using exquisite images (clouds fly out like birds, icicles form like pointed stakes, ice settles on every pool as though the water were putting on a breastplate). In the end he let his thoughts stray across the ocean floor, and marveled at the mysteries lying beyond most people's immediate experience, secrets that have enlisted the aid of seafarers who never tire of recounting the wonders lurking beneath the surging waters. Nevertheless, God's mystery is greater still, and no one can succeed in describing the one who exceeds his works. Straining to sum up the theme of God's majesty, Sirach borrowed a Greek expression: He is all.

A surprisingly polemical note can be heard now and again within this hymn. For example, Sirach seems to have rejected the notion that God consulted Wisdom before creating the world (42:21), and he most likely discounted the claim of some that God could not see through dark clouds. The idea that God's creative act was assisted by a pre-existent primordial entity arose naturally from speculation about Dame Wisdom, which Sirach squelched for the most part by identifying Wisdom with the Torah. As for the denial of God's full knowledge, Sirach made a strong counter claim.

He searches out the abyss, and the hearts of men,
　　and considers their crafty devices.
For the Most High knows all that may be known,
　　and he looks into the signs of the age.
He declares what has been and what is to be,
　　and he reveals the tracks of hidden things.
No thought escapes him,
　　and not one word is hidden from him.

(42:18-20)

Whereas Proverbs had paved the way for the didactic essay and prayer, and the book of Job had adapted hymnic texts to sapiential ends, Qoheleth made use of an ancient debate form which Sirach found particularly helpful in his struggle against those who questioned God's justice.

Say not; "Why were the former days better than these?"
　　For it is not from wisdom that you ask this.

(Ecclesiastes 7:10)

This form can be traced to Egyptian wisdom literature as well.

Do not say, "I am (too) young for thee [thy messenger: Death] to take; for thou knowest not thy death. When death comes, he steals away the infant which is on its mother's lap like him who has reached old age." (Ani)

God is (always) in his success,
whereas man is in his failure;
One thing are the words which men say,
Another is that which the god does.
Say not: "I have no wrongdoing."
Nor yet strain to seek quarreling. (Amen-em-opet)

Do not say: "I have ploughed the field but it has not paid;"
plough again, it is good to plough.
Do not say: "(Now that) I have this wealth
I will serve neither God nor man."
Wealth is perfected in the service of God, the one who causes it to
　　happen.
Do not say: "The sinner against God lives today,"
but look to the end.
Say (rather): "A fortunate fate is at the end of old age."

('Onchsheshonqy)

As in Qoheleth and several Egyptian examples, Sirach used the ancient debate form overwhelmingly within contexts which treated the vexing problem of theodicy. These passages throb with agony brought about by intense soul searching.

> Do not say: "Because of the Lord I left the right way";
>   for he will not do what he hates.
> Do not say: "It was he who led me astray";
>   for he has no need of a sinful man.
>
> (15:11-12)

> Do not say: "I shall be hidden from the Lord,
>   and who from on high will remember me?
> Among so many people I shall not be known,
>   for what is my soul in the boundless creation?"
>
> (16:17)

> Do not set your heart on your wealth,
>   nor say: "I have enough."
> Do not follow your inclination and strength,
>   walking according to the desires of your heart.
> Do not say: "Who will have power over me?"
>   for the Lord will surely punish you.

> Do not say: "I sinned, and what happened to me?"
>   for the Lord is slow to anger.
> Do not be so confident of atonement
>   that you add sin to sin.
> Do not say: "His mercy is great,
>   he will forgive the multitude of my sins;"
> for both mercy and wrath are with him.
>
> (5:1-6)

> Do not say: "What do I need,
>   and what prosperity could be mine in the future?"
> Do not say: "I have enough,
>   and what calamity could happen to me in the future?"
>
> (11:23-24)

In most cases the form consists of (1) the prohibition formula, (2) a direct quotation, and (3) a refutation introduced by *ki* (for). Seven times the prohibition formula (*'al tomar*; do not say) stands in the initial position of the sentence; twice it occurs in the second half of a verse (5:1) or in a parallel verse connected by means of a Hebrew connective (5:6). The *ki* also varies in two instances: once it appears in the second of two verses functioning as a refutation (11:23-26), and once it follows a prohibition which does not occupy the initial position (5:6).

What prompted Sirach's free use of didactic essays and hymns, prayers, and a debate form? One can begin to answer this significant question by learning more about his antagonists. From the content of these different compositions it is clear that certain persons threatened to forsake Judaism because of an inability to believe in God's justice. Again and again Sirach turned to these dissenters with sage counsel and fervent appeal. In doing battle with these individuals, he used the traditional arguments which he gleaned from earlier teachers, but Sirach also developed two wholly new responses to the problem of theodicy.

The old approaches may be conveniently summarized as follows:

1. God knows all things even before they happen and also sees them as they materialize;
2. past experience bears convincing witness to God's justice;
3. every apparent injustice will be set right at the appropriate hour;
4. surrender before the divine imperative of wonder is the ultimate response to creation's grandeur.

To these, Sirach added appeals to psychology and metaphysics. In his view, the real burden of existence was emotional and mental, for sinners' share of anxiety was multiplied sevenfold. For example, God sent nightmares for the wicked, and thus punished them in ways which were not immediately apparent to outsiders. The second answer concerns the structure of the universe. Sirach believed that the universe itself punished vice and rewarded virtue. All things existed in pairs, good things to encourage right conduct and bad things to punish wicked behavior. Like the sages before him, Sirach found it necessary to depart from realms subject to verification when trying to address the problem of evil.

The threat to convictions which Sirach treasured came from other camps too. On the one hand, there were traditional Yahwists who eyed the wisdom literature with suspicion because it lacked specific features which had arisen in and had given distinctive character to Israel's encounter with her God. On the other hand, another group looked upon this lack as the unique strength inherent within the wisdom texts, but saw no reason to prefer such literature over the Greek intellectual heritage with which they had recently come into contact. This noble attempt to find adequate responses to the two groups amounted to a search for continuity, for both Yahwism and the wisdom tradition were at stake.

Sirach's concession to the first group was the extensive integration of sacred traditions into sapiential thought. In this way the chasm separating sages from others became less and less wide, for teachers donned prayer shawls. At the same time, the incorporation of Israel's heroes into wisdom teachings enabled Sirach to defend the Old Testament as God's gift to Israel, and thus to juxtapose divine words and human speculation. In his view, Greek philosophy failed to achieve the heights reached by the Hebrew Scriptures. Nevertheless, he did demonstrate willingness to enrich his own teachings from the scholarly tradition within Hellenism, and thus strengthened his appeal to those who longed for intellectual respectability in the Greek world.

Regardless of the different responses to those who partially shaped the Jerusalem sage's thinking, one fact can hardly escape detection: theology prevailed over the experiential tradition, for a world devoid of divine compassion had been found wanting. Sirach's emphasis upon God's mercy set him apart from the earlier sages whose legacy he inherited; so it is singularly appropriate that his final words combine both emphases with characteristic confidence.

> May your soul rejoice in his mercy,
> and may you not be put to shame when you praise him.
> Do your work before the appointed time,
> and in God's time he will give you your reward.
>
> (51:29-30)

CHAPTER 7

The Widening Hunt:
Wisdom of Solomon,
Wisdom Psalms, and Beyond

The impact of Israel's sages extended far beyond the actual court setting and scribal context, for the major issues with which they struggled were universal ones. The author of Wisdom of Solomon borrowed a new language, Greek, to convey his thoughts, and with that medium came entirely new emphases. Moreover, certain psalmists tried to provide adequate responses to the problem of undeserved suffering and apparent prosperity of wicked persons, and in the process the wisdom tradition merged with the liturgical. Beyond these two significant ventures one may discern various literary works which have been thought to breathe wisdom's atmosphere to a greater or lesser degree.

WISDOM OF SOLOMON

Sirach's emphasis upon divine mercy is carried forward with vigor by the unknown author of Wisdom of Solomon, who lived during the first century before the Christian era.[1] Indeed, this significant theological claim is formulated in a refrain that occurs twice within the work:

> . . . grace and mercy are upon his elect,
>   and he watches over his holy ones.
>
> (3:9 but with uncertain text, 4:15)

If this assertion left any question about God's willingness to forgive those who belong to the chosen people, a further declaration removed even the slightest doubt.

> But Thou, our God, art kind and true,
> patient, and ruling all things in mercy.
> For even if we sin we are thine, knowing thy power;
> but we will not sin, because we know that we are accounted thine.
>
> (15:1-2)

The consciousness of belonging to an elected people pervades this work and the belief that the souls of the righteous rest in God's hand (3:1).

The idea of an elect people scarcely accords with the universalism which dominates ancient Israelite wisdom, but Sirach's praise of past heroes paved the way for the adoption of particularistic thinking. Conscious of the impossibility of defending such a position logically, the author appealed to divine sovereignty (12:12-18). No one, human or otherwise, can call the only God to task for his conduct.

God's compassion expressed itself upon the elect and those not favored by divine choice, according to this author. Even the wicked Canaanites were given ample warning and perished little by little so that they would have an opportunity to repent (12:3-11). The same lenience was granted the Egyptians, whom God could have slain much more dramatically than by sending the plagues (11:15-20). Still, the author seems constrained to point out that God had sufficient foresight to know that these wicked people would never abandon their folly (12:10). Now and again tension exists between this sort of thinking and a desire to emphasize God's love for everyone, particularly since the entire world is no more than a speck of dust that tips the scales (11:22)—an argument that the book of Job expressed with considerable power.

It follows from this divine foreknowledge that God sees and hears everything that takes place within the universe which he fashioned (1:7-8). To be sure, some people draw erroneous conclusions from divine forbearance, viewing delayed punishment as evidence that God does not maintain justice. When this suspicion is strengthened by reflection upon life's brevity, it often leads to a lifestyle in which sensual gratification becomes the highest good. The author of Wisdom of Solomon attacks those who reason in this manner, accusing them of faulty logic (1:16—2:24).[2] In this connection care is taken to place the responsibility for death squarely upon human shoulders—and upon the devil's.

Human perversion expresses itself most visibly in *idol worship*, according to this author (13:1—15:17).[3] He even considers idolatry the beginning, cause, and end of all evil (14:27). Two explanations, perhaps three, are offered for the genesis of idol making: vanity, grief, and aesthetics. Desire to pay proper respect to far-away emperors prompted royal subjects to fashion images in the likeness of their ruler. Alternatively, a grief-stricken father may have shaped a piece of wood to resemble his dead child. Both explanations are reinforced by the desire to make images that please the eye; pride of craft turns idle carving into purposeful design.

The author goes a long way toward condoning the worship of nature, since God is manifest in what has been created. The error lay in a failure to move one step further from the creation to the Creator. The stupidity of idolatry becomes evident in the requests made to lifeless objects: one prays to a dead thing for life, to an inanimate artifact for health, to an idol that cannot take a single step for protection on a journey (13:18). This author finds it ludicrous that people embarking on a voyage by ship will entreat a paltry piece of wood, when God is the helmsman[4] who steers safely into harbor. Perhaps it is significant that precisely at this point the symbol of God as Father surfaces (14:3).

This allusion to God as Father stands alongside mention of wisdom by which the ship was built. In no other book does Wisdom play such a prominent role, and nowhere else does she possess such rich imagery. Here Wisdom goes beyond personification to hypostasis; she becomes a manifestation of God to human beings, an emanation of divine attributes. Futhermore, she is portrayed as Solomon's bride who enables him to rule wisely and justly. In addition, she functions in synonymous parallelism with the divine word, and even seems to be identical with God's holy spirit (6:12—9:18).

Whereas Sirach had identified wisdom and torah, Wisdom of Solomon brings God even closer to humans by understanding wisdom as

> . . . a breath of the power of God,
> and pure emanation of the glory of the Almighty.
>
> (7:25)

As such she mirrors God's eternal light and activity, for she is an image of God's goodness (7:26). For this reason divine attributes are ascribed to her.

> For in her there is a spirit that is intelligent, holy,
> unique, manifold, subtle,
> mobile, clear, unpolluted,
> distinct, invulnerable, loving the good, keen,
> irresistible, beneficent, humane,
> steadfast, sure, free from anxiety,
> all-powerful, overseeing all,
> and penetrating through all spirits
> that are intelligent and pure and most subtle.
>
> (7:22-23)

What is more, she is actually called the orderer and creator of all things (8:1,6). That is why she can also be described as the teacher of the cardinal virtues: self-control, prudence, justice, and courage (8:7).

According to 7:17-22, Wisdom was thought to have provided instruction in the fundamental subjects comprising the curriculum in a Greek school: philosophy, physics, history, astronomy, zoology, religion, botany, medicine.

> For it is he who gave me unerring knowledge of what exists,
> to know the structure of the world and the activity of the elements;
> the beginning and end and middle of times,
> the alterations of the solstices and the changes of the seasons,
> the cycles of the year and the constellations of the stars,
> the natures of animals and the tempers of wild beasts,
> the powers of spirits and the reasonings of men,
> the varieties of plants and the virtues of roots;
> I learned both what is secret and what is manifest,
> for wisdom, the fashioner of all things, taught me.
>
> (7:17-22)

In addition, Wisdom enters holy souls, turning them into prophets (7:27).

In this capacity wisdom guided the chosen people from the very beginning. The author traces this wondrous leadership from the first man to the memorable journey in the wilderness, referring specifically to Adam, Cain (negatively), Noah, Abraham, Lot (and his unfortunate wife), Jacob, Joseph, and Moses. Passing by the narratives from Genesis as hurriedly as possible, the sage dwells at length upon the events surrounding the exodus. Wisdom is even identified as the cloud that accompanied God's people by day and the pillar of fire by night. The final ten chapters (10—19) consist largely of a midrashic[5] exposition on the exodus experience. From 15:18 to 19:22 the contrast between God's manner of dealing with two entities, God's people and the Egyptians, occupies center stage.

Since the book we are discussing purports to come from Solomon's hand, it elevates the *erotic relationship* with Wisdom. In King Solomon's prayer at the sacred place in Gibeon (1 Kings 3:6-9), he requests an understanding mind to enable him to judge his people fairly. That request is amplified by the author of Wisdom of Solomon, who views the young king's prayer as the desire to acquire Wisdom for a bride. Such a wife brings respect, companionship, and freedom from pain. Her dowry includes the finest things one can envision: immortality, wealth, joy, renown, and understanding. Like torah, Wisdom will guard and guide those who love her.

This eulogy of the bride, Wisdom, contains some interesting self-reflections by Solomon. Despite his singular place in Israel's history, Solomon admits that he is mortal like everyone else. Lest the obvious be overlooked, he takes pains to point out that his prayer lacked every vestige of selfish interest. He preferred Wisdom to wealth, health, and beauty, but these accompanied her—to Solomon's utter surprise!

> All good things came to me along with her,
> and in her hands uncounted wealth.
> I rejoiced in them all, because wisdom leads them;
> but I did not know that she was their mother.

> (7:11-12)

Perhaps the most astonishing comment concerning Solomon's unusual status is his remark that a good soul befell him since he was good.

> As a child I was by nature well endowed,
> and a good soul fell to my lot;
> or rather, being good, I entered an undefiled body.
>
> (8:19-20)

To this point we have refrained from identifying *Hellenistic features* in the thought of this author.[6] Since it is well known that our unknown writer thought in Greek categories, although possibly using traditions in Hebrew[7] for sections of chapters 1—9, a few observations about the Greek spirit in the book seem called for at this time.

To begin with, we note a different attitude toward theological doubt, which occupies a prominent place in the Hebrew Bible and functions positively, for the most part. Wisdom of Solomon allows no room for religious doubt, asserting that Wisdom comes only to those who believe fully (1:2-5). Similarly, the Hebraic notion of progeny as an indication of God's favor flies out the window, for this author pronounces the barren, undefiled woman blessed (3:13), extends that honored status to eunuchs who are virtuous (3:14), and extols childlessness with virtue (4:1). To be sure, earlier Israelite sages would probably have agreed that virtue excels vice, even if the latter is accompanied by many children, but the very formulation of the issue in Wisdom of Solomon seems to presage new attitudes. The same goes for the negative attitude toward old age, for now the attainment of advanced years is no longer viewed as reward for a life well-lived.

> For old age is not honored for length of time,
> nor measured by number of years;
> but understanding is gray hair for men,
> and a blameless life is the ripe old age.
>
> (4:8)

This conviction arose from attempts to understand early deaths; the author sees such premature departures as God's gracious removal of persons from the possibility of sinning. An early death prevents worthy persons from defiling themselves, and therefore does not signify God's displeasure. Naturally, Enoch functions as a paradigm for this view.

Another Greek concept occurs in connection with the problem of theodicy; creation itself fights in behalf of the righteous (5:15-23; 16:24). The whole universe has been created so as to defend virtue and punish vice (16:17). The author uses this idea with great effect in discussing the punishment inflicted upon the ancient Egyptians, and in describing God's solicitous care for the elect people. In this connection he also develops a theory concerning psychological fear, according to which the Egyptians suffered more from anxiety than from actual physical causes, whereas the holy people, clothed with impenetrable spiritual armor, confidently relied upon their God for protection.

We have by no means discussed the full extent of Greek influence upon Wisdom of Solomon. Such an analysis would take into consideration the Greek poetic device in 6:17-20, the list of divine attributes in 7:22-23, the cardinal virtues in 8:7, and much more besides. Our intent has been to show the kind of changes that occurred once Hebraic wisdom shifted its locus to Greek soil. The different perspective appears nowhere so dramatically as it does in the following lament over limits imposed upon human knowledge.

> For what man can learn the counsel of God?
> Or who can discern what the Lord wills?
> For the reasoning of mortals is worthless,
> and our designs are likely to fail,
> for a perishable body weighs down the soul,
> and this earthly tent burdens the thoughtful mind.

> (9:13-15)

Qoheleth would gladly have endorsed this sentiment—until an explanation for this ignorance departed completely from the biblical conviction that all things created by God are very good. The distinction between body and soul owes its origin to the Hellenistic environment, not to Hebraic sapiential traditions.

WISDOM PSALMS

It has been said that with Ben Sira Israel's sages became worshipers. Certainly, prayer and praise resound within Sirach to a far greater extent than was true of earlier sapiential works. That inclination to participate in the religious life of the community must surely have found expression within the psalter, which belonged to no special group but voiced the aspirations, fears, and concerns of all people. A few psalms make free use of language and ideas which seem most at home among the sages.[8]

The most striking affinites between psalms and wisdom occur in a group of psalms that belong to the genre which we usually call *discussion literature*. These texts ask the perennial question about divine justice in face of apparent prosperity among the wicked. At least four such psalms merit consideration in this connection: 37, 39, 49, 73.

The first of these, Psalm 37, alerts us to the fact that wisdom is but one of several traditions that enrich this literature. For example, two themes—the land as an inheritance bestowed upon righteous people and divine vengeance upon sinners—belong to ancient sacral traditions. Nevertheless, this psalm does pose the pressing issue of prosperous sinners and resolves that dilemma in ways which recall answers within the book of Proverbs.

> Better is a little that the righteous has
> than the abundance of many wicked.
>
> (37:16)

> Again I passed by, and, lo, he was no more;
> though I sought him, he could not be found.
>
> (37:36)

> The wicked borrows, and cannot pay back,
> but the righteous is generous and gives.
>
> (37:21)

Although the resemblance is not quite so striking, two other verse units in this psalm breathe the same air that flows through Proverbs (37:23-24; 25). The former acknowledges God's control over one's steps, even when calamity strikes. Earlier sages also admitted that righteous persons occasionally fell down, but these teachers insisted that the stumblers would get up again seven times. The last verse cited above uses the literary device that Qoheleth found to his liking:

> I have been young, and now am old;
>> yet I have not seen the righteous forsaken
>> or his children begging bread.
>
> (37:25)

To be sure, Qoheleth never reached this conclusion from observing personal experience.

The next psalm, 39, echoes the voices of Job and Qoheleth. Indeed, the similarities are so close that one is tempted to posit a theory of dependence. Twice the psalmist takes up Qoheleth's motto concerning the vanity of human life.

> Surely every man stands as a mere breath!
>
> (39:5,11; Heb. 6,12)

> Surely man goes about as a shadow!
>
> (39:6; Heb. 7)

In addition he seizes Qoheleth's leitmotif about the inability to know (39:6; Heb. 7). Like Job, this psalmist accuses God of smiting him (39:10-11; Heb. 11-12) and begs his oppressor to avert his watchful eyes.

> Look away from me, that I may know gladness,
>> before I depart and be no more!
>
> (39:13; Heb. 14)

We have already seen how Job parodies Psalm 8, asking that God relinquish his surveillance so that he can die in peace.

The resemblances between Psalm 49 and wisdom literature[9] are less striking, although a common problem provides the subject matter—the prosperity of the wicked. But that problem disturbed prophets as well as sages, and the opening summons seems more at home among the called of God than in wisdom circles (49:1). Still, that summons rapidly becomes one that the sages would readily have owned.

> My mouth shall speak wisdom;
>> the meditation of my heart shall be understanding.
> I will incline my ear to a proverb;
>> I will solve my riddle to the music of the lyre.
>
> (49:3-4)

This psalm employs a form that has been called a "Summary Appraisal," although in this instance it anticipates rather than summarizes.[10]

> This is the fate of those who have foolish confidence,
>> the end of those who are pleased with their portion.
>>>> (49:13).

The psalmist recognizes the impossibility of purchasing life, and therefore he realizes that properous wicked persons will eventually lie in the ground with beasts. Here one encounters a marvelous metaphor: death is a shepherd watching over wicked persons (49:14).

Psalm 73 also wrestles with the problem of prosperous villains, but the resolution achieves startling novelty.[11] The psalm opens with a motto which is promptly put to the test.

> Truly God is good to the upright,
>> to those who are pure in heart.
>>>> (73:1)

The psalmist confesses that he almost betrayed the people of God by envying the prosperity enjoyed by wicked persons, until he went into God's sanctuary and saw their fate. While we cannot be sure what transpired in this setting, we can only note that he suddenly realizes the fleeting character of riches, and he then takes the further step toward cherishing God above all other treasure. The psalm closes with utter confidence that God is continually with the one who has faced doubt squarely. That discovery enabled the psalmist to make one further declaration: "But for me it is good to be near God. . ."(73:28).

Another kind of psalm that shared certain characteristics with wisdom literature is the *torah meditation*. The first psalm employs an image that is also found in Egyptian Instructions.

> He is like a tree
>> planted by streams of water,
> that yields its fruit in its season,
>> and its leaf does not wither.
> In all that he does, he prospers.
>>>> (1:3)

In the psalmist's view those who meditate upon the torah will thrive, whereas whoever neglects God's teaching will be like the chaff which the wind scatters. One wonders why the image of a tree was not used to describe wicked persons, as happens in Egyptian literature. Psalm 19 seems to comprise a riddle about speech that utters no sound,[12] although the text has now become a beautiful reminder that the creation itself proclaims the mysteries of its Creator.

Occasionally, a psalm combines themes and images from the wisdom corpus. For example, Psalm 127 elaborates upon the sages' claim that human plans and activity may ultimately be frustrated by God's contrary intentions (127:1-2). In addition, this psalm uses the image of children as arrows in a quiver (127:4), which also occurs in Sirach in an indirect fashion. In other psalms, only scattered verses seem to derive from wisdom circles or to express concerns similar to those endorsed by Israel's sages. In Psalm 32:8-9, one reads:

> I will instruct you and teach you
> > the way you should go;
> > I will counsel you with my eye upon you.
> Be not like a horse or mule, without understanding,
> > which must be curbed with bit and bridle,
> > else it will not keep with you.

Similarly, Psalm 94:8-11 juxtaposes folly and wisdom in a manner highly reminiscent of the sages.

> Understand, O dullest of the people!
> > Fools, when will you be wise?
> He who planted the ear, does he not hear?
> He who formed the eye, does he not see?
> . . . .
> He who teaches men knowledge,
> > the LORD, knows the thoughts of man,
> > that they are but a breath.

A combination of language and thematic interest gives Psalm 62:8-12 a sapiential character.

> Once God has spoken;
> > twice have I heard this:
> that power belongs to God.

                                                                (62:11)

To this linguistic affinity with Job may be added the emphasis upon life's ephemerality. Perhaps, too, the warning against placing trust in riches echoes the similar piece of advice in Proverbs 23:4-5, but the suspicion that wealth quickly vanishes was probably shared by all segments of Israelite society.

This delineation of wisdom psalms uses formal and thematic criteria, as well as the overall tone which surfaces in a given text. To be sure, other readings of the data have been offered, ranging from the bare admission of wisdom or learned psalmography to a hypothesis of numerous wisdom psalms. The present analysis has looked askance at certain formal and thematic considerations: *'ašre* sayings (Happy the . . .); acrostic (alphabetic) arrangement; anthological composition (made up of selected phrases from various sources); mere didactic intent; themes such as "fear of God," the fate of the righteous and the wicked; and exhortation as such. Should we widen the net to include such texts, we would have difficulty demonstrating their sapiential character. It seems best, therefore, to exercise caution with respect to the incorporation of additional passages into the wisdom category. In any event, we have isolated sufficient evidence to suggest that Israel's sages eventually participated in, or directly influenced, the cultic life which finds expression in the Psalter. Still, we are not justified in taking the further step toward declaring that the sages had a lively interest in the cult from the very beginning.

1 ESDRAS 3:1—5:3

The impact of sapiential thought was also felt in late historiography. The contest of Darius' guards in 1 Esdras 3:1—5:3 concerning the strongest thing in the world makes free use of traditions derived from wisdom literature.[13] A case can be made for direct dependence upon Sirach and Qoheleth, and the matchless description of wine's power over its hapless victims echoes similar observations in Proverbs. Although the final praise of truth has been compared to a passage in Ptahhotep's Instruction,[14] it represents universally acknowledged conviction that the truth alone survives time's passage.

At the same time, the larger context resembles Sirach 43:1-5 and

17:31-32 in so many respects that it is difficult to deny a direct relationship. Both Sirach and 1 Esdras praise the sun, but note that its light pales, so that only truth lasts forever. Each passage concludes with a doxology which lauds the Creator of the sun and Lord of truth. Furthermore, Sirach 17 singles out humans as masters of the earth and contrasts ephemerality and unrighteousness with that which endures, just as 1 Esdras juxtaposes eternal truth with everything which eventually decays because it is unrighteous. On the basis of these striking resemblances, together with evidence within the context itself (1 Esdras 4:2, 14, 37), it appears that a fourth speech has been displaced from the narrative. In it, man was depicted as strongest because he lorded it over the beasts.

The kinship with Qoheleth occurs within the speech concerning the king as strongest. Here the similarities with Ecclesiastes 3:1-9 are remarkable. Only those actions which are not subject to external command (for example, making love, hating, and so forth) are missing from 1 Esdras. Otherwise, essentially the same polarities appear in both texts.

> If he tells them to kill, they kill; if he tells them to release, they release; if he tells them to attack, they attack; if he tells them to lay waste, they lay waste; if he tells them to build, they build; if he tells them to cut down, they cut down; if he tells them to plant, they plant.
> (1 Esdras 4:7-9)

The four answers to the question, "what is strongest?" are defended with remarkable flourish: wine, the king, woman, and truth. The author's fondness for rhetorical questions expresses itself throughout the dialogue, as does conscious humor. Two exquisite examples of humor occur when a man is described as dropping his most cherished possession and gazing *open-mouthed* at a lovely woman, and when the king is reminded of his gazing *open-mouthed* at his playful concubine after she has just slapped him. By this means the king is reduced to the level of ordinary humans, and the final verdict appropriately comes from the people themselves.

That spontaneous celebration of truth introduces a religious dimension into the story, for all eyes turn toward the one before whom even eternal truth does obeissance. Here entertaining dialogue functions in the service of religious instruction; futhermore, nothing demands a hypothesis of Greek origin for this exaltation of abstract truth.[15] The Israelite sages were certainly capable of praising abstract concepts like truth, righteousness, and wisdom.

BARUCH 3:9—4:4

A hymn in praise of wisdom occurs in Baruch 3:9—4:4, a text which probably originated during the first century B.C.E. It draws heavily upon canonical language, imagery, and concepts, particularly Proverbs and Job, but also borrows from Ben Sira. As a consequence of such extensive reliance upon earlier texts, this hymn signals no advance in sapiential reflection.

The similarity with Proverbs extends beyond the reference to the fountain of wisdom.

> Learn where there is wisdom,
>> where there is strength,
>> where there is understanding,
> that you may at the same time discern
>> where there is length of days, and life,
>> where there is light for the eyes, and peace.
>
> (Baruch 3:14)

The connection between the hymn and Deuteronomy 30:12-14 and Job 28 is even more striking.

> Who has gone up into heaven, and taken her [wisdom],
>> and brought her down from the clouds?
> Who has gone over the sea, and found her,
>> and will buy her for pure gold?
> No one knows the way to her,
>> or is concerned about the path to her.
> But he who knows all things knows her,
>> he found her by his understanding.
>
> (Baruch 3:29-32a)

Although wisdom is inaccessible to humans, the God of Israel acquired her and bestowed her upon Jacob, with whom she came to dwell. It follows that those people who claim to have achieved wisdom, the Edomites, for example, have not done so.

Like Ben Sira, this author identifies wisdom with torah.

> She is the book of the commandments of God,
> and the law that endures forever.
>
> (Baruch 4:1)

BEYOND THE APOCRYPHA

Speculation about the accessibility of wisdom increased in the intertestamental period. The author of Enoch alters Sirach's idea that wisdom searched for a place to reside until finally choosing Jerusalem; in the new version she could not find a suitable place anywhere on earth.

> Wisdom found no place where she might dwell;
> Then a dwelling-place was assigned her in the heavens.
> Wisdom went forth to make her dwelling among the children of men,
> and found no dwelling-place:
> Wisdom returned to her place,
> and took her seat among the angels.
>
> (Enoch 42:1-2)

This emphasis upon the hiddenness of wisdom derives from a canonical text (Job 28), and finds expression in 2 Esdras 5:9b-10a.

> Then shall intelligence hide itself,
> and wisdom withdraw to its chamber—
> by many shall be sought and not found.

Philo of Alexandria drew freely upon wisdom literature; his fondness for this section of the Hebrew Bible is rivaled only by the Torah.[16] The similarities between Philo and Wisdom of Solomon are striking, although the resemblances occasion little surprise since both works came from the same general vicinity and date. In Philo's thought reflective mythology was completely at home, and *sophia* was portrayed as mother, wife, lover, virgin, and bride. But this heavenly hostess was also a symbol for evil, seduction, carnal passion—as she was in Proverbs 9.

Within the New Testament, wisdom traditions made a significant impact—from Q, the oldest collection of Jesus' sayings,[17] to hymnic texts in the Pauline corpus. Although Q has been understood against the background of Hellenistic wisdom, there is no need to do so, for Jewish sapiential literature provides an adequate milieu for this material.[18] In this document Jesus and John were viewed as wisdom's sons and prophets. Matthew develops this idea further, interpreting Jesus as the sender of prophets, wise men, and scribes. In short, for Matthew Jesus was the incarnation of wisdom and embodiment of torah. Therefore, he can speak as wisdom does in Sirach 51:26-27: "Come to me, . . . my yoke is easy, and my burden is light" (Matthew 11:28-30).[19]

The Pauline corpus implies that the negative aspects of wisdom threatened the unity of the Christian fellowship. Perhaps an organized school of wisdom at Ephesus introduced excessive rhetoric and uncontrolled speculation, prompting Paul's assertion that God alone is wise (1 Corinthians 1:18ff.).[20] In any event, gnostic speculation certainly surfaces within the early Christian community. From the other perspective, ethical Jewish maxims undoubtedly influenced the author of James, and the Johannine prologue describes Jesus as the *logos* incarnate.

Two early sapiential works merit a few words in this connection: the *Sentences of Sextus*[21] and the *Teachings of Silvanus.*[22] The former consists of over four hundred proverbial type maxims setting forth the ideal life for Christians. These nuggets of learning also functioned to inculcate morals; that is, they served as instruments of moral transformation. Unlike Sextus, Silvanus engages in mystic-theosophical reflection.[23] Both authors are non-Jewish in their inspiration, although similarities with Israelite wisdom certainly occur. Silvanus, like Philo, resembles Wisdom of Solomon; metaphysics, not experience, lies behind his motivation clauses and exhortations. Such sages have come a long way from the early proverbs which drew practical lessons from daily experience. The endless quest has widened its net to feed an unquenchable appetite like Sheol's.

CHAPTER 8

Wisdom's Legacy

The sages of Israel have bequeathed a valuable legacy to posterity. That legacy cannot easily be summarized in the scope of a chapter, but I wish to emphasize three areas in which wisdom made a contribution to ancient Israelite thought. Naturally, these aspects of the sapiential heritage include countless other important contributions which I shall discuss here only by implication.

Perhaps the most noteworthy feature of wisdom's legacy is the capacity to recognize the limits imposed upon human reason and to face reality honestly, submitting every claim about knowledge to this severe judgment. That awareness of human limits also applied to so-called revelatory knowledge. The result was the *growth of skepticism* in ancient Israel. That phenomenon merits our careful analysis and will therefore constitute the bulk of this chapter.

The sages also proclaimed a world view which offered a *viable alternative to the Yahwistic one.* According to the sapiential legacy, creation was the occasion for God's contact with those who bore the divine image. Revelation, that is, was pushed back to the beginning, and humans possessed the necessary means of discovering truth. This positive view of women and men contrasts greatly with the dominant Yahwistic emphasis upon sin and guilt.

A third feature of wisdom's legacy is its *ability to cope* with reality. In a real sense, this aspect of wisdom embraces the other two, for skepticism was her way of dealing with experienced ambiguities, and the formulation of a new world view grew out of the actual practice of coping with events which had rendered traditional religious convictions obsolete.

THE BIRTH OF SKEPTICISM IN ANCIENT ISRAEL

"The deepest, the only theme of human history, compared to which all others are of subordinate importance, is the conflict of scepticism with faith."[1] The author of this astonishing observation, the poet Wolfgang von Goethe, described that antipathy between doubt and a vision of a transformed society with extraordinary power in Faust's final surge of humanitarianism which elicited the fateful request, "Stay, thou art so fair," signaling the loss of his wager with Mephistopheles and, by a curious non sequitur, the ultimate triumph of virtue. This essay will examine that conflict between faith and doubt in ancient Israel.

THE SKEPTIC'S VISION

To begin with, we must distinguish between *skepticism, pessimism,* and *cynicism.* In my view, skepticism includes both a denial and an affirmation. The negative side of a skeptic's mental outlook consists of doubting thought, whereas the positive affirmation of a hidden reality indicated that it is altogether inappropriate to accuse skeptics of unbelief.[2] This powerful vision of a better world inherent within skepticism prompted Blaise Pascal to write that "there never has been a real complete sceptic."[3] The matrix formed by the disparity between the actual state of affairs and a vision of what should be both sharpened critical powers and heightened religious fervor. Doubt, it follows, is grounded in profound faith.[4]

Once skeptics lose all hope of achieving the desired transformation, *pessimism* sets in, spawning sheer indifference to cherished convictions. Pessimists believe chaos has the upper hand and will retain control forever; they lack both a surge for transcendence and faith in human potential. Since they own no vision which acts as a corrective to the status quo, pessimists can muster no base upon which to stand and from which to criticize God and the world. The inevitable result is a sense of being overwhelmed by an oppressive reality.[5]

Cynics go a step further; by their disdain for creaturely comforts and sensual pleasure they show contempt for everything life has to offer. No vision moves them to reject an imperfect present reality while awaiting a more perfect one which God and humans bring into being, and no feeling of helplessness makes them throw up their hands in despair. Instead, they demonstrate an amazing capacity for survival despite outward circumstances to which they are inwardly indifferent.[6]

Skeptics freely raise their voices within the Hebrew Scriptures, and pessimists occasionally add their cry; but we listen in vain for cynics' sighs. The reason is easily perceived: the presupposition of cynicism, contempt for the material world, is wholly alien to Hebrew thinking. In what follows, the area of concentration will be skepticism, though rare expressions of pessimism may surface as well.

Now doubt may be what Jean Jacques Rousseau called "reverent doubt" and skepticism, "unwilling skepticism."[7] That is why Tennyson was on target when observing that there is more faith in honest doubt than in half the creeds. For some reason not yet fathomed by flesh and blood, certain eras lend themselves to wholesale skepticism, eliciting the painful admission that "We of this generation are not destined to eat and be satisfied as our fathers were; we must be content to go hungry."[8] Such deprivation resulting from a complete breakdown in cultural values offers a unique opportunity for fresh breakthroughs[9] which rejuvenate human society. Once dogma freezes, traditions become lifeless fetters, and can only be thrown off by resurging vital faith that dares to challenge the most sacred belief in the name of a higher truth.[10]

It has been said that *skepticism without religion is impossible, and religion without skepticism is intolerable.*[11] To be sure, the skeptic's faith does not necessarily name God as its object. For example, the French Enlightenment was a great age of skepticism in which faith sought new outlets—first nature and after that, men and women. Unwilling to sanction the tyranny of the church any longer, these skeptics found a new and wondrous object of trust in nature, particularly when epochmaking geological discoveries cast serious doubt on established views about divine providence and the date of creation. Futhermore, the complexity of human beings approached the mystery formerly relegated to God as the individual emerged into the limelight and fresh knowledge of previously unknown cultures stirred the imagination. Long before corrupt ecclesiastical officials aroused strong resolve to crush the infamous thing, Israelites, too, chafed under an oppresive yoke. The name of Job suffices to remind readers that religion can easily become an instrument of cruelty unless it is tempered with a skeptic's honesty.

By assisting religion in its endless struggle to prevent belief from becoming hollow testimony to a reality belonging only to the past, skepticism functions as religion's handmaid. Many of Israel's noblest insights resulted from the interplay between faith and doubt. Confronted with the void, her skeptics fought to sustain their vision of an eternal order where justice prevails. Here and there we hear a triumphant shout when skeptics affirm their faith while walking in utter darkness. Perhaps the most moving such expression of confidence occurs in the unparalleled seventy-third psalm, where the poet ultimately feels the touch of a father's hand and knows that God is present to one who has honestly faced doubt.[12]

Skepticism's indispensability may be seen in the fact that the great ideologies correspond to three syntactic moods.[13] *Theology affirms the declarative, humanism informs the imperative, and skepticism supplies the interrogative.* The prominence of narrative in the Hebrew Bible derives from the basic truth that theology is essentially affirmation. Once that declarative statement imposes strong demands upon men and women, humanism intrudes to maintain the dignity of persons upon whom the divine imperative has fallen. Skepticism dares to penetrate beneath the statement and consequent demand; it inquires about the ultimate basis for the declaration and presses toward determining motivation for obedience. Self-knowledge emerges largely through interrogation; for example, the question, "Why am I suffering?" early became a means of dealing with guilt, and eventually revolutionized Israel's understanding of reality itself.[14]

Ironically, this Joban onslaught fought against a world view which resulted directly from the first decisive breakthrough in our intellectual history.[15] That is the principle of universality—the ideal of rationality according to which no individual possessed the truth, the universe was orderly, and human beings were spectators of a powerful drama which God directed toward a distant goal. The assumption of order precipitated crises in Mesopotamia, Egypt, and Israel, as is well documented in the relevant literature.[16] One need not envision mass distribution of these texts in Israel and elsewhere[17] to recognize the revolutionary impact of such thinking, for the doubting thought surfaced throughout recorded memory.

DOMINANT HYPOTHESES

From this observation it follows that one cannot subscribe to the theory that the decisive breakthrough in Israel coincided with the Solomonic empire and constituted a complete break with sacral thinking.[18] Skepticism within the canon can hardly be restricted to an understanding of the manner in which God governs history. Failure to recognize this important fact has seriously distorted analyses of the extent and complexity of Israelite skepticism.[19] This narrow understanding of skepticism has produced three significant half truths which have dominated most discussions of intellectual development in ancient Israel: (1) skepticism signifies a worn out culture;[20] (2) such rejection of established views is an elitist phenomenon;[21] and (3) skepticism arose as a consequence of historical crises.[22]

1. Skepticism Signifies a Burnt Out Culture

To be sure, centuries of affirmation precede significant doubt. Society's givens accumulate slowly; in the beginning sanctions are consciously formulated, and later their acceptance becomes almost as natural as breathing. In this way a world view takes shape,[23] and legitimations reinforce it from every side. Cherished beliefs are promulgated consciously and unconsciously, and daily experience seems to support such values. Only after sanctions for life have evolved and demonstrated their dependability can doubt about their legitimacy arise. Ancient rabbis perceived this fact and applied it to their paragon of wisdom. According to them, Solomon wrote

Song of Songs in his youthful days when desire surges, Proverbs during mature years, and Qoheleth when senility had settled in for good. Like individuals, civilizations grow old and cast off their youthful garments in order to don funeral shrouds.

The denigration of post-exilic Israel as a burnt-out culture may have coincided with prevailing interpretations of late Judaism, to use a term that is itself pejorative, but such a reading of Israelite history belongs inherently to certain streams of canonical tradition. The Deuteronomistic understanding of events as one great failure on Israel's part, with rare exceptions, and the apocalyptic notion of successive ages whose very names imply gradual decay must surely be responsible for the widespread belief that Israelite skepticism arose in the midnight hour of canonical history.

2. Skepticism Is an Elitist Phenomenon

The claim that skepticism is a malaise suffered only by the well-to-do builds upon an assumption about the leisure class as guardians of Israel's intellectual tradition.[24] Acceptance of this plausible hypothesis about the authors of the sapiential corpus may permit one to make significant observations concerning Job and Qoheleth, but the skeptical voice reaches far beyond these dissenting cries. Parallels with neighboring cultures, particularly the Egyptian, are informative, but Israel's sages functioned in an entirely different context from that represented by Egyptian counsellors to the Pharaoh.[25]

3. Skepticism Resulted from Historical Crises

The third misconception, that political catastrophe generates skepticism, possesses an element of truth, as a cursory reading in prophetic literature confirms. Still, various answers to the problem occasioned by defeat on the battlefield readily present themselves and secure faith intact: Israel has sinned; God is testing his people; foreign powers function as God's agents; external events do not accurately reflect true reality.[26] The amazing resiliency of faith enabled men and women to survive events that had the capacity to shatter fondest dreams. Even Josiah's dark fate precipitated no discernible religious revolt against providence.[27]

Having acknowledged the partial truth in each of the three statements, I wish to formulate opposing assertions: (1) skepticism belongs to Israel's thought from early times; (2) it extends far beyond the intelligentsia; and (3) it springs from two fundamentally different sources, which we may call theological and epistemological. In short, skepticism is intrinsic to biblical thinking rather than an intruder who took Israel by surprise; this rich heritage of doubt often took up willing residence among the ordinary people in Judah and Ephraim; and skeptics turned their attention toward human ability to know anything as well as toward theories about God's works.

1. Skepticism Arose Early

Occasional texts confirm the relative antiquity of skeptical outbursts.[28] For instance, Isaiah pronounces a woe upon those who say:

> . . . "Let him make haste,
>   let him speed his work
>   that we may see it;
> let the purpose of the Holy One of Israel draw near,
>   and let it come, that we may know it!"
>
> (Isaiah 5:19)

Similarly, Zephaniah accuses his contemporaries of thinking that God "will not do good, nor will he do ill" (Zephaniah 1:12). Furthermore, an old account of Gideon's encounter with a heavenly visitor bristles with skepticism and describes Gideon as nearly laughing in the angel's face (Judges 6:11-13). When tested in the crucible of experience, the people's miserable circumstances hardly accorded with religious convictions that God actively worked to sustain Israel.

> "Pray, sir, if the LORD is with us, why then has all this befallen us? And where are all his wonderful deeds which our fathers recounted to us?"
>
> (Judges 6:13)

In this case the interrogative mood threatened to swallow up the declarative, and youthful rebellion placed paternal teaching under a dark cloud. A full fledged pragmatist, Gideon insisted on incontroverible proof for theological statements. Naturally, such a one refused to surrender before the divine imperative until convincing demonstration of faith's assertions lay within his grasp. As Jeremiah 44:15-19 shows, such empirical tests cut two ways: here the Jewish refugees residing in Egypt inform Jeremiah that they had prospered so long as they worshiped the queen of heaven, but fell victim to destructive forces when they abandoned their goddess. In their eyes, as in Gideon's too, devotion to Yahweh did not pay sufficient dividends.

Even without this evidence that skeptics came upon the stage long before Job and Qoheleth were written, we could reasonably conjecture that certain features of Yahwism made such doubt extremely probable. To begin with, Israel's understanding of God as one who withholds his name at the very moment of self-revelation openly invites skepticism.[29] Mystery clothes the one who freely makes himself known, whether to Moses as "I AM WHO I AM" (Exodus 3:14) or to Manoah as "wonderful" (Judges 13:18).[30] In the last resort, Israel's sovereign refuses to bow before human manipulation, and thus retains his freedom in all circumstances. As a result, this God gains a reputation as one who comes to assist oppressed peoples, although an occasional suspicion that he is demonic also lingers in the hearts of those who encounter stark mystery.[31] Inherent within such conviction is the belief that God dwells afar off, so that one can know only what he allows humans to perceive. Like Adam long ago, one merely observes the surgeon's finished work. Even the celebrated "mighty acts of God" which generation after generation recited in sacred assembly and in the family circle were inferences drawn from footprints in the Judean hills, for no eyes ever penetrated the veil shielding God from frail creatures.

Naturally, such theology gives rise to emphasis upon creaturely finitude. Between humans and God stretches a vast chasm, and no bridge spans the abyss. The defiant post-deluvian generation was not the only one that dreamed of linking heaven and earth. A favored two, Enoch and Elijah, were thought to have walked hand in hand with God into the sunset or to have ridden a heavenly chariot upon the clouds, but for most mortals access to God was completely circumscribed. It consisted of the divine image which included, among other things, verbal communication; by this means imagistic links occurred—poetic inspiration, prophetic visions, and the sage's intuition. The walls of God's heavenly castle were so steep that even "thoughts slipped below," to quote Goethe once again, and the entire enterprise which aimed at uniting the two realms crashed to the ground like the ill-fated tower of Babel. Those who live on borrowed breath can hardly boast about their strength, especially when events overwhelm human victims and crush them indiscriminately.

The earliest sages also knew that their knowledge came up against limits beyond which it could not go.[32] Careful plans could always clash with God's secret intentions, and in such cases humans proposed but God disposed. When the deity's glory consists in hiding things, the stage is already set for anxiety in the face of apparent injustice. That worry intensifies the moment true wisdom is placed outside human reach, for men and women inevitably ask why God retains her for his private possession.

Given these two extraordinary facts, a God who hides and creatures who are dependent, skepticism's appearance in Israel was no great surprise. Some texts seem almost to encourage expostulation with the deity as if he longed to have probing questions directed his way. For example, the narrative concerning the Lord's destruction of Sodom and Gomorrah pictures the deity standing before Abraham in open invitation to discuss the moral implications of the decision to demolish entire cities. Obviously, God is not the only one who has qualms about wholesale slaughter, for the author of the prose tale allows Abraham to utter his own weighty objections. A single question gathers together the entire moral dilemma into which God has placed himself: "Shall not the Judge of the whole earth do justice?" The skeptic's criticism appeals to a vision of right conduct to which even God's deeds are subject.

2. Skepticism Enjoyed Popular Support

This intrinsic nature of skepticism means that it refused to become the exclusive property of an intellectually elite group of people. Admittedly, breakdowns often fail to achieve decisive breakthroughs for lack of popular support. Such aristocratic revolutions always abort because they do not succeed in capturing the imagination of common people. The mere presence of potentially revolutionary thoughts cannot alter the human situation unless the idea seizes the minds of those who alone can implement lasting change.

Of course, revolutions can be attempted without popular support, but the outcome is predictably disappointing. Akenaton's remarkable break with the past achieved no permanence, despite the powerful sanctions accompanying the reform, and Egypt soon reverted to pre-Amarna thinking. Similarly, the French experiment in recent times collapsed for lack of enthusiasm among the masses.[33] For these people religious belief survived the devastating attack upon faith launched by the intelligentsia. Even widespread clerical corruption failed to convince ordinary church goers that the reality to which they prayed did not deserve their supreme devotion.

Perhaps the most astonishing failure in this regard occurred in ancient Babylonia, where the revolutionary idea of linearity surfaced but became a victim of a more powerful belief in divine caprice. Lacking faith in God's control of human events so as to bring them to a distant goal envisioned by the deity, Babylonian religion failed to achieve the idea of *telos* which shines with such dazzling splendor in the Hebrew Scriptures. No vision of the *eschaton* transformed Babylonian cultic dominance, and no linear purposive progression put an end to circular thinking. Divine caprice turned these people into what has been called the most pessimistic civilization in history.[34]

For several reasons, the hypothesis that Israel's skepticism was elitist misses the mark. Such a restriction of the doubting thought to the perimeters of wisdom ignores the widespread phenomenon of skepticism throughout Israelite society. The author has discussed elsewhere numerous instances of skeptical defiance which confronted canonical prophets and prompted intemperate language and considerable soul searching.[35] To be sure, not all of these antagonists challenged prophetic utterances on the basis of enduring visions of transcendence,[36] but it can hardly be denied that many of them protested against bogus promises and insisted upon complete honesty in assessing the theological situation.

In this respect compilers of canonical psalms displayed considerably more appreciation for those who uttered the perennial interrogative: "How long, O Lord?" In these expressions of lament and praise occurs a mighty crescendo of expostulation with the deity concerning justice above all. It seems that the most devout worshiper cannot decide whether to acknowledge God's justice in the face of evidence to the contrary or to concede divine blindness, nay indifference, as irrefutable fact. Even when the psalmist cites such low opinions of God and attributes them to fools, the very articulation of skeptical views satisfies a need for honesty on the part of the worshiping community.

Within the wisdom corpus itself certain bits of evidence suggest that the skeptical mood threatened to overwhelm the entire sapiential enterprise. The sheer bulk of the skeptical literature, including Job and Qoheleth, must surely have suggested to many that the proper scholarly pursuit comprised the study of comparable texts. More importantly, Ben Sira feels constrained to enter into lively dialogue with a group of skeptics[37] who offered his own students a viable alternative to the confessional theology he had lately interpolated into wisdom's repertoire. In attempting to refute their arguments, he borrowed an old debate form and used it freely. One element of that literary device, the actual quotation of an opponent's argument, permitted skeptical views wide audience, particularly when Ben Sira's teachings became part of the canon. Even though the doubting thought is dismissed for one reason or another, it continues to sink deeply into the minds of all who read Sirach. Perhaps an awareness of this persuasive whisper moved the author of Wisdom of Solomon to register the opinion that doubt's mere presence renders one incapable of receiving divine revelation (1:2). Such warning can only mean that skepticism posed a real threat in the eyes of this sage, and that makes the hypothesis of minimal impact by skeptical literary works wholly unacceptable.

3. Skepticism Flowed from Two Separate Streams

My third assertion, that skepticism arose in two distinct

contexts, requires considerable elaboration. On the one hand, skepticism addresses itself to a specific theological situation; in short, it signifies a crisis of faith in God. On the other hand, the skeptic also isolates a wholly different kind of bankruptcy—the loss of faith in human beings. It will not do to label one stream Yahwism and the other wisdom, although the inclination to do so arises from a valid intuition. Nevertheless, the two streams converge at decisive locations, and in the end both tributaries flow into the same reservoir.

The starting point for an analysis of these streams must surely be the conviction that the cosmos was essentially orderly, which we have earlier called the first decisive breakthrough in our spiritual history. Without a firm sense of predictability, Israel could never have developed certain legitimations that undergirded society. The declaration that the universe could be relied upon (Genesis 9:8-17) bursts upon the scene precisely when the deluge seemed to render life utterly perilous; its formulation constitutes a mighty expression of confidence in God's goodness despite the memory of raging waters. In time that optimism yielded further affirmations, especially the claim that virtue bore rich fruit, just as vice produced its own unwanted harvest. To be sure, minor fissures occurred here and there, but skillful hands nearly always filled those cracks with reliable cement.[38]

Alongside this belief in a calculable universe stood an equally compelling conviction that Israel was a covenant people who enjoyed God's favor. No task was too great, no enemy too powerful, to frustrate this desire on God's part to bestow life upon Israel at any cost. Other nations fell like flies before this covenant God, and not even sin by the favored people could thwart God's purposes. Having established the covenant relationship in the first place, Israel's sovereign was not about to let anything frustrate his designs for her.

The principal arena in which God carried out his hopes for Israel was political, and the decisive medium, the Davidic monarchy. To a large degree, the prophetic witness coincided with the period of the monarchy, a fact that has not been sufficiently appreciated in critical research. Both corporate and individual existence achieved significance in the course of history, upon which the divine word worked with matchless success. Israel's enemies fled when the Lord lifted his mighty arm, and God's people marched joyously from bondage into liberty. Valiant soldiers wasted away when the death angel spread its wings and flew into the midst of God's enemies. So ran the embellished account of Israel's history,[39] a story so far from the truth that it sowed seeds of skepticism at almost every telling. The disparity between present reality and grandiose confessions of God's mighty deeds in the past demanded an adequate explanation lest wholesale abandoning of the Lord take place.

The response to this need succeeded in reducing divine sanctions of society to a book, that is, Deuteronomy. This single event paved the way for crystallized dogma and precipitated a sharp attack on a closed cosmos, an offensive that eventuated in outright skepticism. In Deuteronomy life stands over against death, and individuals are exhorted to choose which of the two they wish to embrace. Any intermediary position has vanished from sight, and the earlier dynamic juxtaposition of the one and the many has likewise disappeared altogether. In the process a decisive shift in ethos occurs. Slowly the family loses its hold over allegiances,[40] and individuality surfaces in a way that was hitherto unknown. Ownership of disposable property, urban concentration of the population, religious syncretism, political violence, and the like both brought this change about and shaped new attitudes that soon became widespread through conscious and unconscious dissemination.

The Deuteronomistic theory of exact retribution encouraged the rapid growth of skepticism by emphasizing human corruption, a theme that permeates the Yahwistic primeval history. Paradoxically, the canonical prophets also stimulated a sense of moral defeatism by repeated denunciations of the people as a *massa damnationis*. Perhaps to a certain extent such indictments became self-fulfilling, and moral impotence resulted since all self-esteem had been stripped away by well-intentioned prophets. Precisely where such thinking leads can be seen in 2 Esdras' lament that it would have been better not to have been born.

Blind bards, like the unknown author of Psalm 37, who had

never seen the righteous forsaken or his descendants begging bread, tried desperately to withstand the tide of skepticism within the populace, and others wrote and rewrote actual history to remove the discrepancy between celebrated story and real fact. In the process the Deuteronomistic national focus vanished in favor of rigid emphasis upon retribution at the individual level.[41] Long before the Chronicler engaged in his effort to formulate an adequate account of earlier history, individual choice played a prominent role in determining destiny. Indeed, in the Yahwist's view, the original sin introduced an alien force which even God could not eradicate. Its effect upon the human will was so irresistible that no righteous person existed throughout the land. Subsequent thinkers like Jeremiah and Qoheleth agreed wholeheartedly with this low estimate of human beings. Lacking both the will and the power to achieve virtue, individuals have no choice but to rely upon God's mercy. Accordingly, they praise God for accomplishing what men and women cannot do. As human potential decreases, divine power increases; nothing exists outside God's sovereignty. Of course, the appropriate human attitude is submission before the Almighty.

The ultimate step is to deny knowledge to humans. Thus we come to the second aspect of my assertion that skepticism has two distinct sources. Theological claims about God that conflict with reality and about humans that degrade them are matched by an epistemological view which encourages skeptical thoughts. The knowledge which humans acquire concerns terrestrial affairs, for Wisdom dwells with God, and none born of woman can approach her house. Once reason surrenders its throne to an alien power, the best the human intellect can do is to teach men and women "to bear in an understanding silence what must be borne." In such a situation, Agur's opening lament functions as a suitable motto: "There is no God at all, and I am powerless."[42]

Since the discussion of theological sources for skepticism has addressed issues as they arose in Yahwism generally, this analysis of the epistemological crisis will concentrate on Israelite wisdom. The earliest collection in Proverbs requires an acknowledgment that the terms theological and epistemological are inadequate, for the sages' subsequent admission concerning a bankruptcy of knowledge rests ultimately upon convictions about God which surface in the very beginning. For example, human preparations for warfare may abort, since the battle belongs to the Lord. All efforts to master the universe labor under a single unknown factor—God's freedom. Thus an element of surprise hovered over every attempt to control fate, and no means of fathoming that secret ingredient presented itself. Still, the sages saw no great threat in that unknown quantity so long as they believed in God's goodness.

A decisive shift occurs in the book of Job, which wrestles with an awareness that God sometimes becomes an enemy to the one who faithfully trusts him. Job complains that God cannot be found, for he is unfathomable and so remote that sin does not affect him in the least. The same note is sounded with greater velocity by Job's three friends and by the youthful intruder, Elihu. In their view, humans are unclean, as are heavenly beings, and God alone possesses innocence. On this fact everyone is agreed except Job, who would prove God guilty to demonstrate his own purity. Job's predicament forces him to abandon the rational principle, although his argument presupposes the truth of exact retribution for good and evil. The divine speeches remind Job of fixed limits which have been imposed upon human knowledge and power.

Qoheleth advances in yet another direction; in his opinion, God is wholly indifferent to human beings, a thesis that picks up one aspect of Job's friends' theology. In addition, knowledge is limited to earthly things, and even there it does not amount to anything permanent. The reason, of course, is that death cancels everything,[43] rendering all human striving a chasing after wind and utterly meaningless. A twisted world mocks all human effort, since none can straighten what God has made crooked; mystery clothes the beautiful creation and prevents men and women from making use of God's gift implanted in their hearts.[44] Moral impotence naturally flows from such a thoroughly pessimistic view.[45]

Sirach internalizes the burden which weighs heavily upon one and all; anxiety functions as a powerful means of equalizing things which otherwise appear to refute any belief in justice. Confronted by divine control over the inner life as well as outward events, men and women rely more and more upon God's mercy. Accordingly, Ben Sira seems never to tire of praising the Lord for compassionate dealings with sinful creatures who repent of their deeds. Earlier sages had remained silent on this theme, for they believed sufficient knowledge and power belonged to them to secure life.[46]

By far the most extreme statement of pessimism comes from Agur, who boldly rejects the theistic hypothesis and concedes that the consequence is devastating.[47] That confession stands at the polar position from earlier optimism; its simplicity and brevity electrify. In a word, "I cannot." Nevertheless, this foreign sage stopped short of the *ennui* which grips the author of the Babylonian "Dialogue of Scepticism." In his chaotic world nothing commends itself sufficiently to stave off a desire to terminate life. Agur, on the other hand, resorts to rhetorical questions which underscore human frailty and ignorance.

> Who has ascended to heaven and come down?
> Who has gathered the wind in his fists?
> Who has wrapped up the waters in a garment?
> Who has established all the ends of the earth?
> What is his name, and what is his son's name:
> Surely you know!
>
> (Proverbs 30:4)

Such cognitive dissonance[48] brings about a wholly new situation with regard to persuasive discourse. The impossible question, saying, and task rapidly come to the forefront in wisdom literature.[49]

> Can a man carry fire in his bosom
> and his clothes not be burned?
> Or can one walk upon hot coals
> and his feet not be scorched?
>
> (Proverbs 6:27-28)

> "Can papyrus grow where there is no marsh?
> Can reeds flourish where there is no water?"
>
> (Job 8:11)

Here the sages argue from what is universally acknowledged to be truth; ironically, they focus upon human inability. In these instances

rhetorical questions function as strong assertions: no one can carry
fire in his clothes without suffering the consequences of stupidity.
The choice of such rhetorical questions as the appropriate language
for God when he finally addresses Job springs from the authority
pervading this type of speech. No stronger statement can be
imagined, particularly since the questions place Job in the
unpleasant role of a student who has stirred up the teacher's ire.

Concomitant with an increasing awareness of human frailty runs
the growing use of such impossible questions, especially in
Qoheleth and 2 Esdras.

> How many dwellings are in the heart of the sea,
> or how many streams are at the source of the deep,
> or which are the exits of hell,
> or which are the entrances of paradise?
>
> (2 Esdras 4:7)

> Consider the work of God;
> who can make straight what he has made crooked?
>
> (Ecclesiastes 7:13)

> That which is, is far off, and deep, very deep, who can find it out?
>
> (Ecclesiastes 7:24)

Similarly, impossible tasks isolate vast areas in which human
strength and ingenuity fail miserably.

> Go, weigh for me the weight of fire,
> or measure for me a measure of wind,
> or call back for me the day that is past.
>
> (2 Esdras 4:5)

> Count up for me those who have not yet come,
> and gather for me the scattered raindrops,
> and make the withered flowers bloom again for me;
> open for me the closed chambers,
> and bring forth for me the winds shut up in them,
> or show me the picture of a voice.
>
> (2 Esdras 5:36-37)

Occasionally, it seems that a numerical proverb has been altered to
conform to this linguistic usage.

> The sand of the sea, the drops of rain,
> and the days of eternity—who can count them?

> The height of heaven, the breadth of the earth,
>> the abyss, and wisdom—who can search them out?
>>> (Sirach 1:2-3)

Impossible sayings function in the same way that related questions and tasks do.

> But a stupid man will get understanding,
>> when a wild ass's colt is born a man.
>>> (Job 11:12)

> My son, if the waters should stand up without earth,
> and the sparrow fly without wings,
> and the raven become white as snow,
> and the bitter become sweet as honey,
> then may the fool become wise.
>> (Ahiqar 2:62)

Such texts could easily be multiplied, but these suffice to demonstrate their power to render a negative judgment on all human striving. Impossible questions, sayings, and tasks went a long way toward impressing upon ancient Israelites the futility of trying to steer their course on the high seas once the divine helmsman had relinquished his post.

CONCLUSION

In summary, Israel's skeptics severed a vital nerve at two distinct junctures. They denied God's goodness if not his very existence, and they portrayed men and women as powerless to acquire essential truth.

> Then I saw all the work of God, that man cannot find out the work that is done under the sun. However much man may toil in seeking, he will not find it out; even though a wise man claims to know, he cannot find it out. . . .
> But all this I laid to heart, examining it all, how the righteous and the wise and their deeds are in the hand of God; whether it is love or hate man does not know. Everything before them is vanity.
>> (Ecclesiastes 8:17—9:1)

Faced with this formidable onslaught, God's defenders removed him from the human scene altogether, or placed sufficient emphasis upon divine mercy to eclipse "the human deed in a time of despair."[50]

What, then, did these skeptics accomplish? Precisely this: they inscribed a huge question mark over that first great revolution in human thinking, and they turned the spotlight upon the cognitive act. That is, they refused to take confessional statements concerning divine control of human events at face value, and they insisted that boasts about human ingenuity also be taken *cum grano salis*. Pressing the interrogative mood thus placed linearity in jeopardy, as the quotation from Qoheleth in the preceding paragraph demonstrates with crushing finality, but it also showed the inadequacy of the critical tool by which divine purpose was discarded.[51]

A VIABLE ALTERNATIVE TO YAHWISM

A second aspect of wisdom's legacy concerns her understanding of the relationship between God and the universe, including its human inhabitants. The sages offered an alternative mode of interpreting reality to the Yahwistic one in which God was actively involved in guiding history toward a worthy goal. The claim that God chose a particular people, fought on their behalf, called prophets, issued legal codes, sent angels to maintain contact with humans, enlisted foreign powers to discipline the chosen race, and promised to bestow a new covenant upon inveterate sinners for the sake of God's honor represents a way of looking at the human situation that is wholly alien to the sapiential one.

This Yahwistic affirmation of faith encountered considerable objection from those who failed to discern evidence that God actually controlled history, on the one hand, and from individuals who preferred a more tolerant religious spirit, on the other. Both criticisms possessed a great deal of weight, inasmuch as Israel's political history depended in large measure upon the strength or weakness of the super powers in Egypt and Mesopotamia, while religious syncretism inevitably occurred as a result of Israel's vulnerable geographical setting, if for no other reason.

The prophetic understanding of God as actively involved in the life of the people imposed a weighty burden upon ancient Israel, since few individuals possessed the moral integrity to achieve the high demands laid upon them, in the view of Old Testament "historians." Defeat on the battlefield easily led to abandonment of faith, for theological conviction had failed to accord with reality. Of course, the easy solution to this problem arose early: God was punishing Israel for her sins. That sort of theological improvisation had permanent effect on the soul of the elect people, who soon lost all self-confidence and depended more and more upon divine assistance.

Perhaps the most vexing problem arising from this Yahwistic view concerns the validation of divine communication with humans. Two opposing messages, each claiming divine origin, left the people confused because they lacked a valid means of determining truth from falsehood. In such a situation the people found it necessary to put an end to this form of communication between God and humans. Thus they discredited prophecy and silenced God's voice.

The sages understood God's relationship with the world quite differently. In their view, revelation took place during the creative act, and when human capacity to discover this hidden mystery seemed inadequate, God continued to make known his will through personified wisdom. In other words, truth was planted within the universe, and humans searched diligently for it by using their intelligence. Still, truth was not entirely disinterested; in some mysterious fashion divine mystery declared itself to the inquiring mind.

The beauty of this view is that it makes no claim about divine control of history. Instead, the sapiential understanding of reality rested upon a universal base: everyone could make contact with transcendent reality regardless of the historical situation. Religious claims were modest ones, and no link existed between God and a particular people or ruling dynasty.

A consequence of this attitude toward reality is its orientation toward immediate experience. Nothing within human experience lacked revelatory capacity. No vision of past glory or future hope robbed the present moment of its importance. For this reason every encounter afforded a bridge into the transcendant realm. The slightest act by an insect, or the behavior of humans, concealed a secret worthy of discovery. In this way all of life became an arena in which divine truth unfolded, and God's truth coincided with human insight.

ABILITY TO COPE

This observation about the intrinsic relationship between human and divine truth marks the arrival of the third facet of wisdom's legacy which will be emphasized: wisdom enabled people to cope. The secret of Wisdom's wide appeal lay in the reward which she bestowed upon those who followed her path.

No situation arose in which the sages found themselves unprepared, for they addressed every conceivable eventuality. Their goal was to know what to do or say on any given occasion. To this end they gathered information and perfected their powers of drawing analogies between different realms and categories. Through centuries of experience the sages acquired valuable insight into personal relationships and human character.

The fact that the sages had proverbial insights for every circumstance does not mean that they reduced life to the little things which could be managed successfully. Life's greatest mysteries constantly drew the sages' attention, and refused resolutely to succumb to rational resolution. Nevertheless, the sages' struggle to understand the problem of suffering and death stands as living testimony that the human spirit can indeed cope, and that we need not despair when kingdoms crumble and temples vanish in flames.

If we keep in mind these three areas in which wisdom's legacy manifested itself, we shall not marvel that the sapiential literary corpus stands in the Hebrew Bible alongside torah and prophecy. The mere attribution of Proverbs and Ecclesiastes to Solomon hardly assured these works a place in the canon. Instead, Job, Proverbs, and Ecclesiastes gave authentic voice to the sages' fundamental understanding of reality, and in so doing, functioned to orient generation after generation with regard to the world into which they had been thrust.

Changing historical circumstances and theological perspectives effected comparable shifts of emphasis within the sapiential corpus itself, as we have seen. Such transitions occurred without suppressing earlier religious views. Although the result lacks uniformity in important respects, the positioning of opposing perspectives and the free use of interpretive statements (for example, the epilogue to Ecclesiastes) permitted later viewpoints to make maximal impact.

Just as private experience confirmed the veracity of innumerable proverbs, encounters with life's ambiguities demonstrated ever anew the essential truth within Job and Ecclesiastes. Undeserved suffering and the specter of death were inescapable realities for which no more satisfactory responses presented themselves than those put forth by the unknown authors of Job and Ecclesiastes.

The situation is hardly different with respect to Sirach, in spite of Ben Sira's pride of authorship. Apparently, this bold attempt to bring together two distinct traditions, wisdom and Yahwism, addressed a real need in the second century B.C.E. Wisdom of Solomon, too, serves to preserve a heritage by transmitting it in a different language and thus a new world view. The fact that later Jewish leaders restricted the age of inspiration to the period from Moses to Ezra, thus excluding Sirach and Wisdom of Solomon from the Hebrew Bible, has nothing to do with the adequacy of the two books, but derives from altogether different circumstances.

In summary, the literary corpus of the sages was placed alongside the Pentateuch and the prophets precisely because wisdom's legacy was no mean achievement. Proverbs enabled the people to cope with life; Job and Qoheleth empowered them to face sickness and death; Sirach introduced hymnic praise as an *essential ingredient* in the discussion of life's enigmas; and Wisdom of Solomon added an erotic dimension to the search for knowledge.

CHAPTER 9

Egyptian and Mesopotamian Wisdom Literature

Israel's ceaseless search for knowledge, divine presence, meaning, and survival was part of a larger quest in the ancient Near East. Scattered allusions within the Hebrew Bible to the wisdom of the Easterners and the Egyptians (Genesis 41:8; Exodus 7:11; 2 Kings 4:30 [Heb. 5:9-10]; Isaiah 19:11-15) have assumed greater force again and again as literature from Egypt and Mesopotamia has come to light. Similarities between Israelite wisdom and that of her powerful neighbors to the south and east abound, but decisive differences also exist.

Those features which distinguish Egyptian and Mesopotamian wisdom literature from similar Israelite texts have prompted caution in using the term "wisdom" with regard to extra-Israelite material. The leading authority on Egyptian wisdom literature has noted that the biblical notion of *ḥokmah* (wisdom) is less appropriate than the descriptive term "instruction" when applied to Egyptian texts.[1] Similarly, the author of the standard treatment of Babylonian wisdom in English writes that " 'wisdom' is strictly a misnomer as applied to Babylonian literature."[2] He goes on to explain that "generally 'wisdom' refers to skill in cult and magic lore, and the wise man is the initiate."[3] Both specialists recognize a significant area of common subject matter, literary form, and world view in Israelite wisdom and in that of Egypt and Mesopotamia.

Inasmuch as at least one ancient writer compared Solomon's wisdom with that of Egypt and "Eastern sages," by which Edomites may have been meant, it seems appropriate here to examine extra-biblical wisdom. When one considers the direct contact between various sections of Proverbs and Egyptian wisdom literature, as well as the amazing resemblances between Mesopotamian wisdom on the one hand, Job and Ecclesiastes on the other, exploration of non-canonical sapiential literature becomes more than a desideratum. Proper comprehension of biblical wisdom depends upon an understanding of related texts in Egypt and Mesopotamia. Only by this means will the distinctive features of Israelite wisdom come to prominence.

EGYPTIAN WISDOM LITERATURE

For convenience, Egyptian sapiential literature may be divided into texts which consciously endeavor to inculcate traditional morals and practical lessons from experience, and those which challenge society's givens because of adverse social changes that have rendered life hazardous at best.[4] Into the former category falls a significant body of literature which has a special title, *sboyet* (teaching). To these may be added various texts which treat the scribal profession as inherently superior to all other tasks and which deal with aspects of that exalted vocation. The second category consists of pessimistic literature in which weightier questions about life's meaning and the conflict between truth and falsehood prompt radical rethinking of established intellectual positions.

A. Instructions and the Scribal Tradition

The Instructions span the period from 2800 to 100 B.C.E. and function as a barometer by which one can determine the religious and social values of ancient Egypt. Their external form remains remarkably consistent throughout this long period; in general, a father offers advice to his son, although these two terms, father and son, soon designate a teacher and his student. Occasionally, the court setting of this counsel is highlighted by attributing the teaching to a pharaoh. Where this is not the case, emphasis falls upon the teacher's role as advisor to the ruler. In short, the teachings are directed at actual or potential bureaucrats.[5] Naturally, certain themes came into prominence as a consequence of this elite clientele, although other people would also profit from such advice: the art of correct speech, proper relations with women, correct dealing with one's inferiors and superiors, rules of etiquette, truthfulness, and the like.

The fundamental concept which underlies these Instructions is *ma'at*,[6] which may be translated as justice, order, truth. No distinction exists between secular and religious truth for this literature. God's will can be read from the natural order, social relations, and political events. Life in accordance with that principle of order paid off in tangible blessings, just as conduct at variance with *ma'at* brought adversity. It follows that pragmatism enjoyed religious grounding; for this reason the utilitarianism which prevails within this literature constitutes an appropriate faith response. Alongside purely utilitarian motivations for conduct lie positive reinforcement in terms of God's will and warnings which emphasize divine wrath arising from certain abominable practices.

A fundamental *conservatism* pervades these Instructions. The teacher transmits to his students the intellectual tradition which has accumulated over the years. In this thought world there is no place for the creative thinker who charts new paths for the imagination. Personal experience that cannot be repeated by everyone rarely surfaces in these texts. The operative word seems always to have been "tradition." Nevertheless, discernible changes do manifest themselves, primarily as a result of widespread political unrest which alters the understanding of divine order itself.[7] In time overt piety of a self-conscious kind penetrates the teachings, whereas the earliest instructions had a powerful religious impulse which lay hidden within the concept of *ma'at*. In a word, for the ancient teachers no chasm separated divine truth from ordinary knowledge.

The goal of this instruction was to enable students to master their lives; the ideal sage was called "the silent one." Those who *heard* their teachers acquired the art of self-control; whoever refused to listen to the voice of experience gave free rein to passions. Naturally, such persons were known as hot-headed or uncontrolled individuals.

Since paternal instruction, and that of teachers generally, could be spurned by rebellious sons, the instructions were presented as attractively as humanly possible. Unable to rely upon supernatural revelation, teachers expended considerable effort toward making their words both pleasing to the ear and intellectually cogent. In addition, appeal was made to paternal authority and to self-interest, for the status of officials within the court was a lofty one indeed.

Turning to the Instructions, we shall attempt to summarize the distinctive characteristics of each. From the period of the Old Kingdom three texts have survived: Ptahhotep, Kagemni, and Hardjedef. The first of these, The Instruction of Ptahhotep, can be dated around 2450 B.C.E. It sets the tone for subsequent teachings, so that closer examination of its contents seems worthwhile.

Ptahhotep

The opening lines strike readers as remarkably similar to the final description of old age in Ecclesiastes.

> O sovereign, my lord! Oldness has come; Old age has descended. . . . The eyes are weak, the ears are deaf, the strength is disappearing because of weariness of heart, and the mouth is silent and cannot speak. . . . Good is become evil. All taste is gone.
>
> (*ANET,* 412)

To be sure, Qoheleth expresses himself much more felicitously, choosing exquisite poetic images to portray time's ravages on the human body. But the bottom line is the same: old age is truly an unwelcome guest.

Ptahhotep counsels eloquence, but warns that it is hidden and must be diligently sought after. Moreover, persuasive speech can be found in wholly unexpected places.

> Good speech is more hidden than the emerald, but it may be found with maidservants at the grindstones.
>
> (*ANET,* 412)

Still, mastering the art of correct speech is no minor task, and eloquence is more difficult than any craft. Success in this important endeavor has its own reward, for courtiers inspire respect by the scope of their knowledge and the persuasiveness of their speech.

Correct speech implies truthfulness as well as eloquence.

According to Ptahhotep, truth alone endures time's passage. So convinced of this intrinsic connection between truth and permanence is he that Ptahhotep denies any future to wrongdoing. Fraud may acquire riches temporarily, but "wrongdoing has never brought its undertaking into port."

The courtier must know when to be silent, particularly in the presence of powerful individuals. Ptahhotep offers advice on the right way to deal with various types of relationships. He seems to consider proper deference at table to be particularly important. The operative word seems to be "caution," and an ability to stay in one's place appears essential, especially in a setting where ambition thrives and suspicion lurks within the minds of rulers who seek to preserve their power in the face of aspiring underlings.

Courtiers seem to have been rather vulnerable on the erotic front; for this reason Ptahhotep issues a strong warning against making overtures toward women.

> One is made a fool by limbs of fayence, as she stands (there), become (all) carnelian. A mere trifle, the likeness of a dream—and one attains death through knowing her.
>
> (*ANET,* 413)

Like Qoheleth, Ptahhotep thinks women have destroyed huge numbers of men; both teachers chose to express the devastating power of women with reference to the number "a thousand." Nevertheless, Ptahhotep recognized the great worth of a wife, whom he likened to a profitable field, a favorite metaphor in the ancient world.[8]

The Instruction of Ptahhotep concludes with a lengthy discussion of the two possible responses to such advice. Naturally, hearing is the desired response; those whom God loves will listen attentively and hearken to their father's advice. On the other hand, failure to hear is an abomination to God; those who refuse to hear find themselves in an existential paradox: "dying while alive every day." Such a one is a fool, and "guilt is his food." The hearer, however, will eventually pass along the teaching to his son, thereby renewing the instruction.

The Instruction for Kagemni

Only the ending of The Instruction for Kagemni has survived. Its contents cover some of the themes already discussed: proper table manners and the pleasing character of wise teaching. Here one is instructed to curb the appetite when dining with a glutton, and the person who pays heed to wise counsel is called a silent one.

The third teaching from the Old Kingdom, that attributed to Prince Hardjedef, has perished except for a few lines which warn against boasting and advise marriage. Frequent mention of this sage in later literature bears witness to the impact of his teaching, a fact which the surviving instruction under the name Hardjedef would hardly have suggested.

From the period of the Middle Kingdom two instructions merit our consideration, although a third has been preserved. These works are The Instruction for King Merikare, The Instruction of King Amen-em-het, and The Instruction of Sehtepibre.

The Instruction for Merikare

Whereas Ptahhotep was a vizier to the pharaoh, and his teaching was directed to his own son, the unknown author of the partially preserved instruction for Merikare was a pharaoh writing for his son who reigned in the twenty-second century. Alongside repeated emphasis upon silence and eloquence there stand words of counsel concerning royal responsibility to ensure justice. At the same time, a certain ruthlessness appears.

> Do not kill a man when thou knowest his good qualities, one with whom thou didst once sing the writings.
>
> *(ANET,* 415)[9]

The implicit becomes entirely explicit in another connection, where Merikare is advised to kill talkers and to banish all memory of excitable persons.

The powerful sanction for behavior inherent within belief in a final judgment at death presents itself for the first time in this teaching, although Ptahhotep's silence in this regard does not appear to be overly significant. A new note is also struck by the claim that "good speech is more valorous than any fighting." In short, self-mastery requires far more effort than conquering enemy soldiers.

The bulk of this instruction concerns advice for the king's conduct with regard to the daily affairs of state. For one brief moment the pharaoh confesses to having done something wrong; such admission of misconduct was a rarity in ancient Egypt. Perhaps it is significant that this teaching values human character above ritual performance.

> More acceptable is the character of one upright of heart than the ox of the evildoer.
>
>   (*ANET*, 417)[10]

Such exalted thinking does not lead beyond self-interest, for the author proceeds to advise careful attention to oblations so that God will be disposed to return the favor. In this teacher's view, the hidden creator whose might repelled the chaos monster is attentive to the tears of human beings. Perhaps it is noteworthy that the scribe who copied this instruction identified himself as the truly silent one, suggesting that the epithet has already become a technical term.

It should be noted that a new tone can be heard in this text: life's shadow-side lurks nearby. God hides from humans, who sin unwittingly if not consciously. Although a judgment is set, one's fate cannot be altered through magical acts which aim at controlling the gods. In addition to this theological shift, another change occurs in the character of teaching, which assumes explicit political ends approaching propaganda.

The Instruction of Amen-em-het

This text consists of advice given by King Amen-em-het I to his son about 1960 B.C.E. Since the pharaoh died as a result of a conspiracy within his harem, the counsel is decidedly pessimistic.[11] In short, Amen-em-het warns against placing trust in anyone. Despite his good works, which the king parades before his son, calamity befell him from trusted servants. Once again private experience provides the lesson by which others may profit; to that end the king tells about that fatal hour when he slept, oblivious to danger from his intimates.

During the New Kingdom a different religious ethos took shape, largely because of the collapse of divine order. Whereas earlier sages thought God was experienced indirectly in the political state, laws, and daily life, scribes now sought to make contact with God more directly through prayer and worship in general. Two instructions from this period manifest this new spirit magnificently: The Instruction of Ani, and The Instruction of Amen-em-opet. A third, The Instruction of Amennakhte, is too fragmentary to throw further light on the picture which these two teachings paint.

The Instruction of Ani

The scribe responsible for this text was a minor official; his son's promise that he will tender an obedient response concludes the work, which strongly endorses passivity, holiness, and religious duty. Considerable attention falls to preparation for marriage and proper conduct toward a wife, as if this instruction actually were written for a young man about to venture forth on his own. Ani's firm reminder that the lad's mother had made innumerable sacrifices in his behalf, particularly by providing daily beer and bread while he was in school, may strengthen this interpretation.

In this text a warning against foreign women occurs, a theme which assumed prominence in biblical proverbs as well.

> Be on thy guard against a woman from abroad, . . . a deep water, whose windings one knows not, a woman who is far away from her husband. "I am sleek," she says to thee every day. She has no witnesses when she waits to ensnare thee.
>
> (*ANET,* 420)

While active resistance of foreign women is necessary, one should not object to *God's* decisions, even when they entail an early death. At all times care should be taken lest God become angry; special attention belongs to the act of transporting the gods in ritual processions. Indeed, the ideal is to be silent, pray, and show respect for older people. Such a cautious lifestyle implies a certain kind of secretiveness, together with a fleeing into one's own inner sanctuary.

The Instruction of Amen-em-opet

The Instruction of Amen-em-opet consists of thirty chapters, which exhibit parallelism and four-line strophes. The introduction has a series of infinitives that underscore the purpose of the teaching; in this respect the text resembles the first collection in the book of Proverbs (1—9). The final chapter of Amen-em-opet describes the contents as entertaining, instructive, and powerful.

> See thou these thirty chapters:
>   They entertain, they instruct;
> They are the foremost of all books;
>   They make the ignorant to know.
> If they are read out before the ignorant,
>   Then he will be cleansed by them.
>
> (ANET, 424)

The fourth chapter contrasts the heated one and silent one; the former resembles a tree growing in the open and experiencing rapid destruction, while the latter is like a tree growing in a garden. Naturally, that tree with such fortunate surroundings flourishes, yielding sweet fruit and pleasant shade. The same imagery occurs in Psalm 1 and Jeremiah 17:5-8.

The similarities between Amen-em-opet and Proverbs 22:17—24:22 are so close that borrowing seems highly likely. Those affinities can be seen in the following comparisons.[12]

> Never make friends with an angry man
> nor keep company with a bad-tempered one.
>
> (Proverbs 22:24, NEB)

> Do not associate to thyself the heated man,
>   Nor visit him for conversation.
>
> (Amen-em-opet 11:13-14; ANET, 423)

> Do not move the ancient boundary-stone
> which your forefathers set up.
>
> (Proverbs 22:28, NEB)

> Do not carry off the landmark at the boundaries of the arable
> land, . . .
>
> (Amen-em-opet 7:12; ANET, 422)

> You see a man skilful at his craft:
> he will serve kings, he will not serve common men.
>
> (Proverbs 22:29, NEB)

> As for the scribe who is experienced in his office,
>   He will find himself worthy (to be) a courtier.
>
> (Amen-em-opet 27:16-17; ANET, 424)

> Do not toil to acquire wealth;
>   be wise enough to desist.

> When your eyes light upon it, it is gone;
>   for suddenly it takes to itself wings,
>   flying like an eagle toward heaven.
>   (Proverbs 23:4-5)

> Do not strain to seek an excess,
> When thy needs are safe for thee.
> If riches are brought to thee by robbery,
> . . . .
> (Or) they have made themselves wings like geese
> And are flown away to the heavens.
>   (Amen-em-opet 9:14—11:5; *ANET,* 422)

> Do not eat the bread of a man who is stingy;
>   do not desire his delicacies;
> for he is like one who is inwardly reckoning.
>   (Proverbs 23:6-7a)

> Be not greedy for the property of a poor man,
> Nor hunger for his bread.
> As for the property of a poor man, it (is) a blocking to the throat.
>   (Amen-em-opet 14:5-7; *ANET,* 423)

In light of these striking similarities, the rendering of Proverbs 22:20 in terms of Amen-em-opet 27:7-10 seems firmly established.

> Here I have written out for you thirty sayings,[13] full of knowledge and wise advice, to impart to you a knowledge of the truth, that you may take back a true report to him who sent you.
> See thou these thirty chapters.
> They entertain, they instruct;
> They are the foremost of all books;
> They make the ignorant to know.
>   (*ANET,* 424)

We have by no means exhausted the possibilities of similarities between this text and Proverbs. Elsewhere we read that humans propose but God disposes; men and women may make elaborate plans, but God's will works itself out even when it goes against human calculations. Again we confront cautious advice not to empty one's soul to every "Tom, Dick, and Harry," but to guard one's innermost thoughts against profanation. In addition, we encounter the usual pleas for responsive listening and obedient action, and we experience the zeal with which instructions were given. To be sure, we must not discount the possibility that some of these similarities between Proverbs and Amen-em-opet represent universal concerns, but this explanation hardly suffices for all the resemblances which we have noted.

With Amen-em-opet we sense a heightening of piety beyond Ani. Worship and morality lie at the heart of the instruction comprising these thirty chapters. Ethical motivation transcends selfish concerns, for right conduct is enjoined because of love for God. At the same time, God's ways are inscrutable, even if he has given *ma'at* for the ordering of life. Despite the fact that all are sinners, lacking essential knowledge, God sails the ship successfully into harbor. Since the all-knowing One has compassion, human beings should practice hospitality toward one another and engage in acts of love that demonstrate self-mastery.

Demotic Instructions

So far we have focused upon instructions from the Old, Middle, and New Kingdoms. Two texts in demotic continue the teaching tradition: *The Instruction of 'Onchsheshonqy*[14] and *Papyrus Insinger*. The former teaching resembles Ahiqar in that it represents instructions transmitted by a wise man who has fallen out of favor with the ruler. The opening narrative states that 'Onchsheshonqy was implicated in a palace revolt and underwent a long imprisonment, during which time he saved the potsherds in which he received his daily wine and managed to copy down on them the teachings which he considered worth preserving. Two things stand out about these sayings: (1) they make use of a simple gnomic form resembling biblical proverbs that have traditionally been considered quite early, and (2) they seem to have been addressed to the populace as opposed to an elite circle.

The scope of 'Onchsheshonqy is quite extensive; it contains more than 550 sayings, many of which are syntactically simple and make up only one line. Synthetic parallelism occurs with greater frequency than antithetic, in sharp distinction from biblical Proverbs. Synonymous parallelism seems to be totally missing in the demotic text; once again the biblical book of Proverbs differs greatly. The rural background of 'Onchsheshonqy is evident in many of the sentences, as is a deep religious sentiment. Again and again these religious and moral statements resemble Proverbs and Ecclesiastes.

Papyrus Insinger, perhaps from the Ptolemaic period (fourth and third century), comprises twenty-five teachings, each of which bears a superscription. The religious grounding of these instructions, which make use of the gnomic form, is pervasive. The earlier ideal of silence is replaced by a concept of equilibrium, by which is meant self-mastery that avoids every extreme. Naturally, sin is a force that disturbs the equilibrium, and God punishes such acts that endanger the balance. Even apparent prosperity of sinners is deceptive, for God is merely allowing sufficient time to elapse for retribution to become effective.

The Scribal Tradition

One further instruction belongs to those texts in which the scribal profession is singled out as more honorable than all other occupations. Already it has been referred to in connection with our discussion of Sirach 38:24—39:11. This Egyptian text, *The Instruction of Khety,* son of Duauf, paints a miserable picture of work in the period between 2150 and 1750. Only the scribal trade is a pleasant one, according to this satire, whereas all other forms of labor are debilitating to mind and body. The author spares no single occupation, but with almost brutal force describes the unwelcome features of the following professions, among others: stoneworkers, goldsmiths, carpenters, barbers, reed-cutters, potters, bricklayers, vintners, weavers, arrow makers, field hands, sandalmakers, fowlers, fishermen. The scribe alone carries out assigned tasks without the hostile eyes of a supervisor nearby, Khety argues, and it follows that nothing surpasses writing—not even affection for one's mother.

A similar note is struck in a number of texts that have survived the ravages of time. *In Praise of Learned Scribes* (c. 1300 B.C.E.) concedes that ancient scribes were unable to construct for themselves lasting pyramids or to preserve their names in progeny, but "they gave themselves [*the papyrus-roll* as a lector] priest, the writing-board as a son-he-loves, (books of) wisdom (as) their pyramids, the reed-pen (as) their child, and the back of a stone for a wife" (*ANET,* 431-432). The author proceeds to call books more effective than houses or stelae, since the constant recitation of scribes' names constitutes a kind of immortality. This text even allocates a magical power to the teachings, and attributes to sages an ability to look into the future with uncanny clarity.

Similarly, *The Instruction of a Man for His Son* mentions the incredible power within the teacher's grasp. In this author's words a scribe "teaches the mute to speak, and he opens the ears of the deaf." Despite this exalted status which befell scribes, considerable evidence points to a certain hesitancy on the part of some students to devote themselves fully to learning. *Papyrus Sallier* (I, 6:9—7:9) alludes to a scribe who has neglected the writings and urges him to look at the sorry lot of field hands. This choice of alternative labor is a clever hint that the lazy scribe will soon be performing such manual work if he does not amend his ways soon. *Papyrus Anastasi* (IV, 9:4—10:1) describes the miserable treatment a soldier undergoes, and pleads with a certain Inena to reconsider his claim that a soldier fares better than a scribe. The argument that lessons are often too difficult fails to convince the author of *Papyrus Anastasi* (V, 8:1—9:1), who observes that even apes can be taught to dance and horses can be tamed. All else failing, prayer to Thot for skill in writing is appropriate *(Papyrus Anastasi* V,9:2—10:2). The ultimate goal is that scribes will embody the traditions they preserve; this sentiment must surely underly Amunnakhte's admonition to his student: "Become like a chest of writings."

We know very little about the actual learning experience in ancient Egypt, although repetition seems to have characterized that setting.[15] Students recited texts from memory, and they copied ancient instructions over and over. It seems that this method of learning continued even after the meaning of the ideograms had long since faded from memory, resulting in copious scribal errors. Perhaps, too, examinations were given—at least one text seems to represent a scribal controversy. Here a sarcastic quiz, possibly imitating tests in schools, is presented to the opponent. In addition, noun lists (onomastica) were compiled, consisting of current encyclopedic knowledge concerning the different professions, flora, fauna, and so forth.

B. Discussion Literature

Radical social changes within the structure of Egyptian life gave birth to a significant protest against earlier expressions of confidence in the way things were. Ranging from pessimistic utterances, complaints, and protests against dominant social forces to hedonistic grasping after life's pleasures at any cost, this literature also manifests a tamer spirit now and again, particularly in debates and fables.

Such pessimism as can be found in *Neferti, Khakheperre-sonbe, Ipuwer,* and *The Dispute of a Man with His Soul* carries a strong element of political propaganda. *Neferti,* for example, maintains the literary fiction of prophecy, whereas it actually looks back upon the immediate past. Accordingly, this text describes the times prior to Ammenemes as chaotic and thereby justifies that king's usurpation of the throne for the purpose of establishing order. Similarly, *Ipuwer* emphasizes the calamities that had befallen the land and lauds the reigning monarch for the restoration of beneficent rule. Things had become so intolerable the "great and small" exclaimed: " 'I wish I might die,' and little children said, 'He should not have caused (me) to live.' " The proverbial hot-tempered man responded to such chaos with a blasphemous retort: "If I knew where God is, then I would serve Him" (Simpson, *LAE,* 215-216).

The Lamentations of Khakheperre-sonbe is couched in the form of a discourse between a man and his other self. The author complains of his own inadequate vocabulary, inasmuch as words have become ineffective through constant use.

> Would that I had unknown speeches, erudite phrases in new language which has not yet been used, free from the usual repetitions, not the phrases of past speech which (our) forefathers spoke.
>
> (Simpson, *LAE,* 231)

The following comment that "whatever has been said has been repeated, while what has been said has been said" recalls Qoheleth's complaint that there was nothing new under the sun, since everything had already been spoken. Nevertheless, Khakheperre-sonbe ventures to utter something new, specifically that things are deteriorating throughout the land. Because of such dire straits the author wishes for additional knowledge, together with an enlarged capacity for suffering. Such endurance is necessary, since "every day one wakes to suffering. . . . Everyone is lying in crookedness. Precision in speech is abandoned" (Simpson, *LAE*, 233). Once again the resemblance with Ecclesiastes is striking, for Qoheleth complained that perversion had occurred so that none did right.

This comparison with Ecclesiastes may extend even further. The opening words of Khakheperre-sonbe sound remarkably like the beginning lines of the epilogue to Ecclesiastes.

> The gathering together of sayings, the culling of phrases, the search for words by an inquisitive mind, which . . . wrote.
>
> (Simpson, LAE, 231)

> Besides being wise, the Preacher also taught the people knowledge, weighing and studying and arranging proverbs with great care. The Preacher sought to find pleasing words, and uprightly he wrote words of truth.
>
> (Ecclesiastes 12:9-10)

Once more we are compelled to ask: Could the enigmatic title Qoheleth have something to do with collecting, that is, gathering together, words of truth?

The dispute over suicide registers some of the same points we have already alluded to, but moves one step further to describe death as highly desirable.

> Death is in my sight today
>   (Like) the recovery of a sick man,
>   Like going out into the open after a *confinement*.
> Death is in my sight today
>   Like the odor of myrrh
>   Like sitting under an awning on a breezy day.
> Death is in my sight today
>   Like the odor of lotus blossoms,
>   Like sitting on the bank of drunkenness.
> . . . .
> Death is in my sight today
>   Like the longing of a man to see his house (again),
>   After he has spent many years held in captivity.
>
> (ANET, 407)

This text constitutes a dialogue between a man and his soul. Weary of life, the man contemplates suicide, but the soul objects at first through anxiety lest there will be no mortuary service for him. As an alternative course of action the soul encourages hedonistic abandon. In the end the soul seems to agree to remain with the man regardless of his ultimate decision.

Echoes of this pessimistic mood can be heard in *The Tale of the Eloquent Peasant,* an entertaining story about abuse of power and its eventual punishment. The simple plot about a corrupt official who robbed a peasant and imprisoned him, but who lived to regret his hasty action against so eloquent an individual, provides an occasion for elaborate discussions of justice's demands. The peasant's articulate defense of his cause supplied excellent entertainment at the royal court. At the same time, the discourses served as models for conduct in office, for they reminded rulers that they had a responsibility for executing justice in behalf of every citizen regardless of social status.

The Song of the Harper urges enjoyment while life lasts, for no one takes anything into the next world and none returns from that place. The author argues that ancient worthies who built elaborate chapels to assure survival after death wasted their time, for those chapels now lie in ruins. The natural consequence of this unhappy disclosure is to seize life's bounty in the present moment.

> Follow your desire while you live. Place myrrh upon your head, Clothe yourself in fine linen, anointed with real wonders of the god's own stores.
>
> (Simpson, *LAE,* 307)

Such reflection upon self-gratification leads the poet to utter the shocking bit of advice: "Do not control your passion until that day of mourning comes for you." How far this thinker has departed from the ancient teacher's admonition to acquire self-control above all else!

In the light of such passionate protest literature those fables and disputes which discuss the advantages and disadvantages of various trees, for example, strike readers as wholly different. What does a dispute between the heart and stomach have to do with pessimistic literature of the sort we have been discussing? Perhaps the most that should be said is that both kinds of literature manifest a contentious spirit. To be sure, they highlight the negative aspects of existence, and for that reason the inclusion of fables and disputes in this discussion of protest literature is not entirely inappropriate.

What impact did ancient instructions and protest literature have on Egyptian society? If we can answer that question on the basis of citations within biographical literature and royal inscriptions the teachers must have wielded unusual power in their own day and for generations afterwards. The very preservation of the names of these ancient teachers, together with their concepts, for more than fifteen hundred years bears convincing testimony to the signal importance of Egyptian teachers. But an even more telling indication of the impact of the instructions can be seen in the adoption of the concept "the silent one" as paradigmatic for "ideal-biographies." In a word, the teachers instructed society with regard to the art of living; that is no small contribution.

MESOPOTAMIAN WISDOM

Unlike the Egyptians, Sumerian scribes arranged proverbs in separate anthologies.[16] At least twenty-four collections have survived, although their meaning is not yet as clear as one could wish. One important text, *The Instructions of Šuruppak*,[17] the survivor of the flood in Sumerian lore, resembles Egyptian teachings, even to the formal feature of father and son as teacher and instructed one.

> My son, let me give you instructions,
> May you pay attention to them!
>
> (Alster, *IS*, 15)

> The instructions of an old man are precious,
> May you submit to them.
>
> (Alster, *IS*, 35)

The counsel pertains to some of the same themes that we have isolated in Egyptian instructions.

> [My] son, do not sit (alone) in a [chamber] with someone's wife.
>
> (Alster, *IS*, 37)

[A man installs] a good woman for a good field.

(Alster, *IS*, 16)

Disputations between two scribes, a schoolboy and his supervisor, two women, a bird and a fish, summer and winter, and various gods resemble the debates in Egyptian literature, although in Sumerian texts a god resolves the issue. Of course, noun lists also were drawn up by these Sumerian scribes, and satires also occur—for example those concerning a thief, a lame man, and a drunkard. In addition, considerable discussion of the scribal profession has survived. These *edubba* (Tablet House) texts describe the various situations accompanying school days in ancient Sumer.

The similarities between Egyptian and Sumerian wisdom extend even farther than use of the same literary forms. Common themes also occur; one Sumerian text gives a powerful description of the aging process. This account is closer to Ecclesiastes than to Ptahhotep in its use of poetic imagery.

(I was) a youth (but now) . . . my black mountain has produced white gypsum . . . my teeth which used to chew strong things can no more chew strong things. . . .

(Alster, *SSP*, 93)

But we turn to another biblical narrative to find a closer parallel to the Sumerian text in its entirety, for the emphasis falls on the mysterious power young girls possess for revitalizing old men. The same assumption underlies the attempt to restore King David's waning life force by allowing him to sleep with the youthful Abishag (1 Kings 1:1-4).

One significant departure from Egyptian wisdom occurs in the Sumerian variation to the biblical Job.[18] For at least two significant reasons the problem of theodicy did not unduly occupy the Egyptian sages' thoughts.[19] Of course, belief in life after death softened any experience of innocent suffering, for everything would be set right in the next life. Furthermore, the absence of legal codes in Egypt meant that humans were less likely to try to subject their gods to rules that applied among men and women. In ancient Sumer the problem of unjust suffering elicited an early protest, in this case an objection that the gods made human beings with a basic flaw.

> They say—the sages—a word righteous (and) straightforward:
> "Never has a sinless child been born to its mother,
> . . . a sinless *workman* has not existed from of old."
>
> (*ANET,* 590)

Nevertheless, the god eventually looked favorably upon the sufferer, granting joy once more as a reward for proper conduct during suffering.

The same theme is taken up again and pursued at great depth in *I Will Praise the Lord of Wisdom*.[20] In this version a noble undergoes a complete reversal in fortune and becomes a social outcast. As if this loss of social status were not sufficient misery, the man also becomes seriously ill. While struggling to understand the reason for this sudden antagonism on god's part, the sufferer dares to think the unthinkable.

> I wish I knew that these things would be pleasing to one's god!
> What is good for oneself may be offense to one's god,
> What in one's own heart seems despicable may be proper to one's
>   god.
> Who can know the will of the gods in heaven?
> Who can understand the plans of the underworld gods?
> Where have humans learned the way of a god?
>
> (*ANET,* 597)

As a consequence of this conviction that values must be reversed where gods are concerned, resignation seizes the sufferer. He attempts a cure through exorcism, wherein he tries to name every conceivable disease, and thus to drive the evil spirit out, and finally confesses abiding trust in his eventual restoration. At this point he experiences three suprahuman visitations and complete recovery follows.

Although the appropriateness of viewing this text as a Babylonian Job has been contested in favor of a kind of "Pilgrim's Progress,"[21] there can be no question at all about the next text we shall discuss—*The Babylonian Theodicy*. Cast in the form of a friendly dialogue between a sufferer and his companion, this acrostic text consists of twenty-seven stanzas of eleven lines each, and dates from about 1000 B.C.E. It, too, emphasizes the remoteness of the gods and the inscrutability of their ways, and complains that they made human beings prone to injustice.

The mind of the god, like the center of the heavens, is remote;
Knowledge of it is very difficult; people cannot know it.
. . . .
Narru . . .
And majestic Zulummar . . .
And goddess Mami . . .
Gave twisted speech to the human race.
With lies, and not truth, they endowed them forever.

(*ANET*, 604)

In the initial stages of the dialogue the companion offers reasonably adequate responses to problems raised by the sufferer, but as the argument intensifies the answers become less satisfactory. At one point he even admits that god-fearing persons may lack sumptuous spreads on the table, but insists that they will not starve to death. Although the sufferer stoutly denies having done anything that deserved such treatment as the gods insist on dishing out, he eventually lowers his head and utters a prayer for help from the god who has temporarily abandoned his cause.

These three attempts to find a satisfactory response to unjust suffering stop short of considering the termination of life, and for that reason they are somewhat tame when compared with *The Dialogue of Pessimism*. This conversation between a master and his servant culminates in a radical answer to the supreme question that sages posed: what is good for men and women? That answer was: "To have my neck and yours broken and to be thrown into the river" (*ANET*, 601). Regardless of how we understand this text—as burlesque (comedy) or as deadly serious (satire)—it testifies to a crippling *ennui* that renders all action totally meaningless.[22] No persuasive argument favors a particular course of action over its exact opposite, and all incentive for behavior vanishes. The result is complete irreverence.

"Do not sacrifice, master, do not sacrifice. You get your god to follow you about like a dog."

(*ANET*, 601)

Small wonder a similar disrespect occurs where women are concerned.

["Do not] make love, master, do not make love. A woman is a
pitfall, a hole, a ditch, a woman is a sharp iron dagger that slits a
man's throat."

(*ANET,* 601)

Such pessimistic literature was by no means the only voice to be
heard in Akkadian circles. The *Counsels of Wisdom* urges love for
one's enemies and enjoins benevolence in language—or silence.

Do not return evil to your adversary;
　Requite with kindness the one who does evil to you,
Maintain justice for your enemy.

(*ANET,* 595)

Do not speak ill, speak (only) good.
. . . .
　Do not express your innermost thoughts even when you are
alone.

(*ANET,* 595)

Among the many disputes, that between the tamarisk and date palm
possesses a feature that occurs far more frequently in biblical
proverbs than in Akkadian literature.

"I am better than you. Six times I excel, seven times I [. . .]"
(*ANET,* 593)

This numerical heightening[23] occurs also in *The Words of Ahiqar,* a
seventh century sealbearer under Sennacherib and Esarhaddon.

Two things [which] are meet, and the third pleasing to Shamash: one
who dr[inks] wine and gives it to drink, one who guards wisdom, and
one who hears a word and does not tell.

(*ANET,* 428)

This advice from one who had been implicated in a palace revolt has
numerous features in common with biblical proverbs, especially the
necessity of using the rod in disciplining children and the
impossibility of recovering a spoken word.

For a word is a bird: once released no man *can re[capture it].* First
co[un]t the secrets of thy mouth; then bring out thy [words] by
number. For the *instruction* of a mouth is stronger than the
instruction of war.

(*ANET,* 428)

Withhold not thy son from the rod, else thou wilt not be able to save [him from *wickedness*].

(*ANET,* 428)

Thus far we have not considered a whole series of texts that represent these sages' attempt to cope with everyday circumstances—omen literature.[24] The search for auspicious signs and the wish to isolate inauspicious omens as completely as humanly possible arose from the magical base upon which Mesopotamian religion was founded. Such omen collections functioned as a means of safeguarding royalty, and thus secured order and continuity from which the populace also prospered. The *Advice to a Prince* goes one step further in protecting the rights of the citizenry with respect to taxation, forced labor, and appropriation of personal property. By imitating the style of omens the author warns the king that retribution will become operative if he abuses his power.

Gleanings from the wisdom of Mari have been meager,[25] consisting of a few popular proverbs, some similes, and the like. These tablets date from 1815 to 1760 B.C.E.

The bitch, in her passing back and forth(?)
    gave birth to lame(?) (puppies).

The fire consumes the reed,
and its companions pay attention.
Under the straw the water flows.

Let him go up to heaven,
let him go down to the netherworld;
nobody must see him!

The first proverb seems to mean that attention to matters of secondary importance during a time for decisive action inevitably leads to unfortunate consequences. The second observes that misfortune does not go unnoticed by those threatened by its presence, and may constitute astute political advice: "kill deserters promptly and others will be less likely to raise their voices against the ruler." The third proverb makes the point that appearances often deceive, while the fourth, which is nothing more than a conventional saying, makes use of polarities to express totality.

From this rapid survey of Sumerian and Babylonian wisdom

literature one can understand the reasons for viewing wisdom as an international phenomenon. The amazing similarities in wisdom thinking throughout the Fertile Crescent do not demand a hypothesis of borrowing, for most resemblances occur where universal problems are being addressed. Still, the increasing religionization of wisdom in Egypt and Mesopotamia may say something about the inability to sustain a high degree of self-confidence when society crumbles.

In Mesopotamia once moral categories replaced natural ones the stage was set for a sharp conflict, for humans confronted the problem of death—an experience that was denied the gods. This fact alone points to gross inequity, and when unjust suffering becomes a reality as well, protests inevitably follow. The astonishing thing is the heightening of religious fervor precisely at a time when one would expect wholesale abandonment of religion.

The close connection between schools and temples is instructive, particularly since learning seems to have been the handmaid of religion during the Cassite period. The scholars of the day were also priestly functionaries. That is why even the strongest protests against divine conduct occur within the context of eventual submission to God's will. In a very real sense, therefore, these texts such as *I Will Praise the Lord of Wisdom* function paradigmatically by demonstrating the way anyone who is stricken by suffering should behave.

Now it is true that the moral ethos in ancient Mesopotamia was nothing to boast about, given the prominence of cultic prostitution and the magical basis of ritual. Still, certain texts like *The Šamaš Hymn* achieve a high level, both in religious sentiment and in ethical sensitivity.

> You stand by the traveler whose road is difficult,
> To the seafarer in dread of the waves you give [. . .]
> A man who covets his neighbor's wife will [. . .]
> before his appointed day.
> A nasty snare is prepared for him. . . .
>
> (Lambert, *BWL,* 131)

Since Babylonian wisdom texts have been found at Ras Shamra,[26] a few words about Canaanite wisdom are in order. One text constitutes a father's advice to his son, who is about to embark on a journey, which symbolizes life itself. The father describes the consequences of obedience or disobedience, and discusses in great detail the dangers confronting the young man: the hazards of travel, the risks of the city, the problems accompanying human relationships, and so forth. The father concludes by recalling life's brevity.

So far no significant wisdom corpus has turned up in ancient Canaan, although Ebla reportedly yielded some such texts.[27] It is difficult to imagine that these people ignored this important body of knowledge, particularly since they knew of its existence. Although they did attribute wisdom to El, that fact alone hardly contributes to our knowledge of Canaanite wisdom literature.

The Hebrew Bible mentions Edomite wisdom as a well-known fact (Jeremiah 49:7), but none has survived to substantiate that tantalizing bit of information. To be sure, Job and certain features of the Yahwistic epic have been viewed as remnants of Edomitic wisdom,[28] but supporting evidence is scant. Perhaps the choice of a geographical setting for Job bears indirect testimony to a vibrant Edomite wisdom tradition.

According to 1 Kings 4:30 (Heb. 5:10) Solomon's wisdom surpassed that of the Easterners and Egyptians. This adulation of Solomon proceeds to name some famous sages (Ethan the Ezrahite, Heman, Calcol, and Darda, the sons of Mahol), the first two of whom are alluded to in the superscriptions to Psalms 88 and 89. In 1 Kings 10:23 Solomon's wealth and wisdom are said to surpass those of all other kings. On the basis of our discussion of Egyptian and Mesopotamian wisdom, it seems altogether proper that Israel reckoned herself among the nations of the earth where wisdom was concerned. To be sure, our survey of the evidence suggests that the Israelite author's enthusiasm threatened to distort the facts greatly, for considerably more modesty was called for. Nevertheless, Israel's sages did not need to hang their heads in shame, for they made a distinctive contribution to ancient sapiential literature.

Conclusion

This pursuit of wisdom began with an analysis of the distinctive sapiential feature of the moral code in Job 31. On the basis of that discussion, the conviction that humans possess the essential means of securing their existence surfaced as characteristically wisdom. Three ingredients went into the definition of wisdom offered in this treatment: a literary corpus, a way of thinking, and a tradition.

The focus upon the world of wisdom yielded evidence that sages saw themselves as a professional class. As such, they developed certain literary forms which functioned to communicate their special traditions. The reader has examined these literary types, without being immersed in the waters that threaten to flood the entire Hebrew Bible, specifically the trend to label everything "wisdom."

The consideration of the traditions concerning Solomon, the central figure in the wisdom tradition, to whom at least three sapiential works are attributed, uncovered meager evidence supporting his actual participation in the wisdom enterprise. The conclusion reached is that his reputation for wealth may have given rise to the further legend concerning extraordinary wisdom. The development from clan wisdom through the royal court and ultimately to scribal schools has seemed to merit considerable discussion. The theme for the analysis of the wisdom corpus came from the sages, for they envisioned their task as the search to uncover hidden mystery.

The pursuit of knowledge gave rise to various collections of proverbs which encapsulate the truths derived from experience. These sentences and instructions reveal a great deal about the values of ancient Israelites, particularly with respect to those things which enhance life, on the one hand, and threaten existence, on the other. Although theological reflection occurs unevenly throughout the several independent collections, and dominates the latest unit, the presence of religious sayings from the very beginning is likely. Eventually, however, Wisdom was personified and became a sort of heavenly mediator. Her opposite, Folly, was also given some consideration, but this idea seems not to have caught on the way personified wisdom did.

The search for God's presence testifies to the sages' willingness to pose profound questions. In Job two issues burn themselves into human consciousness: does disinterested righteousness actually exist? and how does one explain innocent suffering, indeed, how should individuals conduct themselves during such misfortune? The arguments put forth by Job and his friends have astonishingly similar presuppositions and grounding, despite their apparent differences. Only the heavenly speaker sees no need to offer warrants for the speeches from the tempest, even if on the moral plane God's conduct raises painful issues. Perhaps Job's final submission was inevitable, especially if the living God came out of hiding for a fleeting moment.

The transitence of such experiences impressed itself upon Israel's sages, who eagerly sought permanence in human relationships. This chasing after meaning inevitably aborted, inasmuch as Qoheleth never transcended self-interest even when forced by cruel reality to look upon oppression. Death's centrality forever pressed itself upon his thoughts, darkening his countenance at those rare moments when positive advice fell from his lips. The perversion of the universe, and rottenness at the core of society convinced Qoheleth that life was empty, as purposeless and futile as chasing the wind. Neither knowledge nor pleasure made a decisive difference in this situation, since the former could not be attained and the latter was fleeting.

The awful ordeal through which God put Job and the lonely voice of Qoheleth touched Ben Sira deeply, but he also heard ringing testimony from another source: the sacred traditions of Israel. Convinced that the convictions which nourished him belonged together regardless of their separate origins, Ben Sira embarked on a quest for continuity and survival. The attractive Hellenistic context prompted him to demonstrate the intellectual rigor of his own national traditions and to seek answers to the problem of divine injustice from Greek philosophical treatises. A means of linking Torah and sapiential literature in general presented itself to Ben Sira in the idea of Dame Wisdom, who was identified with divine revelation.

This personification of wisdom advanced further still in Wisdom of Solomon, a Hellenistic work from the very first. Here Israel's search widens to embrace alien concepts such as an immortal soul, the dualistic separation of body and soul, barrenness as virtue, and so forth. Greek style prevails in this work, from the literary genre of the entire book to individual units like *sorites*. This widening hunt includes certain wisdom psalms which wrestled with the problems of innocent suffering, divine justice, and life's ultimate meaning. In addition, it extends to other apocryphal literature, like the contest of Darius' guards in 1 Esdras 3:1—5:3, and beyond. That open-ended pursuit pried into doors within the New Testament and early Christian literature, if only momentarily.

From time to time we made theological observations about the evolution of sapiential thought in Israel. It seemed proper, therefore, to attempt to trace the final outcome of such reflection, especially since that intellectual development implies a bankruptcy of the mind and heart. Thus we have examined the birth of skepticism, taking care to indicate the chief factors which led to belief that God could not be known and humans could not secure their existence. In truth, the old conviction that wisdom was wholly inaccessible bore its special kind of fruit. Still, such skepticism was a means of coping for those who proposed a viable alternative to traditional Yahwism.

To be sure, Israel's sages participated in a phenomenon that enveloped the entire Fertile Crescent. Egyptian and Mesopotamian wisdom preceded canonical sapiential literature by nearly two millennia. Furthermore, the non-biblical wisdom influenced Israel's thinking in clearly discernible ways. For this reason, we have taken a close look at Egyptian and Mesopotamian wisdom literature, hoping all the time to allow Israelite wisdom to stand out as a distinct entity. Our aim has been to clarify, not to elevate canonical materials at the expense of texts that inspired Egyptian and Sumero-Babylonian sages for millennia.

In short, we ourselves have pursued knowledge, searched for divine presence, chased after meaning, engaged in a quest for survival, and widened the hunt at every juncture. In doing so, we have labored to carry on the quest which our ancestors began. Like them, we encounter the limits of knowledge precisely at the point where ultimate issues impinge upon the intellect. Like them, too, we confess an inability to know anything that would enable us to master the universe for human good, for God excels at concealing things. Still, we have learned some things—and that is a valuable link connecting us through the centuries with Israel's sages. For that opportunity to think their thoughts, and thus to enrich our own, we owe an immense debt to the wise men and women who ventured forth on an endless search more than three thousand years ago.

Abbreviations

AB	Anchor Bible
AnBib	Analecta Biblica
AJSL	American Journal of Semitic Language and Literature
ANET	J. B. Pritchard, ed., Ancient Near Eastern Texts
ANQ	Andover Newton Quarterly
ASTI	Annual of the Swedish Theological Institute
BA	The Biblical Archaeologist
BBB	Bonner biblische Beiträge
Bib	Biblica
BETL	Bibliotheca Ephemeridum Theologicarum Lovaniensium
BJRL	Bulletin of the John Rylands Library
BKAT	Biblischer Kommentar: Altes Testament
BO	Bibliotheca Orientalis
BS	Biblische Studien
BWANT	Beiträge zur Wissenschaft vom Alten und Neuen Testament
BWL	W. G. Lambert, Babylonian Wisdom Literature
BZAW	Beihefte zur Zeitschrift für die alttestamentliche Wissenschaft
CBQ	Catholic Biblical Quarterly
CBQMS	Catholic Biblical Quarterly Monograph Series
CJT	Canadian Journal of Theology
EF	Erträge der Forschung
Enc Jud	Encyclopedia Judaica
EvT	Evangelische Theologie
ExpT	The Expository Times
FRLANT	Forschungen zur Religion und Literatur des Altes and Neuen Testaments
HO	Handbuch der Orientalistik
HThR	Harvard Theological Review
HUCA	Hebrew Union College Annual
IDB	The Interpreters Dictionary of the Bible
Inter	Interpretation
IS	Bendt Alster, The Instructions of Šuruppak
JAAR	Journal of the American Academy of Religion
JAOS	Journal of the American Oriental Society
JBL	Journal of Biblical Literature
JBR	Journal of Bible and Religion = JAAR
JCS	Journal of Cuneiform Studies
JSS	Journal of Semitic Studies

KAT	Kommentar zum Alten Testament
LAE	W. K. Simpson, ed., The Literature of Ancient Egypt
OLZ	Orientalische Literaturzeitung
Rev Exp	Review and Expositor
RHPhR	Revue d'Histoire et de Philosophie Religieuses
RSR	Religious Studies Review
SAIW	J. L. Crenshaw, ed., Studies in Ancient Israelite Wisdom
SBLDS	Society of Biblical Literature Dissertation Series
SBTh	Studies in Biblical Theology
SOTSMS	Society for Old Testament Studies Monograph Series
SPOA	Les Sagesses du Proché-Orient ancien
SSP	Bendt Alster, Studies in Sumerian Proverbs
SUNT	Studien zur Umwelt des Neuen Testaments
TLZ	Theologische Literaturzeitung
TRev	Theologische Revue
TZ	Theologische Zeitschrift
UF	Ugarit-Forschungen
VT	Vetus Testamentum
VTSup	Vetus Testamentum Supplement
VF	Verkündigung und Forschung
WMANT	Wissenschaftliche Monographien zum Alten and Neuen Testament
ZAW	Zeitschrift für die alttestamentliche Wissenschaft
ZDA	Zeitschrift für Deutsches Alterthum
ZST	Zeitschrift für Systematische Theologie
ZTK	Zeitschrift für Theologie und Kirche

Notes

Introduction
[1] Edinburgh: T. & T. Clark, 1954 (original, 1936).
[2] London: The Epworth Press, 1930.
[3] Chicago: University of Chicago Press, 1946.
[4] Nashville & New York: Abingdon, 1972.
[5] Richmond: John Knox, 1972.
[6] New York: Macmillan, 1971.
[7] *BZAW*, 135 (Berlin & New York: Walter de Gruyter, 1974).
[8] New York: KTAV, 1976 (hereafter *SAIW*). Four other collections of essays on wisdom literature have recently appeared: Martin Noth and D. W. Thomas, eds., *Wisdom in Israel and in the Ancient Near East* (*VTSup*, 3; Leiden: Brill, 1960); *Les sagesses du Proché Orient ancien* (hereafter *SPOA*) (Paris: Presses Universitaires de France, 1963); John Gammie et al., eds., *Israelite Wisdom: Theological and Literary Essays in Honor of Samuel Terrien* (Missoula: Scholars Press, 1978); and Maurice Gilbert, ed., *La Sagesse de l'Ancien Testament* (Gambloux, Belgique: J. Duculot & Leuwen University Press, 1979).
[9] Collegeville, Minn.: Liturgical Press, 1965.
[10] London & Nashville: Lutterworth & Abingdon, 1961. Paterson emphasizes Job and Proverbs to the exclusion of Ecclesiastes.
[11] London: Gerald Duckworth & Co. Ltd., 1967. This study devotes considerable attention to New Testament wisdom.
[12] Princeton: University Press, 1969 (Third edition, with supplement), hereafter *ANET*.
[13] Oxford: Clarendon Press, 1960.
[14] New Haven & London: Yale University Press, 1973.
[15] New York: Harper & Row, 1966.
[16] Walter Harrelson, "Wisdom and Pastoral Theology," *ANQ* 7 (1966): 6-14 demonstrates the universality and contemporaneity of wisdom. He discusses the court jester, political satire, and advice to the lovelorn in modern society. In a sense, Amy Vanderbilt, Ann Landers, Dale Carnegie, and Art Buchwald carry on the ancient sapiential tradition. So did Benjamin Franklin and others like him who collected and composed witty sayings.
[17] E. G. K. Hewat, *A Comparison of Hebrew and Chinese Wisdom*, Edinburgh Diss., 1934 (The author has not seen this volume). John O.

Barksdale, "A Japanese Critic Looks at the Bible," *The Japan Missionary Bulletin* (1970): 541-48 discusses a book by the Japanese literary critic, Akira Honda, *Seisho—Gusha no rakuen (The Bible: Fool's Paradise)* (Kōbunsha; Paperback Kappa Series, 1957) and observes that the wisdom literature alone appealed to this critic. In Honda's view, the rest of the Bible depicts a God who is unworthy of human adulation.

[18] John Mark Thompson, *The Form and Function of Proverbs in Ancient Israel* (The Hague & Paris: Mouton, 1974), 33-34.

[19] *Ibid.*, 29.

[20] M. Kuusi, "Southwest African Riddle-Proverbs," *Proverbium* 12 (1969): 305-11.

[21] Georg Fohrer, "The Righteous Man in Job 31," *Essays in Old Testament Ethics*, J. L. Crenshaw & John T. Willis, eds. (New York: KTAV, 1974), 3-22. On this text see the recent commentaries by Marvin Pope and Robert Gordis (*Job, AB,* 15 [third edition]; Garden City, N.Y.; Doubleday, 1973 and *The Book of Job: Commentary, New Translation, and Special Studies,* New York: Jewish Theological Seminary of America, 5378 = 1978).

[22] Claus Westermann, *Der Aufbau des Buches Hiob* (Stuttgart: Calwer, 1977), original publication, 1956. This new edition has a useful discussion of Joban research since 1956; that essay was written by Jürgen Kegler.

[23] Hartmut Gese, *Lehre und Wirklichkeit in der alten Weisheit: Studien zu den Spruchen Salomos und zu dem Buche Hiob* (Tübingen: J. C. B. Mohr [Paul Siebeck] 1958), 63-78.

[24] H. Bardtke, "Profetische Zuge im Buche Hiob" in *Das Ferne und Nahe Wort: Festschrift Leonhard Rost, BZAW* 105 (1967): 1-10.

[25] On this vexing problem, see my discussion in the Prolegomenon to *SAIW,* 3-5 and "Method in Determining Wisdom Influence upon 'Historical' Literature," *JBL* 88 (1969): 129-142 (also in *SAIW,* 481-94).

[26] On Egyptian wisdom see Hellmut Brunner, "Die Weisheitsliteratur," *HO,* 1, 2 (Brill: Leiden, 1952) 90-110 and Ronald J. Williams, "Wisdom in the Ancient Near East," *IDB, Supplementary Volume* (Nashville: Abingdon, 1976), 949-52.

[27] On Babylonian wisdom, see above all W. G. Lambert, *Babylonian Wisdom Literature* (Oxford: Clarendon, 1960).

[28] Glendon Bryce, "Omen-Wisdom in Ancient Israel," *JBL* 94 (1975): 19-37 can find only traces of omens in canonical proverbs, and these are open to question.

[29] Heinz Richter, "Die Naturweisheit des Alten Testaments im Buche Hiob," *ZAW* 70 (1958): 1-19.

[30] Walther Zimmerli, "Concerning the Structure of Old Testament Wisdom," *SAIW,* 175-207. This significant essay originally appeared in German as "Zur Struktur der alttestamentlichen Weisheit," *ZAW* 51

(1933): 177-204; see also *Old Testament Theology in Outline* (Atlanta: John Knox, 1978), 155-66.

[31] Von Rad, *Wisdom in Israel*, 190-239, emphasizes trust and attack in such a way as to reveal the authentic struggle within the hearts and minds of ancient Israelite sages.

[32] Johannes Fichtner, *Die altorientalische Weisheit in ihrer israelitisch-jüdischen Ausprägung (BZAW,* 62; Giessen: Alfred Töpelmann, 1933) offers an illuminating systematic analysis of the essential ideas which characterize Israel's wisdom.

[33] Bernhard Lang, *Frau Weisheit: Deutung einer biblischen Gestalt* (Dusseldorf: Patmos, 1975).

[34] Roland E. Murphy, "Wisdom—Theses and Hypotheses," *Israelite Wisdom*, 35-42, especially 35-36, expresses caution with regard to emphasizing order. His desire to preserve an understanding of divine freedom is salutary, but I do not think the customary interpretation of order threatens this principle.

[35] Rylaarsdam, *Revelation in Jewish Wisdom Literature.*

[36] On the social world of the sages, see the Ph.D. Dissertation by Brian W. Kovacs, *Sociological-Structural Constraints upon Wisdom: The Spatial and Temporal Matrix of Proverbs 15:28—22:16* (Vanderbilt, 1978). For an earlier discussion of the problem, consult Robert Gordis, "The Social Background of Wisdom Literature," *HUCA* 18 (1943-44): 77-118.

[37] Klaus Koch has edited a valuable anthology on the concept of retribution in the ancient world *(Um das Prinzip der Vergeltung in Religion und Recht des Alten Testament* [Darmstadt: Wissenschaftliche Buchgesellschaft], 1972).

[38] See my treatment of the problem in *Prophetic Conflict (BZAW,* 124; Berlin & New York: Walter de Gruyter, 1971), 116-23.

[39] I have discussed the literary forms characterizing wisdom literature in "Wisdom," *Old Testament Form Criticism*, John H. Hayes, ed. (San Antonio: Trinity University, 1974), 229-62, and "Wisdom in the OT," *IDB, Supplementary Volume*, 952-56.

[40] On this type of interrogative, see my essays "Questions, dictons et épreuves impossible," *La Sagesse de l'Ancien Testament*, 96-111, and "Impossible Questions and Tasks in Israelite Wisdom," forthcoming in *Gnomic Wisdom*, Dominic Crossan, ed. (Missoula: Scholars Press).

[41] Jeremiah's abstention from marriage is a special instance. The prophet believed God had forbade him to take a wife because of the unusual historical circumstances in which he lived.

[42] Trible, *God and the Rhetoric of Sexuality* (Philadelphia: Fortress, 1978) provides a stimulating analysis of positive roles which Israelite women played.

[43] Hartmut Gese, *Zur biblischen Theologie: Alttestamentliche Vorträge* (München: Chr. Kaiser, 1977), 38-53 develops a similar theory concerning

belief in life after death, which he thinks the authors of Job and Psalm 73 broached in a revolutionary way.

[44] Archer Taylor, *The Proverb and an Index to the Proverb* (Copenhagen & Hatboro, Pa.: Rosenkilde & Baggers, 1962), 3.

1 The World of Wisdom

[1] Georg Fohrer, "Sophia," *SAIW*, 63-83 (originally in Kittel's *Theological Dictionary of the New Testament*, vol. 7 [Grand Rapids: Wm. B. Eerdmans, 1971], 476-96), and R. N. Whybray, "Slippery Words, IV. Wisdom," *ExpT* (1978), 359-62. The word "wisdom" *(hokmah)* occurs 147 times in the Old Testament, and the adjective "wise" *(hakam)* appears 135 times. The verb "to be wise" *(hakam)* is used 26 times, and the variant nominal form *hokmot* can be found four times. Over half of the uses of *hokmah* and *hakam* occur in three books: Proverbs, Job, and Ecclesiastes. In this literary corpus and elsewhere a number of additional words occur in parallelism with specific vocabulary for wisdom, thus enriching the discourse about wisdom manifold. The most common such parallels are *bin* (to perceive), *nabon* (perceptive, skillful), *binah* (insight) and *t'bunah* (insight, skill), or *da'at* (knowledge), *yada'* (to know) and so forth.

[2] Whybray, *The Intellectual Tradition in the Old Testament*, 24-31 challenges their conclusion.

[3] Ronald J. Williams, "Scribal Training in Ancient Egypt," *JAOS* 92 (1972): 214-21.

[4] Gese, *Lehre und Wirklichkeit in der alten Weisheit*, 2. H.D. Preuss goes one step further; since wisdom literature lacks salvation history, it is for him devoid of inspiration and belongs alongside pagan texts ("Erwägungen zum theologischen Ort alttestamentlicher Weisheitsliteratur," *EvT* 30 [1970] 393-417, and "Das Gottesbild der älteren Weisheit Israels," *VTSup* 23 [1972] 117-45.

[5] Von Rad, *Wisdom in Israel*, 24-50.

[6] William McKane, *Prophets and Wise Men (SBT*, 44; London: SCM, 1965).

[7] Whybray, *The Intellectual Tradition in the Old Testament*, passim, and von Rad, *Wisdom in Israel*, 17.

[8] Hans Heinrich Schmid, *Wesen und Geschichte der Weisheit (BZAW* 101; Berlin: Alfred Töpelmann, 1966), 155.

[9] George M. Landes, "Jonah: A *Mašal*?," *Israelite Wisdom: Theological and Literary Essays in Honor of Samuel Terrien*, 137-58.

[10] On riddles, see my entry, "Riddle," in *IDB, Supplementary Volume*, 749-50, and *Samson: A Secret Betrayed, a Vow Ignored* (Atlanta: John Knox, 1978), 99-120.

[11] See 7:1-6 in particular, where the infancy of Solomon is recalled, and 9:10-18, where a hellenistic view of the body surfaces.

[12] The Instruction of Ani *(ANET*, 420-21).

[13] On schools in Israel see H. J. Hermisson, *Studien zur israelitischen Spruchweisheit (WMANT* 28; Neukirchen-Vluyn: Neukirchener, 1968), 97-136.

[14] Svend Holm-Nielsen, "On the Interpretation of Qoheleth in Early Christianity," *VT* 24 (1974): 168-77, and G. T. Sheppard, "The Epilogue to Qoheleth as Theological Commentary," *CBQ* 39 (1977): 182-89.

[15] This book, to which I have given the tentative title, *The Art of Persuasion in Israelite Wisdom*, will be published by Fortress Press.

[16] A fuller discussion of these forms appears in my essay, "Wisdom," in *Old Testament Form Criticism* (San Antonio: Trinity University Press, 1974), especially 229-62. See also von Rad, *Wisdom in Israel*, 24-50.

[17] Von Rad, "Job XXXVIII and Ancient Egyptian Wisdom," *SAIW*, 267-77, and Albrecht Alt, "Solomonic Wisdom," *ibid.*, 102-112 (originally published as "Die Weisheit Salomos," *TLZ* 76 [1951] 139-44).

[18] Whybray, *The Intellectual Tradition in the Old Testament*, 155 concedes this danger.

[19] Johannes Fichtner, "Isaiah Among the Wise," *SAIW*, 429-38 (originally published as "Jesaja unter dem Weisen," *TLZ* 74 [1949]: 75-80 and reprinted in *Gottes Weisheit* [Stuttgart: Calwer, 1965], 18-26).

[20] J. William Whedbee, *Isaiah and Wisdom* (Nashville: Abingdon, 1971), and Joseph Jensen, *The Use of Tôrâ by Isaiah (CBQMS*, 3, 1973).

[21] Amos' connection with this town has been interpreted as evidence that he came under the influence of sages. For discussion, see Samuel Terrien, "Amos and Wisdom," *SAIW*, 448-55; Hans Walter Wolff, *Amos the Prophet* (Phildelphia: Fortress, 1973); *Joel and Amos* (Philadelphia: Fortress, 1977), and Crenshaw, "The Influence of the Wise upon Amos," *ZAW* 79 (1967): 42-52.

[22] H. W. Wolff, "Micah the Moreshite—The Prophet and His Background," *Israelite Wisdom*, 77-84. Donald Gowan, "Habakkuk and Wisdom," *Perspective* 9 (1968): 157-66 finds wisdom influence in Habakkuk.

[23] George M. Landes, "Jonah: A *Mašal*?," *Israelite Wisdom*, 137-58; Phyllis Trible, *Studies in the Book of Jonah*, Ph.D. Diss., Columbia University, 1963.

[24] R. N. Whybray, *The Succession Narrative (SBT* 9; London: SCM, 1968) has understood this literary complex as an attempt to illustrate truths resting in canonical proverbs. Wisdom, in his view, provides the impetus for this material.

[25] Hans J. Hermisson, "Weisheit und Geschichte," *Probleme biblische Theologie: Gerhard von Rad zum 70 Geburtstag*, Hans Walter Wolff, ed. (München: Kaiser, 1971): 136-54.

[26] Von Rad, "The Joseph Narrative and Ancient Wisdom," *SAIW*, 439-47.

[27] Shemaryahu Talmon, "Wisdom in the Book of Esther," *VT* 13 (1963): 419-55.

[28] Luis Alonso-Schökel, "Sapiential and Covenant Themes in Genesis 2—3," *SAIW*, 468-80 (originally published as "Motivos sapienciales y de alianza en Gen. 2—3," *Bib* 43 (1962): 295-315).

[29] John McKenzie, "Reflections on Wisdom," *JBL* 86 (1967): 1-9.

[30] R. C. Dentan, "The Literary Affinities of Exod. XXXIV 6f.," *VT* 13 (1963): 34-51.

[31] Moshe Weinfeld, "The Origin of Humanism in Deuteronomy," *JBL* 80 (1961): 241-47; "Deuteronomy—The Present State of Inquiry," *JBL* 86 (1967): 249-62; *Deuteronomy and the Deuteronomic School* (Oxford: Oxford University Press, 1972); C. Brekelmans, "Wisdom Influence in Deuteronomy," *La Sagesse d l'Ancien Testament*, 28-38 takes an opposing view.

[32] Von Rad, *Wisdom in Israel*, 263-83.

[33] The following surveys of research in wisdom literature provide further information about the course of recent scholarship: Walter Baumgartner, "The Wisdom Literature," in *The Old Testament and Modern Study*, H. H. Rowley, ed. (Oxford: Oxford University Press, 1951), 210-37; Crenshaw, "Prolegomenon," *SAIW*, 1-45 (46-60, bibliography); "The Wisdom Literature," in *The Hebrew Bible and Its Modern Interpreters*, D. Knight and Gene Tucker, eds. (Chico, Ca.: Scholars Press, forthcoming); John Emerton, "Wisdom," in *Tradition and Interpretation*, George W. Anderson, ed. (Oxford: Oxford University Press, 1979); Maurice Gilbert, "Avant-propos," *La Sagesse de l'Ancien Testament*, 7-13; Roland E. Murphy, "Assumptions and Problems in Old Testament Wisdom Research," *CBQ* 29 (1967): 102-12 (407-418); and R. B. Y. Scott, "The Study of Wisdom Literature," *Int* 24 (1970): 20-45.

2 The Sapiential Tradition

[1] R. E. Murphy, "Qoheleth's 'Quarrel' with the Fathers," in *From Faith to Faith. Essays in Honor of Donald G. Miller on His Seventieth Birthday*, Dikran Y. Hadidian, ed. (Pittsburgh: Pickwick Press, 1979), 235-45 is the latest of several critics to discuss this important topic.

[2] Lou H. Silberman, "The Queen of Sheba in Judaic Tradition," *Solomon and Sheba*, James B. Pritchard, ed. (London: Phaidon, 1974), 65-84; W. Hertz, "Die Rätsel der Königin von Saba," *ZDA* 27 (1883): 1-33, and Moses Gaster, "Story of Solomon's Wisdom," *Folklore* 1 (1890): 133-35; and E. Ullendorf, *Ethiopia and the Bible* (London: Oxford University, 1968).

[3] *Strassburger Räthselbuch. Die erste zu Strassburg ums Jahr 1505 gedruckte Deutsch Räthselsammlung*, A. F. Butsch, ed. (Strassburg: K. J. Trübner, 1876). This unusual collection of riddles, on which I did considerable study during a sabbatical in Heidelberg from 1972-73, has 326 difficult questions and answers. Although written by a monk, the

riddles are sometimes blasphemous, and often achieve appreciable humor.

[4] R. B. Y. Scott, "Solomon and the Beginnings of Wisdom in Israel," *VTSup* 3 (1955): 262-279 = *SAIW*, 84-101, and E. W. Heaton, *Solomon's New Men: The Emergence of Ancient Israel as a National State* (New York: Pica, 1974).

[5] For a translation of this myth concerning Inanna's descent into the nether world, see James B. Pritchard, *ANET*, 52-57.

[6] An early date for 1—9 has been claimed by Christa Kayatz, *Studien zu Proverbien 1—9 (WMANT*, 22; Neukirchen-Vluyn: Neukirchener, 1966).

[7] Hans-Peter Müller, "Magisch-mantische Weisheit und die Gestalt Daniels," *UF* 1 (1969): 79-94.

[8] Siegfried Herrmann, "Die Königsnovele in Ägypten und in Israel," *Wissenschaftliche Zeitschrift der Universitäts Leipzig* 3 (1953-54): 53-57.

[9] The Egyptian "Instruction of Ptahhotep" concludes with a lengthy pun on the word for hearing (*ANET*, 414).

[10] On this story see Trible, *God and the Rhetoric of Sexuality,* 31-34.

[11] Hugo Gressmann, "Das salomonische Urteil," *Deutsche Rundschau* 130 (1907): 212-28.

[12] George M. Landes, "The 'Three Days and Three Nights' Motif in Jonah 2:1," *JBL* 86 (1967): 446-50.

[13] Henri Cazelles, "Les débuts de la sagesse en Israël," *Les sagesses du Proché-Orient ancien,* 27-39, especially 34-35.

[14] On the basis of this story, Teqoa has been seen as a center of sapiential activity—despite the explicit statement that Joab instructed the woman on what to say to David.

[15] R. N. Whybray, *The Succession Narrative.* Such a negative attitude toward wisdom does not depend upon a technical use of the adjective "wise" in the stories about Abel and the women from Teqoa and Abel.

[16] Martin Noth, "Die Bewährung von Salomos 'Göttlicher Weisheit,' " *VTSup* 3 (1960): 225-37.

[17] Scott, "Solomon and the Beginnings of Wisdom in Israel," *VTSup* 3, 263 cites these opinions and documents them in the writings of Anton Causse and H. Wheeler Robinson.

[18] Johannes Fichtner, *Die altorientalische Weisheit in ihrer israelitisch-jüdischen Ausprägung.*

[19] Heaton, *Solomon's New Men,* and Walter Brueggemann, *In Man We Trust* (Richmond: John Knox, 1972).

[20] W. F. Albright, "Some Canaanite-Phoenician Sources of Hebrew Wisdom," *VTSup* 3, writes that a Solomonic nucleus is probable for Proverbs, but those didactic materials credited to Solomon "failed to meet later standards of literary taste—or were simply so archaic in content that they were no longer understood" (p. 13).

[21] Albrecht Alt, "Solomonic Wisdom," *SAIW*, 102-112 (originally published as "Die Weisheit Salomos," *TLZ* 76 [1951]: 139-44).

[22] Gerhard von Rad, "Job XXXVIII and Ancient Egyptian Wisdom," *SAIW*, 267-80.

[23] Brueggemann, *In Man We Trust*, and Whybray, *The Succession Narrative*.

[24] Von Rad, "The Joseph Narrative and Ancient Wisdom," *SAIW*, 439-47.

[25] The reasons for my misgivings about this phrase appear in an extensive review of von Rad's analysis of Israelite wisdom and in a book on his thought. See *"Wisdom in Israel* by Gerhard von Rad," *RSR* 2, no. 2 (1976): 6-12, and James Crenshaw, *Gerhard von Rad* (Waco: Word, 1978). The latter book has now appeared in a German translation by Jürgen Kegler *(Gerhard von Rad: Grundlinien seines theologischen Werks* [München: Chr. Kaiser, 1979]).

[26] R. N. Whybray, *The Intellectual Tradition in the Old Testament*.

[27] R. J. Williams, "Wisdom in the Ancient Near East," *IDB*, *Supplementary Volume*, 949-52.

[28] Johann Marböck, *Weisheit im Wandel. Untersuchungen zur Weisheitstheologie bei Ben Sira (BBB*, 37; Bonn: Peter Hanstein, 1971).

[29] Bernhard Lang, "Schule und Unterricht im alte Israel," *La Sagesse de l'Ancien Testament*, 186-201.

[30] I have pursued this theme in an article entitled "In Search of Divine Presence (Some Remarks Preliminary to a Theology of Wisdom)," *RevExp* 74 (1977): 353-69; see also Samuel Terrien, *The Elusive Presence* (New York: Harper & Row, 1978).

[31] Von Rad, *Wisdom in Israel*, 232-33.

[32] On the centrality of death to Qoheleth's thought, see my essay, "The Shadow of Death in Qoheleth," *Israelite Wisdom*, 205-16.

[33] Wisdom of Solomon falls into the same category as Sirach.

3 The Pursuit of Knowledge: Proverbs

[1] Von Rad, *Wisdom in Israel*, 115-24.

[2] Landes, "Jonah: A *Mašal*?," 139 and William McKane, *Proverbs. A New Approach* (Philadelphia: Westminster, 1970), 22-33, reject the latter possibility.

[3] Quoted in Aage Bentzen, *Introduction to the Old Testament*, I (Copenhagen: G. E. C. Gad, 1948), 168.

[4] This definition has been attributed to Cervantes.

[5] John Mark Thompson, *The Form and Function of Proverbs in Ancient Israel*, 23.

[6] Roger D. Abrahams, "On Proverb Collecting and Proverb Collections," *Proverbium* 8 (1967): 181-84.

[7] Thompson, *The Form and Function of Proverbs in Ancient Israel*,

59-68, and Scott, *Proverbs. Ecclesiastes (AB* 18; Garden City: Doubleday, 1965), 18-20.

[8] Schmid, *Wesen und Geschichte der Weisheit,* 159, note 69. In many instances, particularly within Qoheleth, a comparison certainly occurs.

[9] Scott, *The Way of Wisdom in the Old Testament,* 59-63.

[10] Von Rad, *Wisdom in Israel,* 53-73.

[11] Georg Sauer, *Die Spruche Agurs (BWANT* 84; Stuttgart: W. Kohlhammer, 1963), and Scott, *The Way of Wisdom in the Old Testament,* 166-70.

[12] Patrick W. Skehan, *Studies in Israelite Poetry and Wisdom (CBQMS* 1; Washington, D.C.: The Catholic Biblical Association of America, 1971), 9-45.

[13] McKane, *Proverbs,* 7, 11.

[14] McKane, *Prophets and Wise Men; Proverbs;* and Whybray, *Wisdom in Proverbs (SBT* 45; London: SCM, 1965).

[15] Hans-Jürgen Hermisson, *Studien zur israelitischen Spruchweisheit,* 113-36; Bernhard Lang, *Frau Weisheit,* passim, and "Schule und Unterricht in alten Israel," *La Sagesse de l'Ancien Testament,* 186-201.

[16] Carol Rader Fontaine, *The Use of the Traditional Saying in the Old Testament,* Ph.D. Dissertation, Duke University, 1979. Ms. Fontaine draws upon paroemiological studies in general to clarify the traditional saying in ancient Israel. She focuses on the following texts: (1) Judges 8:2 ("Is not the gleaning of the grapes of Ephraim better than the vintage of Abiezer?"); (2) Judges 8:21 ("For as the man is, so is his strength"); (3) 1 Samuel 16:7 ("Man looks on the outward appearance, but the LORD looks on the heart"); (4) 1 Samuel 24:14, English 13 ("Out of the wicked comes forth wickedness"); (5) 1 Kings 20:11 ("Let not him that girds on his armor boast himself as he that puts it off"). Other texts are often cited in this connection, for example Ezekiel 18:2 (Jeremiah 31:29), "The fathers have eaten sour grapes, and the children's teeth are set on edge," and Ezekiel 16:44 ("Like mother, like daughter").

[17] Norman Habel, "The Symbolism of Wisdom in Proverbs 1—9," *Int* 26 (1972): 131-57.

[18] Wisdom of Solomon 5:9-14 adapts this saying and suggests that its meaning concerns the absence of any trace of movement.

[19] W. O. E. Oesterley, *The Book of Proverbs* (London: Methuen and Company, 1929), LXXXIV-LXXXVII.

[20] Brunner, "Die Weisheitsliteratur," 96.

[21] Kovacs, *Sociological-Structural Constraints upon Wisdom: The Spatial and Temporal Matrix of Proverbs 15:28—22:16.*

[22] The sexual connotation of eating is also found in Genesis 39:6, 9, for Joseph takes pain to explain that Potiphar's wife is the food which is forbidden the servant. The Joseph narrative has been associated with wisdom by von Rad, "The Joseph Narrative and Ancient Wisdom," *SAIW,*

439-47; George W. Coats, "The Joseph Story and Ancient Wisdom: A Reappraisal," *CBQ* 35 (1973): 285-97; *From Canaan to Egypt: Structural and Theological Context for the Joseph Story (CBQMS* 4, 1976).

[23] *ANET*, 427.

[24] Its power for good and ill is described in 1 Esdras 3:18-24.

[25] Jean Paul Audet, "Origines comparées de la double tradition de la loi et de la sagesse dans le Proché-Orient ancien," *Akten des 25 Internationalen Orientalistenkongresses*, I (Moscow, 1962): 352-57.

[26] W. Lee Humphreys, "The Motif of the Wise Courtier in the Book of Proverbs," *Israelite Wisdom*, 177-90.

[27] McKane, *Prophets and Wise Men*, stresses this fact, although he may press the idea too far.

[28] *Antiquities* VIII, 5.

[29] Von Rad, *Wisdom in Israel*, passim and Christa Bauer-Kayatz, *Einführung in die alttestamentliche Weisheit (BS* 55, Neukirchen-Vluyn: Neukirchener, 1969), 36-92.

[30] From this perspective, one could argue that the author of Job defends God's freedom, just as some interpreters insist that Qoheleth guards divine prerogative.

[31] Egon Pfeiffer, "Die Gottsfurcht im Buche Kohelet," *Gottes Wort und Gottes Land, Festschrift für Hans Wilhelm Hertzberg*, Henning G. Reventlow, ed. (Göttingen: Vandenhoeck und Ruprecht, 1965), 133-58.

[32] Von Rad, *Wisdom in Israel*, 144-76; Lang, *Frau Weisheit*, 168-84; und Burton Lee Mack, *Logos und Sophia: Untersuchungen zur Weisheitstheologie im hellenistischen Judentum (SUNT* 10; Göttingen: Vandenhoeck und Ruprecht, 1973).

[33] Delbert R. Hillers, *Treaty-Curses and the Old Testament Prophets (BO* 16; Rome: Pontifical Biblical Institute, 1964), 28-29.

[34] R. N. Whybray, "Proverbs VIII 22-31 and Its Supposed Prototypes," *SAIW*, 390-400 (originally published in *VT* 15 [1965]: 504-14).

[35] Luis Alonso-Schökel, "Sapiential and Covenant Themes in Genesis 2—3," *SAIW*, 468-80 (original English translation in *Theology Digest* 13 [1965]: 3-10).

[36] William F. Albright, "Some Canaanite-Phoenician Sources of Hebrew Wisdom," *VTSup* 3 (1960):8.

[37] Christa Kayatz, *Studien zu Proverbien 1—9*, 76-134.

4 The Search for Divine Presence: Job

[1] Recent interpretations of Job are reviewed by Hans-Peter Müller, *Das Hiobproblem (EF* 84; Darmstadt: Wissenchaftliche Buchgesellschaft, 1978), and by Jürgen Kegler," Hauptlinien der Hiobforschung seit 1956," in Claus Westermann, *Der Aufbau des Buches Hiob*, 9-25.

[2] For recent analyses, see Pope, *Job;* Gordis, *The Book of Job;* Georg Fohrer, *Das Buch Hiob (KAT* 16; Gutersloh: Gerd Mohn, 1963).

[3] Nahum M. Sarna, "Epic Substratum in the Prose of Job," *JBL* (1957): 13-25.

[4] Georg Fohrer, *Das Buch Hiob,* passim.

[5] Perhaps *yomo* (his day) refers to the sons' birthdays; if so, the feasting was not continuous.

[6] On the divine assembly, see R. N. Whybray, *The Heavenly Counsellor in Isaiah XL 13-14 (SOTSMS* 1; Cambridge: University Press, 1971), 39-53.

[7] Rivkah Schärf Kluger, *Satan in the Old Testament* (Evanston: Northwestern University, 1967).

[8] On the assumption that this proverb derives from pre-yahwistic ideas of Mother Earth, it may be that in Genesis 3 the narrator moves naturally from the notion of nakedness to that of mortality, both with regard to the punishment specified for disobedience and with respect to the tree of life. Perhaps the second tree is less obtrusive than interpreters think.

[9] Although this expression seems to come from the practice of barter, its precise meaning is difficult to ascertain.

[10] I have examined the Joban "drama" from this perspective in "The Twofold Search: A Response to Luis Alonso Schökel," *Semeia* 7 (1977): 63-69.

[11] This language derives from Edwin M. Good, *Irony in the Old Testament* (Philadelphia: Westminster, 1965), 196-97.

[12] Fohrer, "The Righteous Man in Job 31."

[13] Zophar's final speech is missing, unless it has been mistakenly attributed to Job. In any case, Job speaks entirely inappropriate language in 24:18-25; 26:5-14; and 27:13-23.

[14] See my *Hymnic Affirmation of Divine Justice (SBLDS* 24; Missoula: Scholars Press, 1975).

[15] Von Rad, *Wisdom in Israel,* 217.

[16] Robert Gordis, "The Lord Out of the Whirlwind. The Climax and Meaning of Job," *Judaism* 13 (1964): 48-63; R.A. F. MacKenzie, "The Purpose of the Yahweh Speeches in the Book of Job," *Bib* 40 (1959): 435-45; Samuel Terrien, "The Yahweh Speeches and Job's Responses," *Rev Exp* 68 (1971): 497-509; Kenneth Thompson, "Out of the Whirlwind," *Int* 14 (1960): 51-63, and H. D. Preuss, Jahwes Antwort an Hiob und die sogenannte Hiobliteratur des alten Vorderen Orients," *Beiträge zur alttestamentlichen Theologie. Festschrift für Walther Zimmerli zum 70 Geburtstag,* H. Donner, R. Hanhart, and R. Smend, eds., (Göttingen: Vandenhoeck und Ruprecht, 1977), 323-43.

[17] David Neiman, *The Book of Job* (Jerusalem: Massada, 1972), and Robert Gordis, *The Book of God and Man* (Chicago: University of Chicago, 1965).

[18] On theodicy, see my entry "Theodicy," *IDB, Supplementary Volume,* 895-96 (with bibliography).

[19] M. Sekine, "Schöpfung und Erlösung im Buche Hiob," in *Pathos und Humor, BZAW* (1958): 213-23.

[20] John G. Gammie, "Behemoth and Leviathan: On the Didactic and Theological Significance of Job 40:15—41:26,"*Israelite Wisdom*, 217-31.

[21] That includes all attempts to understand God's remarks as irony, such as James G. Williams, " 'You Have Not Spoken Truth of Me': Mystery and Irony in Job," *ZAW* 83 (1971): 231-55; and David Robertson, "The Book of Job: A Literary Study," *Soundings* 56 (1973): 446-69.

[22] Marvin E. Tate, "The Speeches of Elihu," *RevExp* 68 (1971): 487-95; and David Noel Freedman, "The Elihu Speeches in the Book of Job," *HTR* 61 (1968): 51-59.

[23] On the problem of warrants for the sages' teaching, see my essay on "Wisdom and Authority: Sapiential Suasion and Its Warrants," *VTSup* (forthcoming).

[24] Such bold affirmation occurs within the Babylonian parallel to Job ("I Will Praise the Lord of Wisdom") and in the Canaanite Baal epic.

[25] Carl G. Jung, *Answer to Job* (Cleveland and New York: The World Publishing Company, 1970), 20 (originally published in 1954). For a different psychological analysis, see Jack H. Kahn, *Job's Illness: Loss, Grief and Integration: A Psychological Interpretation* (Oxford et al.: Pergamon Press, 1975).

[26] A fuller treatment can be found in my article, "The Human Dilemma and Literature of Dissent," *Tradition and Theology in the Old Testament*, Douglas A. Knight, ed. (Philadelphia: Fortress, 1977), 235-58.

[27] Ludwig Schmidt, *"De Deo": Studien zur Literarkritik und Theologie des Buches Jona, des Gesprächs zwischen Abraham und Jahwe in Genesis 18:22ff. und von Hi 1 (BZAW* 143; Berlin and New York: Walter de Gruyter, 1976) has examined this passage and related ones from the perspective of source criticism, with highly questionable results.

[28] Jim Alvin Sanders, *Suffering as Divine Discipline in the Old Testament and Post-Biblical Judaism* (Rochester, N.Y.: Colgate Rochester Divinity School, 1955).

[29] Johannes Hempel, "Das theologische Problem des Hiob," *ZST* 6 (1929): 638 = *APOXYSMATA (BZAW* 81; Berlin: Alfred Töpelmann, 1961), 128.

[30] Von Rad, *Wisdom in Israel*, 206-226.

[31] Kornelis H. Miskotte, *When the Gods Are Silent* (New York: Harper and Row, 1967), and Samuel Terrien, *The Elusive Presence: Toward a New Biblical Theology*. In the latter work the adjective rarely functions because of the majestic cultic presence which overwhelms modern readers as it surely must have done many ancient worshipers.

[32] MacLeish, *J.B.* (Boston: Houghton Mifflin Company, 1956).

[33] Jung's lack of expertise in biblical training did not prevent him from recognizing the immense theological issues involved in the character of

God as presented in Job and throughout the Bible. Those problems, which Jung treats under the shadow side of God, are irreconcilable with a moral view of deity.

[34] On Ernst Bloch's interpretation of Job, see Dichter Gebracht, "Aufbruch zu sittlichem Atheismus: die Hiob-Deutung Ernst Blochs," *EvT* 35 (1975): 223-37. For a different perspective on Job, see Dermot Cox, *The Triumph of Innocence: Job and the Tradition of the Absurd,* Analecta Gregoriana, 212 (Roma: Universita Gregoriana Editrice, 1978).

[35] Samuel Terrien, "Quelques remarques sur les affinité de Job avec le Deutéro-Esaie," *VTSup* 15 (1966): 295-310.

[36] On these similarities see my *Hymnic Affirmation of Divine Justice* and "The Influence of the Wise Upon Amos," *ZAW* 79 (1967): 42-52.

[37] G. Many, *Der Rechtsstreit mit Gott (rib) im Hiobbuch* (1970). I have not seen this book.

[38] For a different view, see von Rad, *Wisdom in Israel,* 210.

[39] Chaim Zhitlowsky, "Job and Faust," *Two Studies in Yiddish Culture,* Percy Matenko, ed. (Leiden: E. J. Brill, 1968), 152, writes: "His emotional world suddenly assumes a different form. The clouds of darkness are dispersed. A feeling of infinite confidence in the world and its Divine Leader arises in his soul and he laughs at the thousand questions, the hungry wolves with burning eyes, and they disappear from his soul."

[40] Matitiahu Tsevat, "The Meaning of the Book of Job," *SAIW,* 341-74 (originally in *HUCA* 37 [1966]: 73-106).

5 The Chasing After Meaning: Ecclesiastes

[1] Job 39:8 refers to an animal's search for food, and Proverbs 12:26 seems to imply that wise people examine their friends very closely. In both cases *tur* is used, a word that is seldom found in the Hebrew Bible.

[2] For the signal importance of death to Qoheleth, see my essay, "The Shadow of Death in Qoheleth" in *Israelite Wisdom: Theological and Literary Essays in Honor of Samuel Terrien,* 205-16. John J. Collins, "The Root of Immortality: Death in the Context of Jewish Wisdom," *HThR* 71(1978): 177-192 is concerned primarily with Ben Sira and Wisdom of Solomon.

[3] Walther Zimmerli, "The Place and Limit of the Wisdom in the Framework of the Old Testament Theology," *SAIW,* 325-26 (originally published in *SJT* 17 [1964]: 146-58) sees Qoheleth as a guardian of ancient faith concerning divine freedom and human limitation.

[4] R. N. Whybray, "Qoheleth the Immoralist? (Qoh 7:16-17)," *Israelite Wisdom,* 191-204 takes a different view. See also "Conservatisme et radicalisme dans Qohelet," *Sagesse et Religion. Colloque de Strasbourg* (October 1976) (Paris: Presses Universitaires de France, 1979), 65-81.

[5] On this difficult problem, see my essay "The Eternal Gospel (Eccl. 3:11)," *Essays in Old Testament Ethics,* 23-55.

[6] Alternatively, the text may mean that the poor sage was consulted and his advice heeded, but the rescued people soon forgot the one who delivered them from certain death.

[7] Von Rad, *Wisdom in Israel*, 263-83, tries to relate Israel's sages with the ancient interest in determining the times which God has fixed for the universe. The argument fails to convince me.

[8] Hellmut *(sic)* Gese, "Die Krisis der Weisheit bei Koheleth," *SPOA*, 151. Human beings are wholly dependent upon God's disposition, since God alone decides what and when to give away.

[9] "The Instruction of Ani" has the following advice: "And when thy messenger (i.e. Death) comes to thee to take thee, . . . do not say, 'I am (too) young for thee to take,' for thou knowest not thy death. When death comes, he steals away the infant which is on its mother's lap like him who has reached old age . . ." (*ANET*, 420).

[10] Von Rad, *Wisdom in Israel*, 231.

[11] Johannes Pedersen, "Scepticisme israélite," *RHPR* 10 (1930): 348-50, saw this fact with great clarity.

[12] Aarre Lauha, "Die Krise des religiösen Glaubens bei Kohelet," *VTSup* 3, 183-91, contrasts Job and Qoheleth as examples of the differences between religious and secular people.

[13] Robert Gordis, "Quotations in Wisdom Literature," *SAIW*, 220-44 (originally published in *JQR* 30 [1939-40]: 123-47) and Hans-Peter Müller, "Wie sprach Qohälät von Gott?" *VT* 18 (1968): 507-21. While Gordis introduced the principle of quotation and gave the theory credibility in various studies, Müller saw the peculiar manner in which Qoheleth cited positive sayings in order to refute them.

[14] Walther Zimmerli, "Das Buch Kohelet—Traktat oder Sentenzensammlung?" *VT* 24 (1974): 221-30, sees evidence for both understandings of the book—a casual treatise and a careful collection of valuable advice.

[15] The assumption that a single idea gave rise to all instances of that notion (monogenesis) is less likely than independent thinking about universal concerns (polygenesis).

[16] "The Instruction of Ptahhotep" (*ANET*, 412).

[17] It follows that I believe certain words function as ciphers and connote two distinct senses. In this instance, the word usually rendered "your creator" *(bor'eka)* alludes to an erotic usage known to us from Proverbs 5:15-20, but it also provides a grim reminder of the "hole" into which everyone will eventually be laid.

[18] Addison G. Wright, "The Riddle of the Sphinx: The Structure of the Book of Qoheleth," *SAIW*, 245-66 (originally published in *CBQ* 30 [1968]: 313-34). The conclusions in this essay have recently been revised. See "The Riddle of the Sphinx Revisited: Numerical Patterns in the Book of Qoheleth," *CBQ* 42(1980): 35-51.

[19] Holm-Nielsen "On the Interpretation of Qoheleth in Early Christianity," Gerald T. Sheppard, *Wisdom as a Hermeneutical Construct, BZAW*, 151 (Berlin and New York: Walter de Gruyter), 1980, 121-129 and "The Epilogue to Qohelet as Theological Commentary," *CBQ* 39 (1977): 182-189.

[20] Surely everyone would have known that Solomon was David's son and that the place of his rule was Jerusalem.

[21] Hans Wilhelm Hertzberg, *Der Prediger (KAT* 17; Gutersloh: Gerd Mohn, 1963), 28-32 and Aarre Lauha, *Kohelet (BKAT* 19; Neukirchen-Vluyn: Neukirchener, 1978), 7-11.

[22] Charles F. Whitley, *Koheleth: His Language and Thought (BZAW* 148; Berlin and New York: Walter de Gruyter, 1979), argues for a date between 152 and 145 B.C.E.

[23] Paul Jouon, "Sur le nom de Qoheleth," *Bib* 2 (1921); 53-54; Edward Ullendorff, "The Meaning of Qoheleth," *VT* 12 (1962): 215.

[24] Duncan Black Macdonald, *The Hebrew Philosophical Genius: A Vindication* (New York: Russell and Russell, 1965), 36.

[25] 1 Kings 22:17 applies the image to King Ahab.

6 The Quest for Survival: Sirach

[1] Johannes Fichtner, *Die altorientalische Weisheit in ihrer isralitisch-jüdischen Ausprägung,* and Johann Marböck, *Weisheit im Wandel: Untersuchungen zur Weisheitstheologie bei Ben Sira.* Otto Rickenbacher, *Weisheitsperikopen bei Ben Sira,* Orbis Biblicus et Orientalis, 1 (Göttingen: Vandenhoeck und Ruprecht; Freiburg, Schweiz: Universitätsverlag, 1973).

[2] Von Rad, "Gerichtsdoxologie," *Schalom: Studien zu Glaube und Geschichte Israels,* Karl-Heinz Bernhardt, ed. (Stuttgart: Calwer, 1971), 28-37. The pioneer essay on this subject was written by Friedrich Horst ("Die Doxologien im Amosbuch," *Gottes Recht* [Munich: Chr. Kaiser, 1961], 155-66).

[3] On the significance of this increased emphasis upon divine mercy, see Rylaarsdam, *Revelation in Jewish Wisdom Literature.*

[4] Leo G. Perdue, *Wisdom and Cult (SBLDS* 30; Missoula: Scholars Press, 1977) takes a more positive view of the cult than von Rad, *Wisdom in Israel,* 186-89, and J. G. Snaith, "Ben Sira's Supposed Love of Liturgy," *VT* 25 (1975): 167-74.

[5] Although he could easily have chosen heroines for inclusion in this eulogy, Ben Sira did not do so.

[6] Josef Haspecker, *Gottesfurcht bei Jesus Sirach: Ihre religiöse Struktur und ihre literarische und doctrinäre Bedeutung (AnBib* 30; Rom: Päpstliches Bibelinstitut, 1967).

[7] Von Rad, *Wisdom in Israel,* 242-46, subordinates the theme, "fear of the Lord," to that of wisdom.

[8] Von Rad, *Wisdom in Israel,* 246.

[9] Edmond Jacob, "Wisdom and Religion in Sirach," *Israelite Wisdom,* 247-60. J. Marböck, "Sirachlitratur seit 1966. Ein Überblick," *ThRevue* 71 (1975): 177-84 gives a survey of research on Sirach after 1966.

[10] On these hymns see J. Marböck, *Weisheit im Wandel;* Crenshaw, "The Problem of Theodicy in Sirach," *JBL* 94 (1975): 47-64; and Luis Alonso Schökel, "The Vision of Man in Sirach 16:24-17:14," *Israelite Wisdom,* 235-45.

[11] That is, Sirach supplements human inquiry with divine revelation. The Torah thus becomes material with which the sages work in their attempts to master reality.

7 The Widening Hunt: Wisdom of Solomon, Wisdom Psalms, and Beyond

[1] David Winston, *The Wisdom of Solomon (AB* 43; Garden City, N.Y.: Doubleday, 1979), 23-25 argues for a date during the reign of Gaius 'Caligula' (37-41 C.E.).

[2] A different conclusion has been reached by Skehan, *Studies in Israelite Poetry and Wisdom,* 213-36, especially 228 ("Ecclesiastes is not, therefore, the typical hedonist whom Wis is arraigning; nor is there any real warrant from the language employed for supposing that Wis is concerned with deliberate misuse of the doctrine of Eccl").

[3] Maurice Gilbert, *La critique des dieux dans le livre de la Sagesse (AnBib* 53; Rome: Pontifical Biblical Institute, 1973), and von Rad, *Wisdom in Israel,* 177-85.

[4] On this image of God as helmsman, see *The Divine Helmsman: Studies on God's Control of Human Events Presented to Lou H. Silberman,* James L. Crenshaw and Samuel Sandmel, eds. (New York: KTAV, 1980).

[5] Technically, a midrash comments upon another text. For the difficulty involved in using this term, see William H. Brownlee, *The Midrash Pesher of Habbakuk (SBLMS* 24; Missoula: Scholars Press, 1979).

[6] James M. Reese, *Hellenistic Influence on the Book of Wisdom and Its Consequence (AnBib* 41; Rome: Biblical Institute Press, 1970).

[7] Winston, *The Wisdom of Solomon, passim* makes a strong case against the thesis of Hebraic sources for the book.

[8] Roland E. Murphy, "A Consideration of the Classification 'Wisdom Psalms,' " *SAIW,* 456-67 (originally published in *VTSup* 9 [1962]: 156-67); Crenshaw, "Wisdom," *Old Testament Form Criticism,* 249-52; Erhard Gerstenberger, "Psalms," *ibid.,* 218-21; Kenneth Kuntz, "The Canonical Wisdom Psalms of Ancient Israel: Their Rhetorical, Thematic and Formal Dimensions," *Rhetorical Criticism,* Jared J. Jackson and Martin Kessler, eds. (Pittsburgh: Pickwick, 1974), 186-222; and "The Retribution Motif in Psalmic Wisdom," *ZAW* 89 (1977): 223-33.

[9] Leo Perdue, "The Riddles of Psalm 49," *JBL* 93 (1974): 533-42.

[10] Brevard S. Childs, *Isaiah and the Assyrian Crisis (SBT* 3; London: SCM, 1967), 128-136.

[11] Ernst Würthwein, "Erwägungen zu Psalm 73," *Wort und Existenz: Studien zum Alten Testament* (Göttingen: Vandenhoeck und Ruprecht, 1970), 161-78; Martin Buber, "The Heart Determines," *On the Bible* (New York: Schocken, 1968), 199-210; J. Luyten, "Psalm 73 and Wisdom," *La Sagesse de l'Ancien Testament,* 59-81; James F. Ross, "Psalm 73," *Israelite Wisdom,* 161-75.

[12] Harry Torczyner (Tur Sinai), "The Riddle in the Bible," *HUCA* 1 (1924): 125-49.

[13] I have discussed these traditions in "The Contest of Darius' Guards," *The Old Testament as Story,* Burke Long, ed. (forthcoming).

[14] Paul Humbert, "'Magna est veritas et prevalet' (3 Esra 4:35)," *OLZ* 31 (1928): 148-150.

[15] Karl-Friedrich Pohlmann, *Studien zum dritten Esra (FRLANT* 104; Göttingen: Vandenhoeck und Ruprecht, 1970), 37-52.

[16] Jean Laporte, "Philo in the Tradition of Biblical Wisdom Literature," *Aspects of Wisdom in Judaism and Early Christianity,* Robert L. Wilken, ed. (Notre Dame and London: University of Notre Dame, 1975), 135. On Philo in general, see Samuel Sandmel, *Philo of Alexandria: An Introduction* (New York & Oxford: Oxford University, 1979).

[17] James M. Robinson, " 'Logio Sophon': On the Gattung of Q," *Trajectories Through Early Christianity,* Robinson and Helmut Koester, eds. (Philadelphia: Fortress, 1971), 71-113. Also published in *The Future of Our Religious Past: Essays in Honor of Rudolf Bultmann,* James M. Robinson, ed. (New York: Harper and Row, 1971), 84-130 (originally published in *Zeit und Geschichte, Dankesgabe an Rudolf Bultmann zum 80 Geburtstag* [Tübingen: J. C. B. Mohr, 1964]).

[18] M. Jack Suggs, *Wisdom, Christology, and Law in Matthew's Gospel* (Cambridge: Harvard University, 1970), 5-29, especially 12-13.

[19] Suggs, *Wisdom, Christology, and Law in Matthew's Gospel,* 130. Suggs writes: "The Jesus who meets us in Q as *sophos* and 'child of wisdom' brings truth to men; he is the mediator of divine revelation. The Jesus who meets us in Matthew retains his functions as teacher and revealer, but he is no longer merely a prophet (albeit the last and greatest) of Sophia. He is Wisdom and that means, as well, that he is the embodiment of Torah" (p. 127).

[20] Birger A. Pearson, "Hellenistic-Jewish Wisdom Speculation and Paul,"*Aspects of Wisdom in Judaism and Early Christianity,* 43-66.

[21] Robert L. Wilken, "Wisdom and Philosophy in Early Christianity," *Aspects of Wisdom in Judaism and Early Christianity,* 143-68.

[22] William R. Schoedel, "Jewish Wisdom and the Formation of the Christian Ascetic," *ibid.,* 169-99.

[23] Elizabeth Schussler Fiorenza, "Wisdom Mythology and the Christological Hymns of the New Testament," *ibid.*, 17-41.

8 Wisdom's Legacy

[1] Franklin L. Baumer, *Religion and the Rise of Scepticism* (New York: Harcourt, Brace & World, Inc. 1960), 3. If this claim approaches the truth, as I think it does, the silence of contemporary Old Testament theologies with regard to religious doubt represents a serious oversight, for we have not taken the dialogue with doubt half as seriously as Israel's thinkers did.

[2] Baumer, *Religion and the Rise of Scepticism*, 11.

[3] *Ibid.*

[4] Robert Davidson, "Some Aspects of the Theological Significance of Doubt in the Old Testament," *ASTI* 7 (1970): 41-52 takes a significant step toward clarifying the contribution skeptics made to the Hebrew Scriptures. Concerning the Psalms, Davidson writes: "The confession of confidence again and again springs out of a situation where life has called such confidence into question, and where a man or a community has had to walk in a darkness which has all but overwhelmed faith . . . Is there, for example, no evidence that the very challenge to faith is a creative element in the development of faith?" (44).

[5] Two canonical texts, the teachings of Agur and Qoheleth, belong to the category of pessimism. From this observation it follows that I concur in John Priest's judgment that "The skepticism of Koheleth ends, however much some commentators cry to the contrary, as pessimism pure and simple" ("Humanism, Skepticism, and Pessimism in Israel," *JAAR* 36 [1968]: 323-24).

[6] Johannes Pedersen, "Scepticisme israélite, *RHPR* 10 (1930): 360-61 contrasts Qoheleth's exhortation to fear God with world renunciation, and rightly interprets this submission as wholly devoid of love.

[7] Baumer, *Religion and the Rise of Scepticism*, 66.

[8] *Ibid.*, 139-40 (The quotation comes from Olive Schreiner, *Story of an African Farm*, 1883, 151).

[9] Eric Weil, "What Is a Breakthrough in History?" *Daedalus* (Spring 1975): 21-36. The title of this volume is *Wisdom, Revelation and Doubt: Perspectives on the First Millennium* B.C.

[10] See the author's essay entitled "The Human Dilemma and Literature of Dissent."

[11] Priest, "Humanism, Skepticism, and Pessimism in Israel," 326.

[12] Martin Buber, "The Heart Determines."

[13] Priest, "Humanism, Skepticism, and Pessimism in Israel," 326.

[14] Paul Ricoeur, *The Symbolism of Evil* (Boston: Beacon Press, 1969) sheds fresh light on this significant issue.

[15] Weil, "What Is a Breakthrough in History?" 22-24.

[16] Hans Heinrich Schmid, *Wesen und Geschichte der Weisheit.*

[17] Contra von Rad, *Wisdom in Israel,* 237-39.

[18] Although the hypothesis pervades von Rad's literary corpus, it was first expressed in "The Form Critical Problem of the Hexateuch," *The Problem of the Hexateuch and Other Essays* (Edinburgh & London: Oliver & Boyd), 1966 (German edition, 1938 in *BWANT*).

[19] In addition to the aforementioned essays by Pedersen, Priest, and von Rad, one may also consult Martin A. Klopfenstein, "Die Skepsis des Qohelet," *TZ* 28 (1972): 97-109; Robert H. Pfeiffer, "The Peculiar Skepticism of Ecclesiastes," *JBL* 53 (1934): 100-09; Charles Forman, "The Pessimism of Ecclesiastes," *JSS* 3 (1958): 336-43; and Helmut *[sic]* Gese, "Die Krisis der Weisheit bei Kohelet," *Les sagesses du Proché-Orient ancien, SPOA,* 139-51.

[20] Pedersen, "Scepticisme israélite," 331.

[21] Von Rad, *Wisdom in Israel,* 237-39.

[22] Pedersen, "Scepticisme israélite," 347; von Rad, *Old Testament Theology* (Edinburgh and London: Oliver & Boyd, 1962), 453-59.

[23] See *Gerhard von Rad,* 138-60, and Kovacs, *Sociological-Structural Constraints upon Wisdom: The Spatial and Temporal Matrix of Proverbs 15:28—22:16.*

[24] Von Rad, *Wisdom in Israel,* 15-23; Whybray, *The Intellectual Tradition in the Old Testament, passim;* Gordis, "The Social Background of Wisdom Literature," 77-118.

[25] W. Lee Humphreys, "The Motif of the Wise Courtier in the Book of Proverbs," 177-90.

[26] For discussion and bibliography, see the author's "Theodicy," 895-96.

[27] Stanley B. Frost, "The Death of Josiah: A Conspiracy of Silence," *JBL* 87 (1968): 369-82.

[28] Von Rad, *Old Testament Theology,* I, 453 concedes that skepticism crops up now and again as early as the eighth century; in his view, the historiography which produced the Joseph narrative and the succession document removed God from daily events so as to conceal his manipulation of the strings that governed human destiny. Von Rad writes that "the thought of God's eternity [in Ps. 90] was so overwhelming that it swept the imagination away to even greater distances, back to creation and beyond it" (453). But the powerful skepticism in Qoheleth is seen as a marginal note on the farthest frontier of Yahwism approaching the tragic dimension (455-59).

[29] Davidson, "Some Aspects of the Theological Significance of Doubt in the Old Testament," 50.

[30] See my *Samson: A Secret Betrayed, a Vow Ignored,* 44-46, 76-77.

[31] This idea is developed in *Prophetic Conflict.*

[32] Von Rad, *Wisdom in Israel,* 97-110.

[33] Baumer, *Religion and the Rise of Scepticism,* 42.

[34] Besides Weil's essay, "What Is a Breakthrough in History?," see in the same volume Benjamin I. Scwarz, "The Age of Transcendence," 1-8;

A. Leo Oppenheim, "The Position of the Intellectual in Mesopotamian Society," 37-46; and Paul Garelli, "The Changing Facets of Conservative Mesopotamian Thought," 47-56.

[35] *Prophetic Conflict*, 23-38.

[36] Baumer, *Religion and the Rise of Scepticism*, 33 distinguishes various moods in skeptics. He writes that in some "righteous indignation predominates, in others triumphant doubt and a sense of emancipation, and in still others sheer indifference or else the reverse, a longing for a religious faith which seems intellectually unattainable." Similarly, Davidson observes that Old Testament thinkers recognized that some skepticism was inappropriate, for example, the fool in Ps.14:1 who denies God's existence ("Some Aspects of the Theological Significance of Doubt in the Old Testament," 51).

[37] I have examined this confrontation in some detail in an essay entitled "The Problem of Theodicy in Sirach: On Human Bondage," 47-64.

[38] Jerry Gladson, *Retributive Paradoxes in Proverbs 10—29*, Vanderbilt University Ph.D. Dissertation, 1978.

[39] One need only mention the controversy surrounding von Rad's emphasis upon salvation history to see how modern interpreters have also stumbled over the disparity between Israel's celebrated story and actual history. On this problem, see D. G. Spriggs, *Two Old Testament Theologies* (*SBT* 30; Naperville, Illinois: Alec R. Allenson, 1974), and Martin Honecker, "Zum Verständnis der Geschichte in Gerhard von Rad, Theologie des Alten Testament," *EvT* 23 (1963): 143-68.

[40] Pedersen, "Scepticisme israélite," 357.

[41] Both Ezekiel's atomistic thinking and Ben Sira's claim that a single act determined one's destiny carried such individualism to an intolerable extreme, despite good intentions on their part.

[42] I follow Scott, *The Way of Wisdom in the Old Testament*, 166 in interpreting Agur's enigmatic opening words ("I have no God") but depart from his reading of the sequel ("but I can [face this or survive]").

[43] James L. Crenshaw, "The Shadow of Death in Qoheleth," in *Israelite Wisdom: Theological and Literary Essays in Honor of Samuel Terrien*, 205-16; and Priest, "Humanism, Skepticism, and Pessimism in Israel," 324 ("The real crux of his pessimism [is] the immutable fact of death which brings an end to all human aspiration, striving, and realization").

[44] See my article entitled "The Eternal Gospel (Eccl. 3:11)," in *Essays in Old Testament Ethics*, 23-55.

[45] Pedersen, "Scepticisme israélite," 347-49. Many Psalms emphasize human frailty (e.g., 14; 39; 44; 49; 103).

[46] Rylaarsdam, *Revelation in Jewish Wisdom Literature*.

[47] E. J. Dillon, *The Sceptics of the Old Testament* (London: Isbister & Company Limited, 1895), 155 writes that negations in metaphysics were

compensated for amply in Job, Qoheleth, and Agur *by ethics.* I find no such compesation in Agur and Qoheleth.

⁴⁸ Although I do not wish to pursue Festinger's categories in this connection, the idea of cognitive dissonance seems to apply nicely to Israel's skepticism. R. P. Carroll, *When Prophecy Failed: Reactions and Responses to Failure in the Old Testament Prophetic Traditions* (London: SCM, 1979) has demonstrated the usefulness of Festinger's concepts in understanding biblical prophecy.

⁴⁹ I have examined these extraordinary forms in two essays, "Impossible Questions, Sayings, and Tasks in the Old Testament," and "Questions, dictons, et éprueves impossible," 96-111.

⁵⁰ This sentence alludes to Lou Silberman's contribution to *Essays in Old Testament Ethics* under the title "The Human Deed in a Time of Despair: The Ethics of Apocalyptic," 191-202. The present discussion of skepticism also appears in *The Divine Helmsman,* 1-19.

⁵¹ Samuel Terrien, "The Sceptics in the Old Testament and in the Literature of the Ancient Near East," Th.D. Dissertation, Union Theological Seminary, New York, 1941 was not available to the author.

9 Egyptian and Mesopotamian Literature

¹ Brunner, "Die Weisheitsliteratur," 90.

² Lambert, *Babylonian Wisdom Literature,* 1.

³ *Ibid.* Lambert also thinks "a case could be made for including many of the Babylonian epics in the Wisdom category, because they deal with cosmological problems."

⁴ Brunner, "Die Weisheitsliteratur," and Williams, "Wisdom in the Ancient Near East."

⁵ In several instances the addressee is already grown, a fact which has a bearing on the actual social location of wisdom literature. Even in Egypt, the school may not have been the most important context for instruction.

⁶ Aksel Volten, "Der Begriff der Maat in den "Ägyptischen Weisheitstexten," *SPOA,* 73-99; Schmid, *Wesen und Geschichte der Weisheit.*

⁷ Eberhard Otto, "Der Vorwurf an Gott," *Vorträge der orientalistische Tagung in Marburg, 1950* (1951): 1-15.

⁸ See my *Samson: A Secret Betrayed, a Vow Ignored,* 118-20.

⁹ That is, a former school companion.

¹⁰ This text has often been compared with Samuel's rebuke of Saul in 1 Samuel 15:22.

¹¹ Note the literary fiction of posthumous advice.

¹² The pertinent texts can be seen in parallel columns in *ANET,* 424. Glendon E. Bryce, *A Legacy of Wisdom: The Egyptian Contribution to the Wisdom of Israel* (Lewisburg and London: Bucknell University and

Associated University Presses, 1979) has examined this material at great length.

[13] The difficult Hebrew word is thus rendered as *šelošim*.

[14] Berend Gemser, "The Instructions of 'Onchsheshonqy and Biblical Wisdom Literature," *SAIW*, 134-60 (originally published in *VTSup* 7 [1960]: 102-28).

[15] R. J. Williams, "Scribal Training in Ancient Egypt," *JAOS* 92 (1972): 214-21; *City Invincible: A Symposium on Urbanization and Cultural Development in the Ancient Near East*, Carl H. Kraeling and Robert M. Adams, eds. (Chicago: University of Chicago, 1960), 94-122.

[16] Edmund I. Gordon, *Sumerian Proverbs. Glimpses of Everyday Life in Ancient Mesopotamia* (Philadelphia: University Museum, University of Pennsylvania, 1959); "A New Look at the Wisdom of Sumer and Akkad," *BO* 17 (1960): 122-52; "Sumerian Proverbs and Fables," *JCS* 12 (1958): 1-21, 43-75.

[17] Bendt Alster, *The Instructions of Šuruppak: A Sumerian Proverb Collection* (Copenhagen: Akademisk Forlag, 1974), and *Studies in Sumerian Proverbs* (Copenhagen: Akademisk Forlag, 1975).

[18] Samuel Noah Kramer, " 'Man and His God': A Sumerian Variation on the 'Job' Motif," *VTSup* 3 (1960): 170-82.

[19] R. J. Williams, "Theodicy in the Ancient Near East," *CJT* 2 (1956): 14-26, especially 18-19.

[20] Lambert, *Babylonian Wisdom Literature*, 21-62.

[21] *Ibid.*, 27.

[22] Von Rad, *Wisdom in Israel*, 248 and 311, takes *both* views!

[23] W. M. W. Roth, *Numerical Sayings in the Old Testament* (*VTSup* 13; Leiden: E. J. Brill, 1965).

[24] Bryce, "Omen Wisdom in Ancient Israel."

[25] Angel Marzal, *Gleanings from the Wisdom of Mari* (Rome: Biblical Institute Press, 1976); cf. Henri Cazelles, "Les nouvelles études sur Sumer (Alster) et Mari (Marzal) nous aident-elles à situer les origines de la sagesse israélite?," *La Sagesse de l'Ancien Testament*, 17–27.

[26] Jean Nougayrol, "Les sagesses Babyloniennes: Études récentes et textes inédits," *SPOA*, 41-50.

[27] Giovanni Pettinato, "The Royal Archives of Tell Mardikh-Ebla," *BA* 39 (1976): 45.

[28] Robert H. Pfeiffer, "Edomitic Wisdom," *ZAW* 44 (1926): 13-25 and "Wisdom and Vision in the Old Testament," *SAIW*, 305-13 (originally published in *ZAW* 52 [1934]).

Selected Bibliography

Alster, B. *The Instruction of Šuruppak: A Sumerian Proverb Collection.* Copenhagen: Akademisk Forlag, 1974.

————. *Studies in Sumerian Proverbs.* Copenhagen: Akademisk Forlag, 1975.

Andersen, F. I. *Job.* London: InterVarsity Press, 1976.

Barr, J. "The Book of Job and Its Modern Interpreters," *BJRL* 54 (1971): 28-46.

Barton, G. A. *The Book of Ecclesiastes.* Edinburgh: T. and T. Clark, 1908.

Bauer-Kayatz, C. *Einführung in die alttestamentliche Weisheit.* Neukirchen-Vluyn: Neukirchener, 1969.

Baumgartner, W. "The Wisdom Literature," in *The Old Testament and Modern Study,* H. H. Rowley, ed. Oxford: Oxford University Press, 1951, 210-37.

Blank, S. H. "Wisdom," *IDB,* IV. Nashville and New York: Abingdon, 1962, 852-61.

Braun, R. *Kohelet und die Frühhellenistische Popularphilosophie.* Berlin and New York: Walter de Gruyter, 1973.

Brueggemann, W. *In Man We Trust.* Richmond: John Knox, 1972.

————. "Scripture and an Ecumenical Life-Style," *Inter* 24 (1970): 3-19.

Bryce, G. E. *A Legacy of Wisdom.* Lewisburg, Pa.: Bucknell University Press, 1979.

Childs, B. S. *Introduction to the Old Testament as Scripture.* Philadelphia: Fortress, 1979 (chs. xxxiv, xxxv, xxxviii).

Clements, R. E. *One Hundred Years of Old Testament Interpretation.* Philadelphia: Westminster, 1976, 99-117.

Coats, G. W. "The Joseph Story and Ancient Wisdom: A Reappraisal," *CBQ* 35 (1973): 285-97.

————. *From Canaan to Egypt. CBQMS,* 4. Washington: The Catholic Biblical Association of America, 1976.

Collins, J. "Cosmos and Salvation: Jewish Wisdom and Apocalyptic in the Hellenistic Age," *History of Religion* 17 (1977): 121-42.

Cook, A. *The Root of the Thing: A Study of Job and the Song of Songs.* Bloomington: Indiana University Press, 1968.

Crenshaw, J. L. "The Eternal Gospel (Eccl. 3:11)," in *Essays in Old Testament Ethics*, 23-55.

_____. "The Human Dilemma and Literature of Dissent," in *Tradition and Theology in the Old Testament*, ed. D. Knight. Philadelphia: Fortress, 1976, 235-58.

_____. "The Influence of the Wise Upon Amos," *ZAW* 79 (1967): 42-52.

_____. "Method in Determining Wisdom Influence Upon 'Historical' Literature," *JBL* 88 (1969): 129-42.

_____. "Popular Questioning of the Justice of God in Ancient Israel," *ZAW* 82 (1970): 380-95.

_____. "The Problem of Theodicy in Sirach," *JBL* 94 (1975): 47-64.

_____. "In Search of Divine Presence: Some Remarks Preliminary to a Theology of Wisdom," *RevExp* 74 (1977): 353-69.

_____. *Studies in Ancient Israelite Wisdom*. New York: KTAV, 1976.

_____. "Wisdom," in *Old Testament Form Criticism*, J. H. Hayes, ed. San Antonio: Trinity University Press, 1974, 225-64.

_____. *"Wisdom in Israel* by Gerhard von Rad," *RSR* 6, no. 2 (1976): 6-12.

_____. "Wisdom in the OT," *IDB* Supplementary Volume 1976, 952-6.

Davidson, A. B. *The Book of Job*. Cambridge: University Press, 1951 (original, 1884).

Davidson, R. "Some Aspects of the Theological Significance of Doubt in the Old Testament," *ASTI* 7 (1968-69): 41-52.

Driver, S. R. and G. B. Gray. *The Book of Job*. Edinburgh: T. and T. Clark, 1921.

Duesberg, H. and I. Fransen. *Les Scribes Inspirés*. Belgium: Éditions de Marsedsous, 1966.

Emerton, J. "Wisdom," in *Tradition and Interpretation*, G. W. Anderson, ed. Oxford: Oxford University Press, 1979, 214-37.

Fichtner, J. *Die altorientalische Weisheit in ihrer israelitisch-jüdischen Ausprägung*. Giessen: Alfred Töpelmann, 1933.

_____. *Gottes Weisheit*. Stuttgart: Calwer, 1965.

Fohrer, G. "The Righteous Man in Job 31," in *Essays in Old Testament Ethics*, J. L. Crenshaw and J. T. Willis, eds. New York: KTAV, 1974, 3-22.

_____. "Sophia," *SAIW*, 63-83.

_____. *Introduction to the Old Testament*. Nashville and New York: Abingdon, 1968, 304-41.

Foster, B. R. "Wisdom and the Gods in Ancient Mesopotamia," *Orientalia* 43 (1974): 344-54.

Gammie, J., et al., eds. *Israelite Wisdom: Theological and Literary Essays in Honor of Samuel Terrien.* Missoula: Scholars Press, 1978. The following essays appear in this volume:

J. A. Sanders, "Comparative Wisdom: L'Ouvre Terrien," 3-14.

A. Caquot, "Israelite Perceptions of Wisdom and Strength in the Light of the Ras Shamra Texts," 25-33.

R. E. Murphy, "Wisdom—Theses and Hypotheses," 35-42.

H. J. Hermisson, "Observations on the Creation Theology in Wisdom," 43-57.

E. M. Good, "The Unfilled Sea: Style and Meaning in Ecclesiastes 1:2-11," 59-73.

H. W. Wolff, "Micah the Moreshite—The Prophet and His Background," 77-84.

W. A. Brueggemann, "The Epistemological Crisis of Israel's Two Histories," 85-105.

W. McKane, "Jeremiah 13:12-14: A Problematic Proverb," 107-20.

J. M. Ward, "The Servant's Knowledge in Isaiah 40—50," 121-36.

G. M. Landes, "Jonah: A Māšāl?" 137-58.

J. M. Ross, "Psalm 73," 161-75.

W. L. Humphreys, "The Motif of the Wise Courtier in the Book of Proverbs," 177-90.

R. N. Whybray, "Qoheleth the Immoralist (Qoh 7:16-17)," 191-204.

J. L. Crenshaw, "The Shadow of Death in Qoheleth," 205-16.

J. G. Gammie, "Behemoth and Leviathan: On the Didactic and Theological Significance of Job 40:15—41:26," 217-31.

L. Alonso-Schökel, "The Vision of Man in Sirach 16:24—17:14," 235-45.

E. Jacob, "Wisdom and Religion in Sirach," 247-60.

S. J. DeVries, "Observations on Quantitative and Qualitative Time in Wisdom and Apocalyptic," 263-76.

W. Lowndes and J. A. Sanders, "Wisdom at Qumran," 277-85.

Gammie, J. G. "Spatial and Ethical Dualism in Jewish Wisdom and Apocalyptic Literature," *JBL* 93 (1974): 356-85.

Gemser, B. "The Instructions of 'Onchsheshonqy and Biblical Wisdom Literature," *VTSup* 3 (1960): 102-28.

_____. "The Spiritual Structure of Biblical Aphoristic Wisdom," in *Adhuc Loquitur. Collected Essays of Dr. B. Gemser,* eds. A. van Selms and A. S. van der Woude. Leiden: E. J. Brill, 1968, 138-49.

Gerstenberger, E. "Zur alttestamentlichen Weisheit," *VuF* 14 (1969): 28-44.

Gese, H. *Lehre and Wirklichkeit in der alten Weisheit.* Tübingen: Mohr, 1958.

_____. "Die Krisis der Weisheit bei Kohelet," *SPOA,* 139-51.

_____. "Weisheit," *RGG* (3rd edition), VI, 1574-77.

_____. "Weisheitsdichtung," *RGG* (3rd edition), 1577-81.

Gilbert, M. ed. *La Sagesse de l'Ancien Testament.* Gembloux: Duculot, 1979.

The following essays appear in this book:

H. Cazelles, "Les nouvelles études sur Sumer (Alster) et Mari (Marzal) nous aident-elles à situer les origines de la sagesse israélite?" 17-27.

C. Brekelmans, "Wisdom Influence in Deuteronomy," 28-38.

J. Vermeylen, "Le Proto-Isaïe et la sagesse d'Israel," 39-58.

J. Luyten, "Psalm 73 and Wisdom," 59-81.

J. P. M. van der Ploeg, "Le Psaume 119 et la sagesse," 82-87.

N. J. Tromp, "Wisdom and the Canticle. Ct., 8, 6c-7b: text, character, message and import," 88-95.

J. L. Crenshaw, "Questions, dictons et épreuves impossibles," 96-111.

S. Amsler, "La sagesse de la femme," 112-16.

P. É. Bonnard, "De la Sagesse personifiée dans l'Ancien Testament à la Sagesse en personne dans le Nouveau," 117-49.

R. N. Whybray, "Yahweh-sayings and Their Contexts in Proverbs 10, 1-22, 16," 153-65.

W. McKane, "Functions of Language and Objectives of Discourse According to Proverbs 10—30," 166-85.

B. Lang, "Schule und Unterricht im alten Israel," 186-201.

M. Gilbert, "Le discours de la Sagesse en Proverbs, 8. Structure et cohérence," 202-218.

G. Fohrer, "Dialog und Kommunikation im Buche Hiob," 219-30.

J. Lévêque, "Anamnèse et disculpation: la conscience du juste en Job, 29-31," 231-48.

D. Lys, "L'Être et le Temps. Communication de Qohèlèth," 249-58.

N. Lohfink, "War Kohelet ein Frauenfeind? Ein Versuch, die Logik und den Gegenstand von Koh., 7, 23-8, la herauszufinden," 259-87.

J. Coppens, "La structure de l'Ecclésiaste," 288-92.

J. Marböck, "Sir., 38, 24-39, 11: Der schriftgelehrte Weise. Ein Beitrag zu Gestalt und Werk Ben Siras," 293-316.

G. L. Prato, "La luminère interprète de la sagesse dans la tradition textuelle de Ben Sira," 317-46.

P. Beauchamp, "Épouser la Sagesse—ou n'épouser qu'elle? Une éngima du Livre de la Sagesse," 347-69.

F. Raurell, "The Religious Meaning of 'Doxa' in the Book of Wisdom," 370-83.

J. M. Rose, "Can Paul Ricoeur's Method Contribute to Interpreting the Book of Wisdom?" 384-96.

Ginzburg, C. D. *The Song of Songs and Coheleth.* New York: KTAV, 1970 (original, 1857).

Glatzer, N. ed. *The Dimensions of Job.* New York: Schocken, 1969.

_____. "The Book of Job and Its Interpreters," in *Biblical Motifs* A. Altmann, ed. Cambridge: Harvard University Press, 1966, 197-220.

Godbey, A. H. "The Hebrew Mašal," *AJSL* 39 (1922-23): 89-108.

Gordis, R. *The Book of Job*. New York: The Jewish Theological Seminary of America, 1978.

_____. *The Book of God and Man*. Chicago and London: University of Chicago Press, 1965.

_____. *Koheleth: The Man and His World*. New York: Schocken, 1951.

_____. "The Social Background of Wisdom Literature," *HUCA* 18 (1943/44): 77-118.

Gordon, E. I. *Sumerian Proverbs: Glimpses of Everyday Life in Ancient Mesopotamia*. Philadelphia: Westminster, 1959.

Gray, J. "The Book of Job in the Context of Near Eastern Literature," *ZAW* 82 (1970): 251-69.

Habel, N. "The Symbolism of Wisdom in Proverbs 1—9," *Inter* 26 (1972): 131-56.

Harrelson, W. "Wisdom and Pastoral Theology," *ANQ* (1966): 3-11.

Haspecker, J. *Gottsfurcht bei Jesus Sirach*. Rom: Päpstliches Bibelinstitut, 1967.

Hausen, A. *Hiob in der französischen Literatur: Zur Rezeption eines alttestamentlichen Buches*. Bern und Frankfurt/M.: Herbert und Peter Lang, 1972.

Heaton, E. W. *Solomon's New Men*. New York: Pica Press, 1974.

Hermisson, H. J. *Studien zur israelitischen Spruchweisheit*. Neukirchen-Vluyn: Neukirchener, 1968.

_____. "Weisheit und Geschichte," in *Probleme biblischer Theologie*. H. W. Wolff, ed. München: Kaiser, 1971, 136-54.

Hertzberg, H. W. *Der Prediger*. Gutersloh: Gerd Mohn, 1963.

Holm-Nielsen, S. "The Book of Ecclesiastes and the Interpretation of it in Jewish and Christian Theology," *ASTI* 10 (1975-76): 38-96.

Horton, E. Jr., "Koheleth's Concept of Opposites," *Numen* 19 (1972): 1-21.

Irwin, W. A. "The Wisdom Literature," *IB* 1. Nashville: Abingdon, 1952, 212-19.

Jensen, J. *The Use of Tōrâ by Isaiah*. Washington: The Catholic Biblical Association of America, 1973.

Jung, C. G. *Answer to Job*. Cleveland and New York: World Publishing Company, 1970.

Kayatz, C. = C. Bauer-Kayatz. *Studien zu Proverbien 1—9*. Neukirchen-Vluyn: Neukirchener, 1966.

Kovacs, B. W. "Is There a Class-Ethic in Proverbs?" *Essays in Old Testament Ethics*, 171-89.

Kroeber, R. *Der Prediger.* Berlin: Akademie-Verlag, 1963.

Lambert, W. G. *Babylonian Wisdom Literature.* Oxford: Clarendon, 1960.

Lang, B. *Frau Weisheit.* Dusseldorf: Patmos, 1975.

Larcher, C. *Études sur le Livre de la Sagesse.* Paris: Librarie Lecoffre, 1969.

Lauhe, A. *Kohelet.* Neukirchen-Vluyn: Neukirchener, 1978.

Loader, J. A. *Polar Structures in the Book of Qohelet. BZAW* 152; Berlin and New York: Walter de Gruyter, 1979.

Loretz, O. *Qohelet und der Alte Orient: Untersuchungen zu Stil und theologischer Thematik des Buches Qohelet.* Freiburg, Basel, Wien: Herder, 1964.

MacDonald, D. B. *The Hebrew Philosophical Genius.* New York: Russell and Russell, 1965 (reprint).

Mack, B. L. *Logos und Sophia: Untersuchungen zur Weisheitstheologie im hellenistischen Judentum.* Göttingen: Vandenhoeck und Ruprecht, 1973.

_____. "Wisdom Myth and Mytho-Logy," *Inter* 24 (1970): 46-60.

Marcus, R. "On Biblical Hypostases of Wisdom," *HUCA* 23 (1950/51): 157-71.

Marböck, J. *Weisheit im Wandel: Untersuchungen zur Weisheitstheologie bei Ben Sira.* Bonn: Peter Hanstein, 1971.

_____. "Sirachliteratur seit 1966. Ein Überblick," *ThRevue* 71 (1975): 177-84.

Marzal, A. *Gleanings from the Wisdom of Mari.* Rome: Biblical Institute Press, 1976.

McKane, W. *Prophets and Wise Men.* London: SCM, 1965.

_____. *Proverbs.* Philadelphia: Westminster, 1970.

Meinhold, H. *Die Weisheit Israels in Spruch, Sage und Dichtung.* Leipzig: Quelle und Meyer, 1908.

Middendorp, T. *Die Stellung Jesu ben Siras zwischen Judentum und Hellenismus.* Leiden: E. J. Brill, 1973.

Momigliano, A. *Alien Wisdom: The Limits of Hellenization.* Cambridge: University Press, 1975.

Müller, H. P. "Altes und Neues zum Buch Hiob," *EvTh* 37 (1977): 284-304.

_____. *Das Hiobproblem.* Darmstadt: Wissenschaftliche Buchgesellschaft, 1978.

_____. "Die Weisheitliche Lehrerzählung in Alten Testament und seiner Umwelt," *Die Welt des Orients* 9 (1977): 77-98.

Murphy, R. E. "Assumptions and Problems in Old Testament Wisdom Research," *CBQ* 29 (1967): 102-12.

_____. "Form Criticism and Wisdom Literature," *CBQ* 31 (1969): 475-83.

_____. "The Hebrew Sage and Openness to the World," in *Christian*

Action and Openness to the World. Villanova University Symposium, II-III, 1970, 289-301.

――――――. *Introduction to the Wisdom Literature of the Old Testament.* Collegeville, Minn.: Liturgical Press, 1965.

――――――. "Qoheleth's 'Quarrel' with the Fathers," in *From Faith to Faith.* Pittsburgh: Pickwick, 1979, 235-45.

Nel, P. "The Concept 'Father' in the Wisdom Literature of the Ancient Near East," *JNorthwestSemLit* 5 (1977): 53-66.

Oesterley, W. O. E. *The Book of Proverbs.* London: Methuen and Company, 1929.

――――――. *The Wisdom of Jesus the Són of Sirach or Ecclesiasticus.* Cambridge: University Press, 1912.

Oliver, J. P. J. "Schools and Wisdom Literature," *JNorthwestSemLit,* 4 (1975): 49-60.

Otzen, B. "O.T. Wisdom Literature and Dualistic Thinking in Late Judaism," *VTSup* 28 (1974): 146-57.

Paterson, J. *The Wisdom of Israel.* London and Nashville: Lutterworth and Abingdon, 1961.

Peake, A. S. *Job.* Edinburgh: T. C. and E. C. Jack, 1905.

Pedersen, J. "Scepticisme israélite," *RHPR* 10 (1930): 317-70.

――――――. "Wisdom and Immortality," *VTSup* 3 (1960): 238-46.

Perdue, Leo. *Wisdom and Cult.* Missoula: Scholars Press, 1977.

Pope, M. *Job.* Garden City: Doubleday, 1973.

Porteous, N. W. "Royal Wisdom," *VTSup* 3 (1960): 247-61.

Priest, J. F. "Humanism, Skepticism, and Pessimism in Israel," *JAAR* 36 (1968): 311-26.

――――――. "Where Is Wisdom to Be Placed?" *JBR* 31 (1963): 275-82.

Preuss, H. D. "Alttestamentliche Weisheit in Christlicher Theologie," *BibEphTheolLov* 33 (1974): 165-881.

――――――. "Erwägungen zum theologischen Ort alttestamentlicher Weisheitsliteratur," *EvTh* 30 (1970): 393-417.

――――――. "Das Gottesbild der älteren Weisheit Israels," *VTSup* 23 (1972): 117-45.

Rad, G. von. *Wisdom in Israel.* Nashville and New York: Abingdon, 1972.

――――――. "The Joseph Narrative and Ancient Wisdom," in *The Problem of the Hexateuch and Other Essays.* Edinburgh and London: Oliver and Boyd, 1966, 292-300.

――――――. "Some Aspects of the Old Testament World View," *ibid.,* 144-65.

Rankin, O. S. *Israel's Wisdom Literature.* Edinburgh: T. and T. Clark, 1936.

Ranston, H. *The Old Testament Wisdom Books and Their Teaching.* London: The Epworth Press, 1930.

Reese, J. M. *Hellenistic Influence on the Book of Wisdom and Its Consequences.* Rome: Pontifical Institute, 1970.

Roberts, J. J. M. "Job and the Israelite Religious Tradition," *ZAW* 89 (1977): 107-14.

Rowley, H. H. *Job.* London: Thomas Nelson, 1970.

Rubenstein, R. L. "Job and Auschwitz," *New Theology* 8 (1971): 107-14.

Ruprecht, Eberhard. "Leiden und Gerechtigkeit bei Hiob," *ZThK* 73 (1976): 424-45.

Rylaarsdam, J. C. *Revelation in Jewish Wisdom Literature.* Chicago: University of Chicago Press, 1946.

Sanders, P. S., ed. *Twentieth Century Interpretations of the Book of Job.* Englewood Cliffs, N.J.: Prentice Hall, 1968.

Sawyer, J. F. A., "The Ruined House in Ecclesiastes 12: A Reconstruction of the Original Parable," *JBL* 94 (1975): 519-31.

Schmid, H. H. *Altorientalische Welt in der alttestamentlichen Theologie.* Zurich: Theologischer Verlag, 1974.

_____. *Wesen und Geschichte der Weisheit.* Berlin: Töpelmann, 1966.

Scott, R. B. Y. *Proverbs. Ecclesiastes.* Garden City: Doubleday, 1965.

_____. "Folk Proverbs of the Ancient Near East" in *Transactions of the Royal Society of Canada* 15 (1961): 47-56.

_____. "Priesthood, Prophecy, Wisdom, and the Knowledge of God," *JBL* 80 (1961): 1-15.

_____. "Solomon and the Beginnings of Wisdom in Israel," *VTSup* 3 (1960): 262-79.

_____. "The Study of Wisdom Literature," *Inter* 24 (1970): 20-45.

_____. *The Way of Wisdom in the Old Testament.* New York: Macmillan, 1971.

_____. "Wise and Foolish, Righteous and Wicked," *VTSup* 23 (1972): 146-65.

_____. "Wisdom; Wisdom Literature," *EncyJud* 16 (1971): 557-563.

Sheppard, G. T., "The Epilogue to Qoheleth as Theological Commentary," *CBQ* 39 (1977): 182-89.

Sheppard, G. T. *Wisdom as a Hermeneutical Construct, BZAW,* 151. Berlin and New York: Walter de Gruyter, 1980.

Skehan, P. W. *Studies in Israelite Poetry and Wisdom.* Washington: The Catholic Biblical Association of America, 1971.

Snaith, N. H. *The Book of Job: Its Origin and Purpose.* London: SCM, 1968.

Terrien, S. *Job: Poet of Existence.* New York and Indianapolis: The Bobbs-Merrill Inc., 1957.

_____. *The Elusive Presence*. New York: Harper and Row, 1978.

Thomas, D. W. ed. *Wisdom in Israel and in the Ancient Near East*. Leiden: Brill, 1960.

Thompson, J. M. *The Form and Function of Proverbs in Ancient Israel*. The Hague and Paris: Mouton, 1974.

Toy, C. H. *Proverbs*. Edinburgh: T. and T. Clark, 1899.

Trible, P. "Wisdom Builds a Poem: The Architecture of Proverbs 1:20-33," *JBL* 94 (1975): 509-18.

Tur-Sinai, N. H. *The Book of Job*. Jerusalem: Kiryath Sepher Ltd., 1967.

Wendel, F. et al. eds. *Les sagesses du Proché-Orient ancien*. Paris: Presses Universitaires de France, 1963.

Westermann, C. *Der Aufbau des Buches Hiob* (2nd edition). Stuttgart: Calwer, 1977.

_____. "Weisheit im Sprichwort," in *Schalom* (Festschrift A. Jepsen). Stuttgart: Calwer Verlag, 1971, 73-85.

Whedbee, J. W. *Isaiah and Wisdom*. Nashville: Abingdon, 1971.

Whitley, C. F. *Koheleth: His Language and Thought*. Berlin and New York: Walter de Gruyter, 1979.

Whybray, R. N. *The Intellectual Tradition in the Old Testament*. Berlin and New York: Walter de Gruyter, 1974.

_____. *Wisdom in Proverbs*. London: SCM, 1965.

Wilken, R., ed., *Aspects of Wisdom in Judaism and Early Christianity*. Notre Dame: University of Notre Dame Press, 1975.

Williams, J. G. "Deciphering the Unspoken: The Theophany of Job," *HUCA* 49 (1978): 59-72.

Williams, R. J. "Wisdom in the Ancient Near East," in *IDB*, Supplementary Volume. Nashville and New York: Abingdon, 1976, 949-52.

Winston, D. *The Wisdom of Solomon*. Garden City: Doubleday, 1979.

Wisdom, Revelation, and Doubt: Perspectives on the First Millennium B.C. Daedalus (Spring), 1975.

Wood, J. *Wisdom Literature*. London: Gerald Duckworth and Co., Ltd., 1967.

Zhitlowsky, C. "Job and Faust," *Two Studies in Yiddish Culture*, P. Matenko, ed. Leiden: Brill, 1968.

Zimmerli, W. "Concerning the Structure of Old Testament Wisdom," *SAIW*, 175-207.

_____. "The Place and Limit of the Wisdom in the Framework of the Old Testament Theology," *SAIW*, 314-28.

_____. *Old Testament Theology in Outline*. Atlanta: John Knox, 1978, 155-166.

Index of Biblical Passages*

*Indexes prepared by Victoria L. Garvey.

Index of Authors

Index of Subjects

Index of Hebrew Expressions